THE ORDEAL OF

PAUL

CÉZANNE

by

JOHN REWALD

PHOENIX HOUSE

LONDON

ALSO BY JOHN REWALD:

The History of Impressionism

Pierre Bonnard

Georges Seurat

Maillol

Gauguin

EDITED BY JOHN REWALD:

Paul Cézanne, Letters

Paul Gauguin,
Letters to A. Vollard and A. Fontainas

Camille Pissarro,
Letters to his son Lucien

The Woodcuts of Aristide Maillol
(A Complete Catalogue)

The Sculptures of Edgar Degas
(A Complete Catalogue)

Renoir Drawings

MADE 1950 IN GREAT BRITAIN

Printed at Ipswich by W. S. Cowell Limited for

PHOENIX HOUSE LIMITED

38 WILLIAM IV STREET, LONDON

First published in Great Britain in 1950

I. SELF PORTRAIT (DETAIL), *c.*1880

TO THE MEMORY OF
MY FATHER

Translation by Margaret H. Liebman

*Published in the United States under the
title 'Paul Cézanne'*

CONTENTS

ILLUSTRATIONS

COLOUR

MONOCHROME

ix

86. Photograph of Cézanne in his studio at Les *After p.* 144
Lauves, sitting in front of his 'Bathers' (small
version, now in the Barnes Foundation, Merion)
Taken by Emile Bernard, 1904

87. *Cézanne:* Bathers (large version), 1902–6. ,,
Painting [719]
Pennsylvania Museum of Art, Philadelphia

The photographs 56, 58, 60, 62, 64, 70, 81, 83 and 85 were taken by the author.

ILLUSTRATIONS IN TEXT

The numbers in square brackets are those given in
Lionello Venturi's catalogue *Cézanne, sa vie, son œuvre*

INTRODUCTION

In *The History of Impressionism*, published in 1946, I endeavoured to give a detailed account of the artistic movement of which Cézanne was, at least for some time, a member. The present biography may be considered as a subsequent attempt to detach a single figure from the general background described in the larger book. Actually, however, this life of Cézanne was written more than a decade ago. After several years of research, it was first published in 1936 in Paris as a Sorbonne thesis, under the title *Cézanne et Zola*. A second edition, expanded to almost twice its original size and with a slightly different title, appeared in 1939 on the occasion of the one-hundredth anniversary of Cézanne's birth. Since then I have been able to add some new material to the book and to reshape it into its present form; from a study of the friendship between the painter and the novelist the emphasis has been shifted to Cézanne alone.

The method by which this biography has been put together over a period of years does not differ from that adopted for *The History of Impressionism*. It presents another attempt to let the facts speak for themselves, to rely chiefly on documents and witness accounts, to quote from the originals wherever possible, and thus bring the reader into direct contact with the historical evidence. It again assigns to the author mainly the role of co-ordinating this evidence and of presenting it in the most effective and also the most scrupulously exact way.

Not all the documents assembled here are new, of course. Since this book first appeared, the collected *Letters of Cézanne* have been published both in French and in English. The several score letters which Cézanne addressed to Zola during almost thirty years have thus been made available to the public. Yet Zola's papers, now at the Bibliothèque Nationale in Paris, have also yielded numerous documents which had hitherto escaped the attention of Cézanne's biographers. They include, for one thing, the notes which the novelist made for his books, notes that often contain the name of Cézanne. Even more important, however, are the letters received by Zola from a number of friends, mostly companions of his youth, who furnish a great wealth of information about the painter.

II. HILLS NEAR PONTOISE, *c.*1880

For having been allowed to consult these all-important sources, I am deeply indebted to Zola's daughter and to her husband, the late Denise Le Blond-Zola and the late Maurice Le Blond, who in every possible way facilitated my research. I am equally grateful to the son of the painter, the late M. Paul Cézanne, for the warm sympathy with which he assisted me. I was fortunately able to gather some first-hand information from Paul Signac, Maxime Conil, Maurice Denis, and Hermann-Paul, all of whom are now dead, as well as from Mme Marie Gasquet and MM. Louis Le Bail, Charles Camoin, Rodo Pissarro, and Albert André. The painter Leo Marschütz assisted me with generous advice.

In the United States I have received encouragement and help from my friend Gerstle Mack, himself the author of the first comprehensive biography of Cézanne published in English; from Margaret Scolari and Alfred H. Barr, Jr., who discovered and published the invaluable correspondence between Marion and Morstatt; and from Mrs Adelyn D. Breeskin, to whom I owe the communication of the unpublished letter by Mary Cassatt. Last but not least, I owe a debt of gratitude to all the collectors and museum officials who authorized me to reproduce works from their collections.

At a time when there appear every few months more or less well assembled albums of plates in colour or in black-and-white after the works of the great French nineteenth-century masters, there seems to be no need of acquainting the reader with the major paintings of Cézanne. The reproductions in this volume have therefore been assembled from a purely documentary point of view. Rather than to show once more his famous works, the illustrations were selected so as to supplement the text with visual references. These include a number of photographs of Cézanne himself, of his family and his friends, and of some of the landscapes that were so dear to him; while among Cézanne's works the choice often fell on little-known paintings and drawings.

Since, for the sake of unity, the present biography does not always follow a strictly chronological pattern, the reader may refer for dates and summary information to the biographical outline that follows the last chapter.

The belief that the average reader dislikes footnotes has led to the almost complete suppression of such references. The student will find these in the two French editions of this book. As to the bibliography, it has been limited to the more important among the several hundred books and articles on Cézanne: it includes, above all, publications of documentary interest and those from which the material here presented has been gathered. A more complete bibliography will be found in Lionello Venturi's masterly catalogue, *Cézanne, sa vie, son œuvre.*

I wish to express here my profound gratitude to Miss Louise Salm for the patience and skill with which she has assisted me in the final revision of the translation from the French and in preparing the index.

J.R.

New York, December 1949

I

YOUTH IN AIX

AIX-EN-PROVENCE is a small town in southern France that seems
to have been by-passed by progress. Time appears to have stood
still there for many decades, and life today is almost as peaceful and
quiet as it was some hundred years ago. No large highway touches
the town, and the express from Paris to near-by Marseilles passes by
its old and sleepy station. A few buses and an obsolete train connect
Aix with the outer world, but their incredible slowness discourages
what traffic might disturb the pace of the town.

Nothing ever seems to happen in Aix, and even the seasons succeed each other without much altering its aspect. The countryside
with its pines and cypresses remains green throughout the winter
and the many warm springs that cascade over mossy stones or run
into baroque basins at practically every street corner never interrupt
their flow all the year round. The town is rich both in beautiful foun-
tains and in churches, whose often clumsy towers or picturesque
belfries dominate the yellow and red tiled roofs. Crowded together
so as to provide cool shadows, the old houses, with their shuttered
windows, stone caryatids, and graceful ironwork, have seen few
changes during the past century. The people who live in them were
born there and will die there, ignorant of the world at large, perfectly contented with their retired existence.

Many of the streets are still cobble-stoned and almost every one
of them leads into the open, into a beautiful country of hills and
vineyards, crossed by rivulets that often dry out in the summer's
heat. Wherever one finds oneself, there appears in the distance the
large and grey wall of Mount Sainte-Victoire, rising abruptly above
the undulating valley. At its foot Marius defeated the Teutons one
hundred years before Christ, and the reddish earth of the fields is
said to have retained its colour from the blood with which it was
drenched. Since then, however, eternal peace has reigned over the
valley; grapes, olives, and almonds ripen in the torrid sun and even
clouds seem banned from the blue sky. No sooner do they appear
than a violent sirocco, blowing from the Mediterranean, chases
them beyond Sainte-Victoire.

In the rocks near Sainte-Victoire lies hidden a large dam, designed by one François Zola in order to provide the town with water during the summer months. And not far from there is a strange old quarry from which a warm-coloured, soft stone has been extracted since Roman times. Most of the houses in Aix are built of this stone and seem to retain some of the yellow glow of the sun. The Bourbon School, however, is not one of them; it is one of the few buildings which do not partake of the silent charm of Aix.

In this quiet, sun-filled town, remote in its own concerns, and behind the austere walls of this school, two young boys met in 1852. Paul Cézanne was then thirteen and a boarder in the sixth class; Emile Zola, who was a year younger, was a part-time boarder in the seventh. Both boys were unconventional in different ways, and a close friendship immediately grew up between them. 'Opposites by nature,' as Zola later remembered, 'we became united forever, attracted to each other by secret affinities, the as yet vague torment of a common ambition, the awakening of a superior intelligence in the midst of the brutal mob of dreadful dunces who beat us.'

Paul Cézanne, who was big and strong, took the somewhat puny Zola under his protection when the younger boy was sneered at as 'Parisian'. Born in Paris and brought up in Aix, Zola was part-orphan. His father, Italian by birth, was an engineer and a former officer of the Foreign Legion. He had died in 1847, soon after beginning the construction of the dam, and his young widow lost her whole fortune in law suits concerning the estate. She lived in straitened circumstances with her parents and her son Emile.

Cézanne, too, was probably of Italian ancestry. His forebears came from a small town near the French frontier and had moved to Briançon.* His father, born in a village in the Var, set up business in Aix as a dealer and exporter of hats. In 1848 he was rich enough to buy the only bank in town, and by this means gained a considerable fortune.

At the Bourbon School, Cézanne and Zola extended their friendship to include a third schoolmate, Baptistin Baille, who later became an engineer. The three friends found themselves closely drawn together by a number of unusual interests and ambitions, and at school they came to be known as the 'inseparables'. They took long walks together over the countryside around Aix, and passed the time in fishing, swimming, and reading verses by Homer and Virgil. They felt, as Zola told Cézanne, 'all three rich in hope, all three equal by virtue of our youth and our dreams'. Artistic questions particularly absorbed them and they discussed everything that

---

*The name *Cézanne* or *Cézane* has been found in the records of the town hall of Briançon as early as 1650 and in those of Aix-en-Provence since about 1700. Paul Cézanne's grandparents had left Aix for a neighbouring township, Saint-Zacharie, where Louis-Auguste Cézanne, the painter's father, was born 28 June, 1798.

was on their minds, persuading each other that they had a great and extraordinary destiny. Zola wrote poetry which he read to his friends, and they in turn wrote verses. Zola found Cézanne's more poetical than his and encouraged him to continue his efforts. 'What we were seeking,' Zola later wrote to Baille, 'was richness of heart and spirit, and especially the future which our youth made us see as so brilliant.'

It is impossible to say who was the most enthusiastic and animated of the three, but it is certain that Cézanne was the least sure of himself. He lost his temper easily and was prone to deep depressions which alarmed his two friends. Nevertheless they did not bear a grudge against him when he insulted them during his fits of rage; Zola, always conciliatory, told Baille: 'When he hurts you, you must not blame his heart, but rather the evil demon which beclouds his thought. He has a heart of gold and is a friend who is able to understand us, being just as mad as we, and just as much of a dreamer'.

When this 'demon' haunted him, Cézanne would say: 'The sky of the future is very dark for me!' When, on the other hand, he was light-hearted, no reasoning could prevent him from carrying out some crazy ideas. For example, when he had money he usually hastened to spend it before going to bed. When Zola questioned this extravagance, Cézanne replied; 'By Jove! If I died tonight, would you want my parents to inherit from me?'

The interests of the friends were many. Henri Gasquet, a schoolmate at St Joseph's School, where Cézanne had studied before entering the High School, tells that Cézanne and Zola used to serenade a pretty girl of the neighbourhood whose only fortune consisted of a green parrot. Zola played the cornet, Cézanne the clarinet, both with more enthusiasm than skill, and the parrot, driven crazy by their cacophony, made an indescribable racket. The two friends also belonged to a musical club which participated in all local ceremonies and gave a warm reception to every official who returned from Paris with the red ribbon of the Legion of Honour. Occasionally they played in religious processions.

On the third floor of Baille's house the friends had found a large workroom full of old newspapers, pictures lying on the floor, chairs with broken straw seats, and rickety easels. There they exercised their talents still further and made chemical experiments, heated retorts, and wrote three-act comedies in rhyme.

Later on they indulged in 'the healthy debauchery of the fields and of long walks. . . . In the morning we left before daybreak,' as Zola used to tell. 'I went under your windows to call you in the middle of the night, and we hurried out of the town, game-bag on back and gun in hand. . . . The game-bag was empty on our return, but the mind was full and so was the beast.'

3

Zola later recollected with emotion this happy period of their youth:

'It was about 1856; I was sixteen. . . . We were three friends, three scamps still wearing out trousers on school benches. On holidays, on days we could escape from study, we would run away on wild chases cross-country. We had a need of fresh air, of sunshine, of paths lost at the bottoms of ravines and of which we took possession as conquerors. . . . In the winter, we adored the cold, the ground hardened by frost which rang gaily, and we went to eat omelettes in neighbouring villages. . . . In the summer all our meetings took place at the river-bank, for then we were possessed by the water. . . . In the autumn, our passion changed, we became hunters; oh! very innocuous hunters, for the hunt was for us only an excuse to take long strolls. . . . The hunt always ended in the shade of a tree, the three of us lying on our backs with our noses in the air, talking freely about our loves.

'And our loves, at that time, were above all, the poets. We did not stroll alone. We had books in our pockets or in our game-bags. For a year, Victor Hugo reigned over us an absolute monarch. He had conquered us by his powerful demeanour of a giant, he delighted us with his forceful rhetoric. We knew entire poems by heart and when we returned home, in the evening at twilight, our gait kept pace with the cadence of his verses, sonorous as the blasts of a trumpet. . . .

'Victor Hugo's dramas haunted us, like magnificent visions. When we came out of classes with our memories frozen by the classical tirades which we had to learn by heart, we experienced an orgy replete with thrills and ecstasy when we warmed ourselves by memorizing scenes from *Hernani* and *Ruy Blas*. How often, after a long swim, the two or three of us performed whole acts on the bank of the little river!

'Then, one morning one of us brought a volume of Musset. . . . Reading Musset was for us the awakening of our own heart. We trembled. . . . Our cult of Victor Hugo received a terrible blow; little by little we felt ourselves grow chilled, and his verses escaped our memories. . . . Alfred de Musset alone reigned in our game-bags. . . . He became our religion. Over and above his laughter and school-boy buffoonery, his tears won us over; and he only became completely our poet when we wept on reading him.'

Those were strange hunting parties, indeed. Paul Alexis, another schoolmate, gives this description of the three friends' expeditions: 'At three in the morning, the first to awaken threw pebbles at the shutters of the others. They left immediately, their provisions having been packed in their game-bags the previous day. By sunrise they had already walked several kilometres. About nine o'clock when the sun became hot, they sat in the shade of a wooded ravine. And lunch was cooked in the open air. Baille had lighted a fire of dead wood in front of which a leg of mutton seasoned with garlic hung from a string, which Zola flipped from time to time. Cézanne prepared the salad in a damp napkin. Then they took a nap. Then they set off again, their guns on their shoulders for a great hunt, perhaps to shoot a snipe. A league farther on, they put down their guns and sat under a tree, taking a book out of the game-bag. . . .'

'Sometimes,' Zola remembered later, 'when an inquisitive bird perched at a suitable distance, we thought ourselves obliged to take a shot at it; fortunately we were wretched shots and almost always the bird shook its feathers and flew away. This barely interrupted the one of us who was reading aloud, perhaps for the twentieth time, *Rolla* or *Les Nuits!* I have never had any other conception of the hunt. . . .'

Back in town the irrepressible interests of the three friends did not lag. During the Crimean War, when numerous regiments passed through Aix on their way to the Orient, the 'inseparables' rushed on to the Cours Mirabeau, the main avenue of the town, as early as four o'clock in the morning to watch the departure of the troops and accompanied the soldiers for a little way on the road to Marseilles.

Their excursions did not make them neglect their studies, however. Cézanne was a diligent student, especially interested in dead languages. For two sous he would turn out a hundred lines of Latin, and during his school years he frequently won prizes for calculus, Greek and Latin, science, and history. Several times he won the prize for general excellence, but only once, in 1854, did he receive an award in painting here. In the same year, however, he attended Professor Gibert's classes at the free drawing academy, where he won second prize. Zola distinguished himself more easily in drawing and won a prize for it each year.

In February 1858 the life of the friends together, with its excursions, painting, music, and poetry, was suddenly interrupted by Zola's departure for Paris to join his mother, who had been forced to go there for financial reasons. Although Zola regretted leaving Aix, he felt a sense of adventure in going to Paris and thought his new life would hold promise for the future. Both Cézanne and Baille promised to come to Paris as soon as their examinations were over, and to resume their life together. Deep in their hearts the two friends who remained in Aix envied Zola, who left 'to find the reward and the lover which God keeps for us at twenty'.

II

FIRST CORRESPONDENCE

WITH ZOLA

1858 – 1859

THEIR letters exchanged after Zola's departure show how much Cézanne and Zola suffered by their separation. Not being sociable, neither succeeded in making new friends and as a result they missed each other more keenly than might otherwise have been the case. In one of his very first letters, Cézanne complains to Zola: 'Since you left Aix, my dear friend, a deep melancholy weighs upon me; I do not lie about this—I no longer recognize myself; I am heavy, stupid, and slow'.

Cézanne's letters contain long poems, short bits of rhyme, Latin verses, an occasional rebus, drawings, and watercolours, as well as detailed and often ironical accounts of school and local events, of his examinations, studies, and personal adventures. The hand-writing is full of verve, there is little space between the lines, many words are scratched out, and the margins are filled with comments which often have no bearing on the rest of the letter. The tone of these letters is not always the same. Sometimes they are full of vitality, sometimes frivolous, sometimes melancholy, and only seldom completely serious. As one of his friends remarked, Paul wrote letters only when he felt depressed. Thus a gay letter ends resignedly: 'When something new occurs, I will write you. Until now a habitual and regular calm envelops our dull city in its sullen wings'.

There is no evidence in his letters that Cézanne felt attracted at that time either to painting or to writing. Only once, in June 1859, did he say that he dreamed of pictures and of a studio in Paris; in general he did not even employ the words 'painting' and 'poetry', and if he painted and wrote verse it was more or less as a pastime. 'Are you swimming?' Zola asked him in one of his letters. 'Are you going on sprees? Are you painting? Are you playing the horn? Are you writing poetry? In sum, what are you doing?' In truth, Cézanne seems to have been doing nothing that was purposeful.

The poems Cézanne sent Zola nearly always contained some mocking lines, even if only at the end. Although Zola admired his friend's verses and found his soul 'tenderly poetic', Cézanne refused to take his literary production seriously and it is apparent that he wrote verse only to please himself and Zola. Convinced of Cézanne's talent, Zola tried to make him stop being a dilettante and to guide him toward serious artistic effort:

'You sing for the sake of singing, and carelessly use the strangest expressions, the most facetious locutions of Provence. Far be it from me to call this a crime; on the contrary, it pleases me, especially in our letters. You write for me and I thank you for it; but the herd, my dear old friend, is more demanding; it does not suffice to express, it is necessary to express well. . . . I have asked myself what this good Cézanne lacks for becoming a great poet. Purity? He has good ideas; his form is vigorous and original, but what spoils it and the whole thing are the provincialisms, the solecisms, etc. . . . Yes, old man, you are more of a poet than I. My verse may be purer than yours, but yours is certainly more poetical, more true; you write with the heart; I, with the mind. . . .'

But Cézanne was not moved by Zola's advice, or concerned with the demands of the herd. That which he lacked 'for becoming a great poet' was chiefly the will to become one. The sheer pleasure of making rhymes and giving play to his ironical wit inspired his pen and his letters in verse, but these were unimportant to his ambitions.

A large part of the friends' correspondence deals with love, and though Zola's opinions appear to be based on numerous experiences, he nevertheless admits: 'I have never loved except in dreams, and I have never been loved, even in dreams.' Cézanne's life in this respect was no doubt similar, as can be seen in one of his first letters to Zola: 'Your letter not only gave me pleasure but even a feeling of well-being. A certain inner sadness fills me and, by God, I do nothing but dream of the woman I spoke to you about. I know not who she is; sometimes I see her passing in the street on my way to the monotonous seminary. I have reached the stage of heaving sighs, but sighs that do not betray themselves externally—they are mental sighs.'

Later Cézanne wrote his friend: 'The love known to Michelet, pure, noble love, may exist, but you must admit that it is very rare'. And Zola, far from discouraging him in this platonic love, advised him to persevere. He even wrote him: 'I am glad to know you, you who do not belong to our century, you who would invent love were it not a very old invention'.

In one of his letters to Zola, Cézanne speaks at length about a new love as enthusiastic as it was fleeting:

'I felt a passionate love for a certain Justine who is really *very fine*;* but as I have not the honour to be *of a great beautiful*,* she

*These expressions appear in the text in English.

7

always turned her head away from me. When I cast my peepers in her direction, she dropped her eyes and blushed. And I thought I detected that when we were in the same street she made as if it were a half-turn and dodged away without looking backwards. I am not happy *quanto a della donna* [sic] and to think that I run the risk of meeting her three or four times a day! And better still, dear fellow: one fine day a young man accosted me—Seymard, whom you know. 'My dear friend,' he said, taking my hand, and then hanging himself on my arm and continuing to walk toward the Rue d'Italie, 'I am about to show you a sweet little thing whom I love and who loves me!'

'I confess that instantly a cloud seemed to pass before my eyes. I had, so to speak, a presentiment that fortune was not going to smile at me, and I was not mistaken, for midday having just struck, Justine emerged from the dressmaker's shop where she works and Seymard, as soon as we caught sight of her, said to me, "Here she is". At this point I saw nothing more, my head was spinning, but Seymard dragging me along with him, I brushed against the little one's frock. . . .

'Since then I have seen her nearly every day and often Seymard has been following her. . . . Ah! what dreams I have not built up, the maddest ever, but you see, things are like that. I said to myself, if she did not detest me, we should go to Paris together and there I should become an artist, we should be happy. I dreamed of pictures, a studio on the fourth floor, you with me—how we should have laughed! I did not ask to be rich; you know how I am—with a few hundred francs I thought we could live contentedly. By God, it was really a great dream, and now I, who am lazy, am happy only when I have drunk; I can hardly go on, I am an inert body, good for nothing.

'My word, old man, your cigars are excellent! I am smoking one while writing you. They taste of caramel and barley sugar. But oh! look, look, here she is, she, how she glides and sways. Yes, it is my little one; how she laughs at me; she floats on the clouds of smoke; there, there, she rises, she descends, she frolics, she turns over, but she is laughing at me. O Justine, at least tell me that you do not hate me. She laughs. Cruel one, you enjoy making me suffer. Justine, listen to me! But she is disappearing, ascending, ascending, ever ascending until at last she fades away. The cigar drops from my mouth, whereupon I fall asleep. For a moment I thought I was going mad, but thanks to your cigar my mind is reasserting itself. Another ten days and I shall think of her no longer, or else I shall see her only on the horizon of the past as a shadow of which I dreamed.'

* * *

Zola went to Aix in the summer of 1858 to spend his vacation with Cézanne and Baille, and despite Cézanne's project of writing a five-act drama to be entitled *Henry VIII of England*, no work of any kind was undertaken because their time was consumed by walks and talks. Once again they read, they spent hours bathing and lying in the sand, 'wrestling, throwing stones at posts, catching frogs in their hands'. They passed entire days on the banks of the Arc, not far from the 'Jas de Bouffan', an estate rented by Cézanne's father.

After Zola's return to Paris, Cézanne and Baille prepared for their baccalaureate examinations, which worried Cézanne a great deal. Baille had already passed his examinations when Cézanne, who had failed in July, passed his on 12 November 1858, with the *mention* 'fair'.

Complying with his father's wishes, Cézanne now registered as a student at the law school of the University of Aix; but his studies did not appeal to him at all; bitter references to this subject are found in his letters. He devoted a minimum of time to his law study and used his leisure to draw and to write poetry as before. Painting attracted him increasingly and he began to feel vaguely that it was his real vocation. He was not yet concerned about the future and continued to have fantastic dreams and to compose interminable poems on historical or eerie themes.

In Paris, Zola, too, continued to write verse. He began the outline of *La Chaîne des Etres* in three cantos: Past, Present, Future. He wrote long poems, *L'Aérienne, Paolo*, etc. Whereas Cézanne was not at all concerned with form, Zola cultivated a gentle and flowery language, but the result was what de Maupassant later tactfully described as 'poetry without definite character'.

When Zola read his verses to his classmates in Paris, he received small praise. This roused Cézanne's ire, and he wrote his friend: 'I am hurling this apostrophe, the terms of which are all too feeble to characterize these boasting, abortive, literary penguins, these asthmatic mockers of your honest rhymes. Pass on my compliment to them if you think it wise and add that if they have anything to say, I am here ready for them all as long as they are ready, waiting to box the first who comes within striking distance of my fist.'

On his return to Aix in July 1859, Zola needed a rest after the strain of his baccalaureate examinations; he had passed the written ones but failed in the orals in German, history, and literature. He, who had suffered in Paris from his isolation, was happy to return even though he found Cézanne complaining about his law studies. Forgetting all their troubles, they went on outings with Baille and his young brother. They went to the dam, to Sainte-Victoire, whose grey wall rises above the village of Le Tholonet, and to the Pilon du Roi, a peak near the small town of Gardanne. Cézanne brought his paint-box and at Les Infernets, between the dam and Sainte-

Victoire, his friends, rigged out in rags, posed for the picture of 'The Brigands', which was retouched by Cézanne twenty times. The painter was in contagiously gay mood and would recite verses by Alfred de Musset.

The relationship between the friends had somewhat changed, however. Zola, though the youngest, had had a considerably harder experience of life and he was perforce the most earnest of the three. On his return to Paris after his stay in Aix, his life continued to be not only lonely, but also poor. Already he was beginning to look for a way to earn his living. In the meantime, he was again studying for his examinations, but when the time came he even failed in his written ones and in discouragement he gave up trying for his baccalaureate. He was filled with the desire to work and to become independent so that he might devote himself entirely to literature. Several years later when he wrote his first novel, *La Confession de Claude*, he recalled this last summer spent with his friends in Provence:

'Brothers, do you remember the days when life was for us a dream? We had friendship, we dreamed of love and glory. . . . The three of us let our lips say what our hearts felt and, naïvely, we loved queens, we crowned ourselves with laurels. You told me your dreams, I told you mine. Then we deigned to touch earth again. I told you about my pattern of life, devoted to work and struggle, and about my great courage. With a sense of the richness of my soul I liked the idea of poverty. Like me, you climbed the staircase to the attics; you hoped to nourish yourself on great thoughts. Because of your ignorance of reality, you seemed to believe that the artist, in his sleepless nights, earns the morrow's bread.'

III

CÉZANNE DREAMS OF PAINTING

1860

IN 1859 Cézanne's father bought the 'Jas de Bouffan', thus following the custom set by so many of the rich bourgeois citizens of Aix
who had a country seat where they passed the summer as well as a
house in town. The 'Jas de Bouffan', about two kilometres west of
Aix, is a thirty-seven-acre estate with a farm and a large, beautifully
proportioned eighteenth-century manor. The wide façade, with
tall and regular windows, overlooks a big garden set with ancient
trees. It was originally the residence of the Governor of Provence,
but when Cézanne's father bought it, for 90,000 francs, the house
was in a deplorable state. A large salon on the ground floor and
several rooms in the upper storeys were in such a dilapidated
condition that they were uninhabitable. They were locked up, and
at first nothing was restored.

The purchase of this property was generally considered ostenta-
tious, 'the whim of a parvenu'. This was not a surprising reaction
in the natives of Aix; they had several reasons for prejudice. One
must not forget that the banker, Louis-Auguste Cézanne, was not
a native of Aix; he had come there in 1825 at the age of thirty. He
had started as a dealer and exporter of hats, for the felt industry was
flourishing in Aix at that time. On 29 January 1844, he had married
Anne-Elisabeth-Honorine Aubert, one of his employees, but by her
he had already had a son, Paul, born 19 January, 1839, and a
daughter, Marie, two years younger. Ten years after their marriage
another daughter, Rose, was born. The humble beginnings of the
elder Cézanne, his marriage to a working girl, and the illegitimacy
of his first two children were reason enough for society in Aix to
keep him at a distance. Because these people did not associate with
him, they did not know him. Some thought of him as a sort of Père
Grandet: authoritarian, shrewd, and stingy. Others considered him,
on the contrary, a man of great humanity. An inveterate republican,
he took an interest in public affairs, and after the fall of Louis-
Philippe in 1848 had tried for election to the municipal council of
Aix, as twenty-second on a list of twenty-seven candidates, advocat-
ing a 'fusion of classes and parties'. He obtained only a very few
votes, however, and was defeated.

The kind of ostracism to which the Cézanne family was subjected left its mark on Paul Cézanne, who was proud and sensitive, and accentuated his introspective tendencies. Later, when he reached manhood, Cézanne avoided society and found it very difficult to make friends.

The 'Jas de Bouffan' was to play a great part in the life of Paul Cézanne. Nowhere else did he work as often. In a great many of his paintings one can recognize the big house, the two rows of chestnuts, the square pool with its stone dolphin and lions, the farm, and the low walls surrounding the property. Yet in his letters to Zola, written in the year the 'Jas' was acquired by his father, Cézanne makes no allusion to the place.

Although Cézanne did not discuss painting in his letters, it is apparent from those written by Zola after December 1859 that he had decided to become a painter. The desire to devote his life to art appears to have developed slowly, however, and he had not yet obtained the consent of his father, who urged him to 'think of the future, for one dies with genius but one eats with money'.

At that time Cézanne often worked at the Aix museum. Here he copied a picture by Dubufe, 'The Prisoner of Chillon', and 'The Kiss of the Muse', by Frillie, two dull, academic works without any artistic interest. The latter copy was his mother's favourite picture and hung in her room; she always took it with her when the family moved between town and country. About this time Cézanne also painted a large mural in the salon of the 'Jas de Bouffan', a fishing scene at sunset.

To satisfy his father, Cézanne continued his studies, but he hated law. His desire to paint grew and made him dream of going to Paris and dedicating himself to art. Meanwhile he enrolled at the free drawing academy of Aix for the school year November 1858 to August 1859. He enrolled again in November 1859 and 1860, and thus copied plaster casts or studied the living model from 1858 to 1861. In the academy he met Numa Coste, Chaillan, Joseph Huot, Honoré Gibert, son of the drawing master and curator of the museum, as well as Villevieille, Truphème, Philippe Solari, and many others.

Doubtless Zola had encouraged him during his visits to Aix; in any case, Cézanne continued trying to persuade his father to let him take up painting as a career. Little by little he succeeded, and he was able to inform Zola in February 1860 that his father was no longer opposed to his departure but wished first to consult Monsieur Gibert, his drawing master. Zola, delighted, immediately outlined a budget, telling Cézanne that one hundred twenty-five francs a month would be just adequate for his expenses in Paris and adding that it would be a good way for his friend to learn resourcefulness and the value of money. He also sent Cézanne a schedule to be followed during his stay in Paris: 'From six to eleven you will go to a studio to paint from the living model; then you will lunch; then, from noon to four you will copy, either at the Louvre or the Luxembourg . . . which will make nine hours of work'.

But Cézanne's trip kept being postponed. First his little sister fell ill; then his drawing teacher advised him to remain in Aix to study from models or plaster casts. As Zola had predicted, 'Master Gibert regretfully sees a pupil escape him'. Cézanne's father was only too glad to follow the advice of the teacher and for the moment there was no longer any question of the trip to Paris. Zola wrote to his disappointed friend: 'You must satisfy your father by studying the law as diligently as possible. But you must also work tenaciously at your drawing'.

Cézanne seemed to yield to this reasoning, and Zola answered one of his letters in these words: 'You are right not to complain about your luck: because, after all, as you say, with two loves, the love of woman and the love of the beautiful, it would be a mistake to despair. . . .' But Zola added: 'One sentence in your letter made a bad impression on me. It was this: "Painting which I love, even though I am not successful, etc., etc." You, not to be successful, I think you deceive yourself! I have already told you: in the artist there are two men, the poet and the workman. One is born a poet, one becomes a workman. And you who have the spark, who possess what cannot be acquired, you complain when all you need to succeed is to exercise your fingers, to become a workman!'

A few days later, Cézanne referred to the subject again: 'When I have finished my law, perhaps I shall be free to do what I think best; perhaps then I can join you'. To this Zola replied: 'Be firm without being disrespectful. Realize that it is your future which is being decided and that all your happiness depends on it'.

However, Cézanne's mood of discouragement and sadness grew to such an extent that he even considered remaining in Aix to study law and giving up all his dreams. He no longer dared ask his father to let him go to Paris, for he had doubts about his own talent and no longer felt himself possessed by the desire to paint. Once again Zola tried to encourage him:

'In your last letter you seem to be depressed; you even speak of throwing your brushes away. You bewail your solitude. You are bored. Isn't this the sickness of all of us, this terrible boredom? Is this not the evil of our century? And isn't discouragement a result of this despondency which chokes us? As you say, if I were with you, I would try to console you, to encourage you. . . Regain your courage; take up your brushes again, and let your imagination wander freely. I have faith in you, and if I push you toward misfortune, may this misfortune fall back on my own head. Courage, above all, and before you embark on this, consider carefully the thorns you may find in your path.'

In face of the inertia with which Cézanne met his advice, Zola, so gentle and patient with his friend until now, finally got angry. An end must be made to all these evasions; Cézanne must get the permission to go to Paris and there become an artist. And Zola demands:

'Is painting only a whim which took possession of you when you were bored one fine day? Is it only a pastime, a subject of conversation, a pretext for not working at law? If this is the case, then I understand your conduct; you are right not to force the issue and make more trouble with your family. But if painting is your vocation—and that is how I have always envisaged it—if you feel capable of achieving something after having worked well at it, then you are an enigma to me, a sphinx, someone indescribably self-contradictory and obscure. One of two things is true: either you do not want to, and you are realizing your purpose admirably; or you do want to, and in that case I don't understand it at all. Sometimes your letters give me a lot of hope, sometimes they take even more away, like the last one in which you almost seem to say farewell to your dreams which you could so well convert into reality. In this letter occurs this sentence which I have tried in vain to understand: "I am going to talk without saying anything, for my behaviour contradicts my words". I have constructed many hypotheses on the meaning of these words, but none satisfies me. What, then, is your behaviour? That of a lazy person, no doubt; but what is surprising about that? You are forced to do work which is distasteful to you and you want to ask your father to let you come to Paris to become an artist; I see no contradiction between this request and your actions. You neglect the law, you go to the museum, painting is the only work you find acceptable; there I find an excellent agreement between your wishes and your actions. Do you want me to tell you? —but be sure not to get angry—you are lacking in character; you dread fatigue of any kind, in thought as well as in action; your main principle is to let things take their course and to leave yourself at the mercy of time and chance. . . . I have thought it my duty to repeat here for the last time what I have often told you: my capacity as your friend excuses my frankness. In many respects, our characters are similar; but by Jesus, if I were in your place, I would want to have the answer, to risk all to gain all, and not to float vaguely between two such different futures, the studio and the Bar. I am sorry for you, because you must suffer from this uncertainty, and this would be for me another incentive to tear the veil. One thing or the other, really be a lawyer, or else really be an artist, but do not remain a creature without a name, wearing a toga dirtied by paint.'

Yet nothing could rouse Cézanne from his apathy, and Zola renewed the attack: 'If you keep silent, how do you expect to progress and reach a conclusion? It is substantially impossible. And note that it is not the one who makes the most noise who is right; speak softly and wisely, but by the horns, the feet, the tail, and the navel of the Devil, speak, go ahead and speak! . . .'

*   *   *

Zola's letters to Cézanne in 1860 were prompted not only by his interest in his friend but also by his eagerness to be with him again, for Zola did not like Paris and he missed his comrades. Unfortunately, Zola was unable to visit Aix during either the summer or the autumn, though there were so many things he wanted to see: 'Paul's panels and Baille's moustache'. Zola's life in Paris was hard. After working on the docks as a clerk for several weeks and earning only sixty francs a month, he had enough of it. Thus he remained without money or hope. Nevertheless he thought of nothing but literature and even in his dreams he saw Cézanne's name joined with his. 'I had a dream the other day,' he wrote Paul. 'I had written a beautiful book, a wonderful book, which you had illustrated with beautiful, wonderful pictures. Both our names shone in letters of gold on the first page and, inseparable in this fraternity of genius, passed on to posterity.'

Zola was desperate at his increasing isolation in Paris, the more so as Cézanne's letters were fewer than before. Their content often worried Zola, who was also upset by what Baille wrote him. A certain coolness seemed to have developed between Cézanne and Baille. The latter, who was studying in Marseilles, complained to Zola of an inhospitable reception at the 'Jas de Bouffan', and when Zola reproached Cézanne for this, he received this reply: 'You fear lest our friendship for Baille weaken. Oh, no, for he is a nice fellow, by Jove; but you well know that with my character I am not too aware of what I do and so if I did him wrong, well then, he should forgive it.'

Cézanne suggested a truth, here; because he and Zola were both artists, they were bound by an affinity which did not tie them to Baille. Memories of their boyhood spent together and a real friendship united all three, but Baille was not of the same breed and this became increasingly apparent. As Zola wrote Cézanne: 'He is not like us, his skull is not cast in the same mould; he has many qualities we lack, and many faults also. . . . What difference does it make to us, his friends? Does it not suffice that we have judged him to be a good fellow, superior to the crowd, or at least more able to understand our heart and mind?'

Nevertheless, from 1860 on, a lack of understanding is apparent in their correspondence. The tact Zola employed in writing Cézanne is missing in his relations with Baille, and when Baille reproached him for 'not facing reality courageously, of not making a position for himself', Zola replied: 'The word "position" smacks of the rich grocer in a way which gets on my nerves.' Baille's answer expressed his contempt for 'crazy' poets and their 'false glory', and concluded by saying that he would 'not be as stupid as they and, for the sake of applause, die in an attic'.

Zola and Baille ended by tacitly avoiding any personal references in their letters and discussed only abstract subjects such as the Ideal or Reality, Shakespeare, George Sand, etc. Zola expounds his ideas in letters which are essentially literary and it is with nostalgia that he remembers their last vacation in Aix: 'Only a year has passed and yet how many changes have taken place in our characters, in our thoughts! Our minds are perhaps on a higher level now and our horizons wider, but we have lost our joyous carefree spirit, we want to solve the problems of life and with this seeking begin our doubts and tears.'

*   *   *

Little by little Cézanne had given up his law studies to devote himself to painting. He still sketched at the drawing academy and described the model there as either taking a pose in the shape of an X or holding her belly. Zola reassured him on the subject of Parisian models: 'The description of your model amused me very much—Chaillan claims that here the models are adequate without, however, being in their first youth. One sketches them in the daytime and caresses them at night (the word caress is a little weak). As to the fig leaf, it is unknown in the studios.'

Cézanne not only worked in Professor Gibert's classes but also outdoors, even in winter, when he would sit on the frozen ground without heeding the cold. Zola approved with all his heart: 'This news delighted me because such steadfastness denotes your love for the arts and the tenacity with which you apply yourself to your work.'

Work, indeed, had given Cézanne courage and confidence and he again tried to get his father's consent to go away. Madame Cézanne took her son's part, saying: 'He is named Paul, like Rubens and Veronese, and is no doubt predestined to paint.' But her husband preferred to give their son only the sage advice he enjoyed dispensing: 'Don't get too excited, take your time and act with caution!' or 'Whenever you go out, know where you are going', etc.

Louis-Auguste Cézanne was sure that Zola was responsible for his son's 'unhealthy' ideas and held this against him. When Baille informed Zola of this, Zola replied:

'I felt that I had an opponent, almost an enemy, in Paul's family; our different ways of looking at things, of understanding life, made me sense how little sympathy M. Cézanne must have for me. . . . This seems to me to be the question: M. Cézanne has seen his son disrupt the plans he made for him. The future banker finds himself to be a painter and, feeling an eagle's wings on his back, wants to leave the nest. Surprised at this metamorphosis and this desire for liberty, M. Cézanne cannot understand that it is possible to prefer painting to the bank and the air of the sky to his dusty office, so M. Cézanne has decided to solve the riddle. He is not able to see that it was thus because God intended it to be, because God, having created him a banker, created his son a painter. But having examined the question thoroughly, he finally understands that I am responsible for it, that it is I who made Paul what he is today, that it is I who has robbed the bank of its dearest hope. The words "bad company" were no doubt used, and that is how Emile Zola, man of letters, became an intriguer, a false friend, and I don't know what else. It is all the more sad because it is ridiculous. Fortunately Paul has doubtless kept my letters: it is evident from them what my advice was and whether I ever sent him on the wrong path. On the contrary, I repeatedly pointed out to him all the disadvantages of his trip to Paris and especially urged him to handle his father with care.

'I cannot be blamed for the influence of these words on Paul's career. Without wishing to, I excited his love for the arts; no doubt I only developed the latent germs, a result which any other external cause could have produced.'

At last Cézanne's father ended by giving in, for his home life had become unbearable. Paul stayed away from home as much as possible and did not talk at all when he was there. M. Cézanne finally put an end to this unpleasant state of affairs and gave his son permission to leave for Paris, but he felt sure that Paul would be bored in Paris once he had had his way and would hurry back to Aix to resume his studies or to go into the bank.

This time Paul Cézanne actually left Aix, and so suddenly that he did not even have time to notify Zola. Towards the end of April 1861, he took the train for Paris with his father and his sister Marie, who both returned to Aix after helping Paul find suitable lodgings. Cézanne was at last in Paris, free to realize his dreams.

IV

CÉZANNE IN PARIS

AND HIS RETURN TO AIX

1861 – 1862

CÉZANNE's first stay in Paris was one of the most unhappy periods of his life. Barely twenty-two, he had come there full of hope and with a great desire to work. Shortly after Cézanne's arrival, Zola informed Baille that Cézanne was working very hard and added rather regretfully that they seldom saw each other. Yet the meeting of the two friends had been extremely cordial. It was even apparent from the way in which Cézanne's father greeted Zola that he no longer felt any animosity towards him. After M. Cézanne's departure, Zola showed Paul the city and took him to admire the paintings of Ary Scheffer, of which he was especially fond, as well as the fountain of Jean Goujon, another of his enthusiasms. Together they visited art exhibitions and made plans for Sunday excursions to the outskirts of Paris—plans which they were unable to realize for financial reasons. Paul received from his father a monthly allowance of one hundred twenty-five francs and presumably his expenses conformed to those outlined in a budget made by Zola. Cézanne's room, which cost twenty francs, and his meals (twenty-seven francs for lunch and thirty-three for dinner) consumed more than half his monthly allowance. In addition he needed ten francs for the studio where he sketched from life and the same amount for all his supplies. The remaining twenty-five francs had to pay for laundry, tobacco, and miscellaneous expenses.

As for Zola, he had not found a job since leaving the docks and he spent the whole year of 1861 without work, without money, with no foreseeable future, doing nothing. Cézanne had found him quite depressed.

In Cézanne's case, his father's predictions were coming true, one after the other. He had hardly been in Paris a month when he wrote to his friend Joseph Huot:

'I do not wish to write elegies in these few lines, but yet must admit I am none too cheerful. I fritter away my life on all sides. The Atelier Suisse keeps me busy from six in the morning until eleven. I have some sort of a meal for fifteen sous; it is not very grand, but what can you expect? And I am not dying of hunger.

'I thought that by leaving Aix I should leave behind the boredom that pursued me. Actually I have done nothing but change my abode, and the boredom has followed me. I have left my parents behind and my friends and some of my habits, that is all. And yet to think that I roam about almost the whole day. I have seen—it is naïve to say this—the Louvre and the Luxembourg and Versailles. You know them, the boring things housed in these admirable monuments: it is astounding, startling, overwhelming. . . . Don't think that I am becoming Parisian. . . .

'I have also seen the Salon. For a young heart, for a child being born to art who says what he thinks, I believe that this is what is really best, because there all tastes, all styles, meet and clash. I could give you some beautiful descriptions and put you to sleep. Be grateful to me for sparing you.'

Despite his admiration for the masters of official art, in spite of his walks, his frequent visits to the Louvre, and the hours spent with Emile Zola, the boredom which 'pursued' Cézanne increased and he was becoming disgusted with Paris, with his friends, and, what was more serious, with his own work. He spoke of returning to Aix and of becoming a clerk in a business. Exasperated by this unhappy result of so many years of effort and so many letters, Zola wrote to Baille on 10 June:

'I rarely see Cézanne. . . . In the mornings he goes to the Atelier Suisse while I stay in my room and write. . . . He then spends the rest of the day sketching at Villevieille's. Then he eats supper, goes to bed early, and I don't see him. Is that what I had hoped for? . . . Paul is still the same fine and strange fellow I knew at school. As evidence that he loses none of his originality, I need only tell you that no sooner had he arrived here than he spoke of returning to Aix. To have fought for his trip for three years and now not to give a straw for it! Confronted with such a character and such impulsive and unreasonable changes of behaviour, I admit that I keep silent and suppress my logic. Proving something to Cézanne would be like trying to persuade the towers of Notre Dame to dance a quadrille. He might say yes, but he would not budge an inch. And note that age has developed his obstinacy without giving him rational grounds for it. He is all of a piece, stiff and hard. Nothing bends him, nothing can force him to make a concession. He does not even want to discuss what he thinks; he abhors discussion, because to talk is tiring, and also because it would be necessary to change his opinion if his adversary were right. There he is, thrown into the middle of life, bringing with him certain ideas, unwilling to change them except on his own judgment, nevertheless the nicest fellow in the world, always agreeing with you, result of his aversion to argument. . . . If, by chance, he advances a contrary opinion and you dispute it, he flies into a rage without wishing to examine, screams that you know nothing about the subject, and jumps to something else. Go ahead and argue—what am I saying?—simply converse with a fellow of this sort and you will not gain an inch of ground but you will have observed a most unusual character. I had hoped that age would make some changes in him. But I find him the same as I left him. My plan of conduct is therefore very simple: never to check his whims; to give him at most very indirect advice; to put myself at the mercy of his good nature as regards the continuation of our friendship, and never to force his hand to shake mine; in a word, to efface myself completely, always receiving him gaily, seeking him out without importunity, and permitting him to determine the degree of intimacy which he desires to have between us. Perhaps my way of speaking surprises you, but it is logical. To me Paul is always a good-hearted friend who knows how to understand and appreciate me. Only, since everyone has his own particular nature, out of wisdom I must conform to his moods if I do not wish to put his friendship to flight. In order to keep your friendship, I must use reason; with him, it would cause everything to be lost. Do not believe that there is any cloud between us; we are very close and everything I have just said is due rather unfortunately to chance circumstances which separate us more than I might wish.'

Cézanne's queer moods reacted on his friend, and the tone of Zola's letters followed Cézanne's mental state. Thus, only a few days after his letter of 10 June, Zola again writes to Baille, who was then planning to join them:

'I attempted to judge him and despite my good faith, I regret having drawn a conclusion which is not, after all, the right one. No sooner had he arrived from Marcoussis than Paul came to see me and was more affectionate than ever. Since then we spend six hours a day together. His little room is our meeting place, and there he paints my portrait while I read or we chat together and then, when we have had enough of work, we usually go to smoke a pipe in the Luxembourg gardens. Our conversations touch on all subjects, especially painting, and on our memories of the past. As for the future, we skim over it with a word in passing either to express a desire for our complete reunion or to pose ourselves the terrible question of success. . . .

'I should like to give you still more details. Cézanne has many fits of discouragement; despite the somewhat affected scorn with which he speaks of fame, I see that he would like to gain it. When he does badly he speaks of nothing less than of returning to Aix and of becoming a clerk in a business firm. Then I have to give him long lectures to convince him of the folly of returning there; he readily agrees and goes back to work. Nevertheless, this idea consumes him; twice he has been on the verge of departure; I fear that he may escape me any moment. If you write him, try to speak to him in the most glowing terms of our forthcoming reunion; it is the only means of holding him.

'To sum up all this, I must say that, notwithstanding its monotony, the life we are leading is not dull; work prevents us from yawning; and the exchange of our memories gilds everything with a ray of sunshine.

'Come, and we shall be still less bored.'

Zola had to exert his ingenuity to find ways of keeping his friend in Paris. One day he caught Cézanne preparing to leave, his trunks already packed, and suggested sitting for a portrait as a means of delaying him. 'He accepted this idea joyfully,' Zola wrote to Baille, 'and this time there was no longer any question of returning.' But the letter continues thus, speaking of this 'damn portrait which was to detain him in Paris':

'Having begun it twice, still dissatisfied with himself, Paul wanted to finish it and asked me for a final sitting for yesterday morning. Yesterday, then, I went to his place; when I enter I see the trunk open and the drawers half empty; Paul, with a gloomy face, is piling objects into the trunk in disorder. Then he tells me quietly:

' "I am leaving tomorrow."

' "And my portrait?" I ask him.

' "Your portrait," he replies, "I have just smashed. I wanted to retouch it this morning and as it was getting worse and worse, I destroyed it; and I am leaving."

'I still refrained from comment. We went to lunch together and parted only that evening. In the course of the day he became more reasonable and at last, when he left me, he promised to remain. But that is only a stop-gap; if he does not leave this week he will go away next week; you may expect to see him leave any day. I even think he would do well to do so. Paul may have the genius of a great painter, but he will never have the genius to become one. The least obstacle makes him despair. I repeat that he should go if he wishes to avoid a lot of worry.'

*　　*　　*

As one can see from Zola's letter, Cézanne did not work during the sittings exclusively but even more after the model had left. While the model was there he studied colour and expression; only from time to time did he touch the canvas. Once the model had left, however, Cézanne really began to work, and painted until another sitting became necessary. Apparently the presence of a living person disturbed him and hindered him, up to a point, from working during the sittings. Indeed, in his still lifes and landscapes he adopted an entirely different approach, never painting without observing his subject.

Of the various portraits which Cézanne painted of Zola at this period only one has been preserved (Pl. 18). It is a sketch showing Zola in profile; a study in chiaroscuro. The forehead, which is strongly lighted, detaches itself from the dark background, while the black beard stands out against the whiteness of the collar. The effect is somewhat harsh.

A self portrait which dates from this period is more interesting than the sketch of Zola, for it reveals Cézanne's mental state. It is fairly certain that Cézanne painted the portrait from a photograph, but he managed to change the general effect while preserving the details (Pls. 1, 2). By lengthening his chin and making his cheeks more prominent, by accentuating his eyebrows and completely changing the expression of his eyes, Cézanne gave to the gentle and quiet young man of the photograph a menacing face with a sharp and piercing expression. This look animates strangely the lifeless image which he used as a model. The rather commonplace subject of the photograph seemed a stranger to Cézanne, who was a prey to perpetual doubts, disillusioned by everything and everybody, sad and in a state of revolt against others as well as himself. In this portrait he appears as he visualized himself. It is the portrait of a man who paid for each hour of hope with days of despair.

Cézanne was less dissatisfied with Paris than with himself and possibly also with Zola. The complete harmony which they so much hoped for and needed in order not to feel lonely had not been established between them. Zola was involved in his own projects, in the books he was planning to write, and felt bitterly disappointed in Cézanne. 'Does our friendship need the sun of Provence in order to exist joyously?' he later was to ask Cézanne. He made a great effort and even succeeded in obtaining Cézanne's promise to stay until the autumn. 'But is that his final decision?' he wrote to Baille. 'I am in hopes that he will not change his mind.'

Indeed Cézanne remained in Paris until September and only then left for Aix. The separation seems to have been cold; the two friends did not correspond for some time. Though Zola had known all along that after all his efforts Cézanne's victory could not be completed without new battles, he never had doubted that his friend would eventually be able to overcome his difficulties. When he had urged Cézanne to join him, he had certainly not expected that some day Paul would leave Paris with the decision to renounce painting to enter his father's bank.

But no sooner had Cézanne taken a job in his father's office than the demon of painting took possession of him again. Aversion to business was enough to make him forget his doubts; his need to paint once more became imperative. It was then that he wrote on the ledger of the Banque Cézanne & Cabassol this verse:

> *The banker Cézanne does not see without fear*
> *Behind his desk a painter appear.*

Cézanne's father was beginning to realize that he would never be able to make his son either his successor at the bank or a prominent lawyer. He again permitted Paul to follow his inclinations and Cézanne enrolled as usual with Coste, Huot, and Solari at the art school for the year 1861–2, thus rededicating himself to painting.

* * *

The correspondence of the two friends was renewed after a lapse of several weeks by a letter from Cézanne written at the beginning of 1862, to which Zola replied assuring Cézanne of his continued friendship despite the temporary coolness in their relationship during Cézanne's stay in Paris. By that time Zola was no longer alone in Paris. Baille had just arrived and had been admitted to the Ecole Polytechnique. They saw each other regularly every Sunday and Wednesday.

It seems that Zola spent the summer of 1862 with Baille and Cézanne in Aix and there worked on his first novel, *La Confession de Claude*. This strange and violent book is a typical work of a beginner and full of unassimilated romanticism. Zola wrote it in the form of a 'confession' for his two friends, to whom he dedicated the book. It was finished three years later and was published in October 1865.

Zola's productivity made Cézanne eager to join him again in Paris. Apprehensive because of his first failure there, he now submitted to Zola a programme to which he wished to conform in the future. Zola replied: 'I approve entirely of your idea of coming to Paris to work and of subsequently returning to Provence; I think it is a way to free oneself from the influence of the schools and to develop whatever originality one has.'

Cézanne expected to remain in Aix until the end of the year and then leave for Paris. He was engaged in painting a 'View of the Dam', the dam which bears today the name of the engineer François Zola. Cézanne had often gone there with Emile Zola to watch the work progress and to swim in the big rock-bordered lake. This was one of their favourite outings. They followed the Tholonet road which crosses the tiny river of the Torse and skirts the property of Chateau Noir, where Cézanne was to return to paint toward the end of his life. Then they crossed the Domaine

St Joseph on the so-called 'Colline des Pauvres', occupied at that time by the Jesuits, who offered them agreeable hospitality.

Zola having left, Cézanne became more intimate with Coste, several years younger than he. Together they attended the evening classes at the drawing academy, where Cézanne had painted a nude of the guardian of the dam, or they went to paint in the countryside.

Before leaving again for Paris, in November 1862, Cézanne probably had to promise his father to present himself to the Ecole des Beaux-Arts. His father believed that since his son was going to become a painter, it was best for him to study seriously in the official school.

V

THE SALON DES REFUSÉS

1863

As soon as Cézanne returned to Paris he began to work again at the Atelier Suisse on the Quai des Orfèvres. He went there 'as formerly . . . in the morning from eight to one and evenings from seven to ten'. This institute offered artists male and female models for a moderate monthly fee. Their work was not supervised here, but Cézanne had a friend, M. Chautard, who corrected his sketches. 'I work calmly and eat and sleep likewise,' he wrote Numa Coste.

Sundays were devoted to long excursions with Zola. 'We used to leave on the first Sunday train,' Zola wrote later, 'in order to be outside the fortifications by early morning. Paul carried an entire artist's equipment while I had only a book in my pocket.' On these excursions they would get out at Fontenay-aux-Roses and cut cross-country to the left of Robinson. Here they would walk through great fields of strawberries before reaching Aulnay, where the famous Loups valley begins. Once they got lost in the forest; Cézanne climbed a tree to try to find the way, but he only scratched his legs and saw nothing but the tree tops.

'One morning,' Zola later recalled, 'while wandering through the forest we came across a pond, far from any path. It was a pond filled with rushes and slimy water which we called "the green pond", not knowing its real name; I have since heard that it is called "the Chalot Pond". "The green pond" finally became the destination of all our walks—we felt for it the affection of a poet and a painter. We loved it dearly and spent our Sundays on the thin grass surrounding it. Paul had begun a sketch of it, the water in the foreground with big floating reeds, with the trees receding like the wings of a theatre, draping the curtains of their branches as in a chapel, with blue holes that disappeared in an eddy when the wind blew. The thin rays of the sun crossed the shadows like balls of gold and threw on the lawns shining quoits whose round discs travelled slowly. I remained there for hours without boredom, exchanging an occasional word with my companion, sometimes closing my eyelids and dreaming in the vague and rose-coloured light which bathed me. We camped there, we lunched, we dined, and only the twilight chased us away.'

In January 1863, Cézanne's father came to Paris, making the trip, which then took about thirty hours, more for business reasons than to see his son. He probably availed himself of this opportunity to remind Paul of his wish to see him admitted to the École des Beaux-Arts, but Cézanne was already contemptuous of official art and artists. He wrote in a letter to Numa Coste:

'About a month has gone by since Lombard returned to Paris. I heard not without regret that he attends the studio of Signol. This worthy gentleman instructs after a conventional pattern destined to lead to an exact copy of his own; it is very beautiful, but not admirable. To think that an intelligent young man had to come to Paris to lose himself. . . .

'I also like Félicien, who boards with Truphemus. The dear boy sees everything in relation to his illustrious friend and shades his opinions to match the latter's colours. According to him, Truphème surpasses Delacroix: he alone can produce colour; also, thanks to a certain letter, he goes to the Beaux-Arts. *Don't think that I envy him.*'

If Cézanne entered the competition for admission to the Ecole des Beaux-Arts, it must have been to satisfy his father. He was rejected.

At the Atelier Suisse, Cézanne had become acquainted with several young painters, including Antoine Guillemet, with whom he later worked in the outskirts of Paris and who was to visit him in Aix. He also met Armand Guillaumin and a Cuban painter, Francisco Oller. They introduced him to Camille Pissarro, who was not then working at the Atelier but who occasionally came to visit his friends there. As early as 1861, during Cézanne's first stay in Paris, Pissarro had noticed at the Atelier Suisse the 'strange Provencal' whose drawings from life (Pl. 3) were ridiculed by everyone. He was the first to recognize the personality of the young artist, and a firm friendship soon united them.

Camille Pissarro, ten years older than Cézanne, had already exhibited once at the Salon without arousing the slightest public interest. In 1863 his entry was rejected along with the works of many other painters, among them Claude Monet and Edouard Manet, whose 'Guitar Player' had obtained a certain success at the previous Salon. In fact, the jury was so severe this time that even the critics took the part of the painters and protested at the numerous exclusions. But it was to be Zola's mission, three years later, to attack the prejudices of the jury and for the first time reveal to the public the abuses involved in having artists as judges of other artists. He was to expose the bickering and jealousy between different groups who tried to hide their opportunism behind moral convictions. Zola was to explain how, from the time they entered the Ecole des Beaux-Arts, where they received general instruction, and the Ecole de Rome, where their training was perfected, the young artists were led to take success for granted. They became convinced that 'the State owes them everything, the lessons to teach them, the Salons to display their work, the medals and money to reward them'. According to Zola, this system was responsible for their pretensions and intolerance of anything which did not conform to their despotic concepts of art. But when the jury of 1863 showed itself to be even more severe than its predecessors, the indignation of the rejected artists produced a furore of protest. The Emperor thereupon issued on April 24 a proclamation stating that the rejected works would be exhibited in another section of the Palais de l'Industrie, so as to 'let the public judge the validity of these protests'.

*　　*　　*

Unfortunately, the public was by no means prepared to play the role of judge. It saw nothing but a practical joke in this exhibition of rejected works. Its inability to appreciate the efforts of unconventional artists may be explained in part by the fact that the bourgeoisie had only recently supplanted the aristocracy and the Church as patrons of the arts. Concerned with stabilizing its general position and extending its influence, it cared little for this new burden which it inherited along with all the others from those who preceded it in power. More interested in the development of science, the bourgeoisie assigned a completely new place to the artist. Instead of working for one patron he had to work for an unknown public, with the result that besides the sincere art, much was produced simply for the sake of achieving mass popularity. Unable to distinguish one type of art from the other, the public taste remained keyed to the pompous and artificial standards of the immediate past. Thus Delacroix, Daumier, Courbet, and other innovators encountered strong opposition, for the irrational admiration of the past precluded an understanding of the present.

In his treatise *Vom Nutzen und Nachteil der Historie für das Leben*, written about ten years later, Nietzsche describes the danger inherent in this 'commemorative contemplation of the past'. It applies to the situation prevailing at the time Edouard Manet exhibited his work in the Salon des Refusés. Nietzsche writes:

'Let us take the simplest and most common example and imagine natures which are anti-artistic or endowed with a weak artistic temperament, armed and equipped with ideas borrowed from the commemorative history of art. Against whom will these natures direct their arms? Against their hereditary enemies: artistic temperaments which are strongly gifted, consequently against those who alone are capable of learning something from the historical events thus presented, capable of drawing from them what is applicable to life and of transforming what they have learned into improved justice. It is to them that the road is barred, the atmosphere darkened, whilst others dance slavishly and with zeal around a glorious monument of the past no matter what it is and without even understanding it, as though to say: "See, here is true and genuine art. What do you care about those who are still prisoners of development and will!" This dancing crowd even possesses, in appearance, the advantage of "good taste", for the creator has always been at a disadvantage with respect to the person who only observes without himself creating. If one thinks of transferring to the realm of art general suffrage and the rule of the majority in order somehow to force the artist to defend himself before a forum of idle aesthetics, one can swear beforehand that he will be condemned. Not, as one might think, in spite of the canon of commemorative art, but because the judges have solemnly affirmed this canon (that of the art which, in accordance with the explanations given, has always "made an impression"). On the other hand, as concerns art which is not yet commemorative, that is to say which is contemporary, they lack, in the first place the need, in the second place the vocation, in the third place precisely the authority of history. On the contrary, their instinct tells them that art can be killed by art. For them the commemorative must at no cost be produced again and their argument stems from those who derive authority and commemorative character from the past. In this way, they appear to be connoisseurs of art, because they would like to suppress art; they mask themselves as doctors; whereas actually they behave like poisoners. Thus they develop their senses and taste in order to explain, by their behaviour of spoiled children, why they so insistently reject everything which is offered them in art as real nourishment. For they do not want anything great to be produced; their method is to state: "See, that which is great exists already!" To tell the truth, this great thing which already exists concerns them just as little as that which is in the process of formation. Their life bears witness to this. Commemorative history is the garb worn by their hatred of the great and powerful of their own time, the garb which they try to palm off as admiration for the great and powerful of yore. This mask permits them to change the true meaning of this conception of history into a meaning diametrically opposed to it. Whether or not they realize it, they always act as though their motto were "Let the dead bury the living." '

The public endorsed this grave-digger attitude with the collaboration of those artists who had already gained its favour and who stopped at nothing to prevent others from gaining the same honours. These artists succeeded in hiding their pettiness and poverty of spirit behind an academic correctness devoid of life. With untiring effort they supplied the public with historical paintings, or, like Cabanel and Bouguereau, with female nudes—maidens or Hebes, Springs or Truths—without a wrinkle of the skin, without any quivering of the flesh, too pink, with no inner movement of the forms, but always with curves. Their art had become the negation of nature. The tendency to prettify forms and colours, the choice of so-called noble subjects and picturesque scenery, had killed any feeling for things actually seen.

The catalogues of the Salons of this period bear witness to the mediocre trend of officially approved art. They contain titles such as, 'The Little Bird's Nester', 'First Caresses', 'The Sugar-Plums of the Baptism', 'A Good Mouthful', 'Grandmother's Friends', 'First Shave', etc. Some paintings have a long legend, such as the following:

'Woman Tied to the Tree from Which Her Husband Had Been Hanged by Order of the Bastard of Vanves, Governor of Meaux in the XVth Century, Devoured by Wolves.'

or:

'Meeting of Francis I and His Fiancée, Eleanor of Austria, at Illescas (Spain). "She Knelt and Asked to Kiss His Hand, and the King Replied: 'I Will Only Give You My Mouth,' Raised Her Up, and Kissed Her".'

It was thought that the subject matter of a painting was more important than its aesthetic value, that striking colour effects were more to be sought after than harmony, and that drawing was independent of colour.

Those who disagreed with these ideas had to fight three enemies: the public, the critics, and the official artists. These latter headed all committees and juries and were thus in a position to exclude all nonconformers from public exhibitions. Even if the work of an independent artist was not 'judged unworthy of being condemned by the public' and was consequently admitted, it was hung in a distant corner where it attracted no interest and received no mention in the interminable articles of the critics. The Salon des Refusés did not alter this situation much. Although the arbitrary decisions of the jury had been circumvented, the public and critics remained hostile to new trends. However, they flocked to the exhibition, and its successs was sufficient, because of the novelty of the event, to inspire caricaturists with jokes of this kind: 'The accepted artists being little noticed, and jealous of the exhibition of those rejected, plan to be rejected themselves next year.'

*   *   *

The catalogue of the Salon des Refusés is very incomplete. Among those listed are Manet with three paintings, Jongkind with three canvases, and Pissarro with three landscapes. Fantin–Latour had works both in the Salon and in the counter-exhibition. Not listed, though exhibiting, were Cézanne and his friend Guillaumin. Neither the titles nor the number of the paintings shown by Cézanne are known. Not one of the numerous reviews seems to have mentioned his work.

The focal point of the Salon des Refusés was Manet's 'Déjeuner sur l'herbe'. It became the target of indignant visitors and critics. Its artistic value being ignored, the indignation centred on the subject: a nude woman in the company of men wearing clothes. No one seemed to remember that Giorgione's painting, 'Rustic Concert', in the Louvre, contained a similar group. (Zola was to mention this later in his pamphlet on Manet.) If Manet had surrounded the woman with nude men, calling it 'A Scene of Fauns and Nymphs', the public would doubtless have been less shocked, but would still have refused to accept his style, which it found most disturbing. Indeed, the difference between the prize-winning pictures and the 'Déjeuner sur l'herbe' was enormous. Manet had not based his painting on any anecdote or given it an 'atmosphere', either sad or gay, to transpose it from reality into the world of pleasant illusions.

'The first impression produced by a canvas of Edouard Manet is a little harsh,' Zola later wrote. 'One is not accustomed to see such simple and sincere renderings of reality.' The violence with which the 'Déjeuner sur l'herbe' contrasted with the historical and allegorical paintings in the careful technique and pretentious banality of the followers of Ingres, led the public to believe that Manet was not master of his brush, that its effects were accidental, that his colours were dirty and his draftsmanship non-existent. He was reproached for not having given his subjects contours which are 'the natural limits of colour'. Censured for the 'banality' of his composition, Manet was discovered only fifty years later to have based his composition on an engraving after Raphael. Nobody saw the qualities of his canvas because everybody sees through glasses of convention, believing that only this convention is true and natural.

This bourgeoisie, so receptive to innovation in the field of science and technology, disliked Manet, who, himself bourgeois and inspired by the same fever of conquest which shook his century, was trying, in his sphere, to make creative discoveries worthy of the era. But, as one of the few critics to appreciate him observed: 'Every artist, every author of a new work done outside the realm of routine and convention is almost always rejected. He wounds the majority too much not to have his own individuality repudiated. Stupid people want others to resemble and imitate them.'

Though rejected by the public, Manet had nevertheless awakened the enthusiasm of those young painters who were striving to escape from academic insipidity. Cézanne and Zola were deeply moved by Manet's painting, but for different reasons. Cézanne admired Manet's canvas because it revealed a new conception which was both sober and ardent and a new technique which seemed accidental but was actually extremely refined and full of virtuosity. He also admired the new use of colour, its subtle oppositions and frank contrasts. Although none of this conformed to Cézanne's passionate temperament, or to his own work up to now, these new elements were to make an impression on him because he was seeking a new means of expression. However, no direct influence of Manet may be found upon Cézanne's palette, which did not become brighter as a result of that impression.

Zola looked at the 'Déjeuner sur l'herbe' from quite another point of view. It conveyed to him 'a feeling of unity and strength'. He found it human and above all original. What Zola primarily sought in a canvas was 'a man and not a painting'.

'What I ask of an artist,' he wrote a little later, 'is not to give me tender visions or dreadful nightmares; it is to render himself, heart and flesh; it is boldly to express a powerful and individual mind, a nature which broadly takes nature in his grasp and plants it before us, just as he sees it. In a word, I have the most profound contempt for petty cleverness, for opportunistic flatteries . . . for all the historical dramas of this gentleman and all the perfumed dreams of that one. But I have the deepest admiration for individual works, for those which burst forth in one spurt, from a vigorous and unique hand.'

These qualities, which Zola had sought everywhere in vain, he found in Manet's picture, and the public ridicule directed against it prompted him to study more carefully this proud protest against academic prejudice. It was doubtless Cézanne who initiated Zola into the hidden beauties of this painting and who pointed out to him 'the delicate exactitude of the inter-relationships of tones'. Twenty years later, when Zola was recollecting memories of his youth in order to put them in his novel *L'Œuvre*, he still remembered Cézanne's enthusiasm and noted: 'The Salon des Refusés. Great discussions with me.'

It was due to these discussions and to love of sincerity that Zola became a fervent admirer of Manet, whom he 'loved instinctively'. As it was not in keeping with Zola's character to conceal his admiration, he soon began a violent campaign in Manet's favour. Though Zola lacked sensitivity of observation and taste, and doubtless was unable to find complete satisfaction in a painting, he had the fine vehemence of an avant-garde fighter and a loud voice capable of drowning out detractors. The new school which was born of the

Salon des Refusés, and which assembled around Manet a group of young painters, could not have found a better champion than this young journalist who, renouncing any delicacy of language or aesthetic terminology, spoke his mind crudely and sincerely. 'I had the passion of my opinions,' he later explained, 'and would have forced my convictions down the throats of others.'

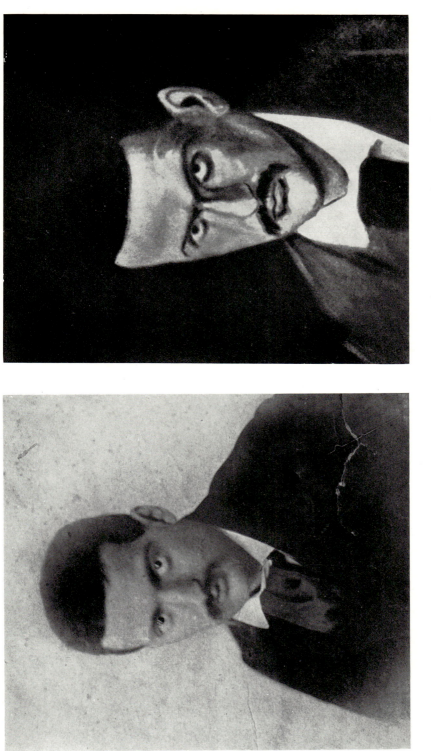

2. Cézanne: Self Portrait, 1861

1. Photograph of Paul Cézanne in 1861

3. *Cézanne: Study of a Nude, probably drawn at the Atelier Suisse, c.1865*

5. *Cézanne: Marion and Valabrègue Setting Out to Paint a Landscape*, 1866

4. *Cézanne: Portrait of Uncle Dominique*, c.1866

7. *Cézanne: Portrait of the Artist's Sister Marie, c.1866*

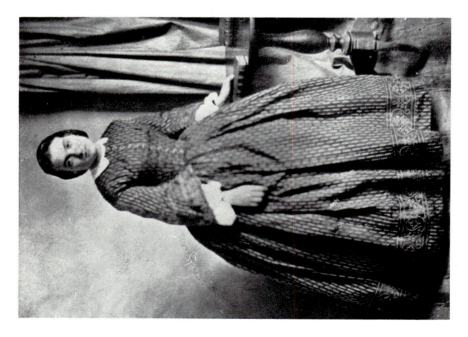

6. *Photograph of Marie Cézanne, c.1870*

9. *Cézanne: Portrait of Fortuné Marion, c.1866*

8. *Photograph of Fortuné Marion, c.1866*

10. *Cézanne: Portrait of Antony Valabrègue, c.1866. Probably rejected by the Salon of 1866*

11. *Cézanne: Overture to Tannhäuser, c.*1866 *(The artist's sister Marie and his mother)*

12. *Cézanne: L'Enlèvement,* 1867. *Formerly Coll. Emile Zola*

13. *Cézanne: Portrait of the Painter Achille Emperaire, c.*1868

14. *Cézanne: Portrait of the Artist's Father reading L'Evénement*, 1866

15. *A corner of Cézanne's studio, c.1866. Formerly Coll. Emile Zola*

16. *Cézanne: The Rape, c.*1870

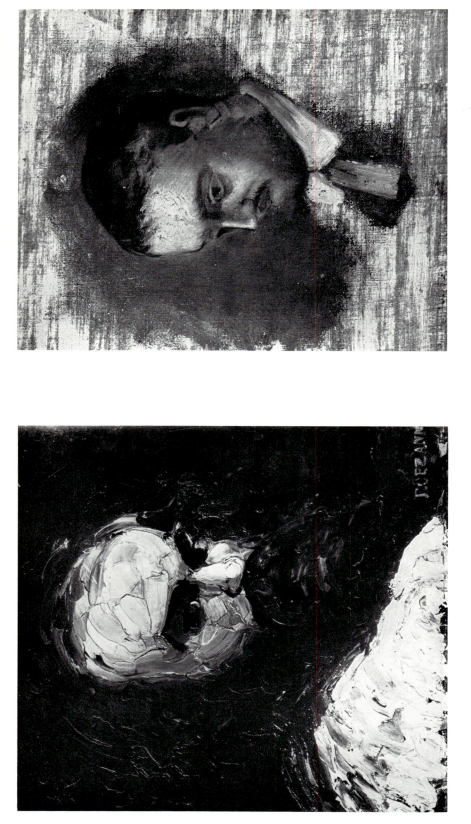

18. *Cézanne: Portrait of Emile Zola, c.1862*

17. *Cézanne: Self Portrait, c.1865*

19. *Cézanne: Still Life with Black Clock, c.1869. Formerly Coll. Emile Zola*

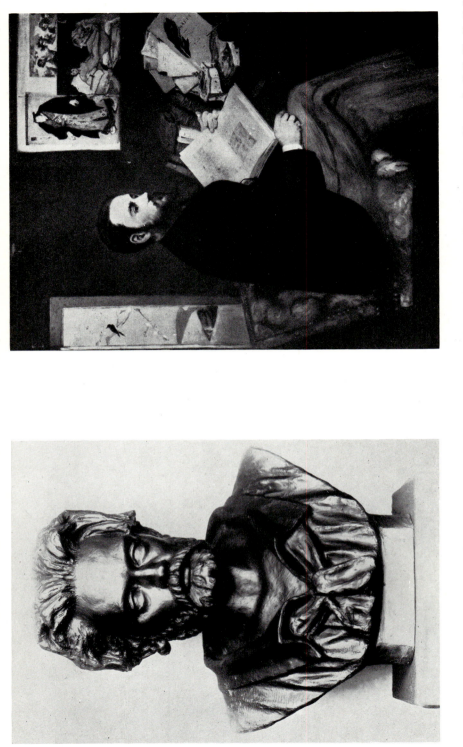

21. *Manet: Portrait of Emile Zola, 1868. Formerly Coll. Emile Zola*

20. *Solari: Bust of Emile Zola, c.1866. Formerly Coll. Emile Zola*

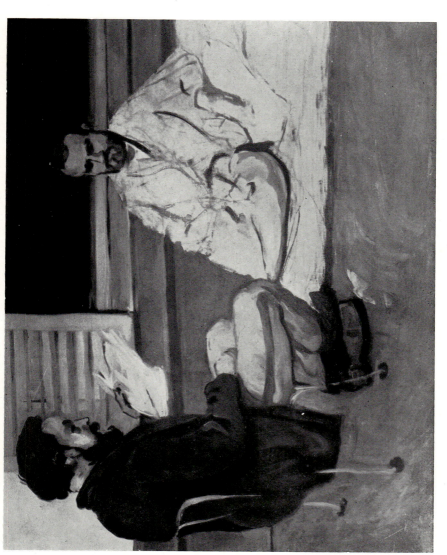

22. *Cézanne: Paul Alexis reading to Emile Zola, c.1869. Formerly Coll. Emile Zola*

23. *Cézanne: Mount de Cengle near Aix, c.*1870

24. *Cézanne: View of L'Estaque, c.*1870. *Formerly Coll. Emile Zola*

VI

EARLY WORKS

1863 – 1866

AFTER the Salon des Refusés, Cézanne took Zola round the studios; there they met the painters Béliard, Pissarro, Monet, Degas, Renoir, Fantin-Latour, and others. Later on Antoine Guillemet and the critic Duranty introduced Zola to Manet. Around that same time Zola also met Gabrielle Meley, whom he married in Paris several years later. It is believed that Cézanne introduced them to each other, but nothing definite is known about it.

Cézanne had become particularly friendly with Pissarro, Bazille, Guillemet, Renoir, Monet, and Armand Guillaumin. They did not see each other constantly, however, because from 1863 to 1870 Cézanne spent part of each year with his family in Aix.

At the beginning of 1864, Cézanne was in Paris and frequently met Baille. Their friend Coste, then still in Aix, wrote to inform Cézanne that he had drawn an unlucky conscription number (which meant seven years of military service). Cézanne, who had not had to serve, his father having bought him a substitute, consoled his friend in a long letter in which he advised him to volunteer immediately and try to be stationed in Paris:

'One can make some progress, while being a soldier. I see some soldiers here who attend courses in anatomy at the Beaux-Arts. Lombard draws, paints, and whirls about more than ever; I have not yet been able to go to see his drawings with which he tells me he is satisfied. For two months I have not touched my [illegible word] after Delacroix. I shall retouch it, however, before leaving for Aix where I will only go in July unless my father sends for me. In two months, in May, there will be an exhibition like the one last year. If you were here we would go to see it together.'

Cézanne was mistaken in believing that the Salon des Refusés, to which he refers, would be held again, for the hostile attitude of the public had endorsed the jury's verdict. Thus there was no reason for exhibiting the rejected canvases of that year.

Numa Coste followed Cézanne's advice and soon appeared in Paris where, in uniform, he joined the circle of Zola's friends. This group was composed mostly of comrades from Aix. Besides

Cézanne and Baille, there were the sculptor Philippe Solari; Chaillan, a painter whose work Zola did not admire; and later Antony Valabrègue and Paul Alexis. With those who could not yet come to Paris, Zola kept up a regular correspondence, as with Fortuné Marion, who was studying in Marseilles to become a naturalist; Marguery, who published insipid novels in the local press; and Marius Roux, who was trying his hand at literary criticism.

Among Cézanne's Parisian friends who remained close to Zola as well were Camille Pissarro and Antoine Guillemet. Both Cézanne and Zola seem to have felt a real affection for Pissarro; as to Guillemet, particularly lively and gay, full of amusing ideas and ever good-natured, his company was always appreciated. Cézanne liked him so much that he even accepted his occasional gibes without ill feeling. Guillemet is credited with having supplied many a canvas by Cézanne with more or less fancy titles. Thus he christened one of his paintings: 'The Wine Grog' or 'Afternoon in Naples', and another: 'The Woman with the Flea'.

At that time Zola was putting the finishing touch to his novel *La Confession de Claude*, the background of which is Paris during the unhappy period of the author's first years there. In this book he realizes an idea which had been forming in his mind and which he had already mentioned in a letter to Baille in 1860—the 'mad idea of bringing back to decent life an unfortunate woman, by loving her, by raising her up from the gutter'. This love story, set in a frame of personal recollections, reveals how painful Zola's early years in Paris must have been, those years during which the will to work and confidence in his vocation were his only refuge. Now, in contrast, Zola had a great deal to do and was beginning to make money. When the book appeared at the end of 1865, the critics condemned its 'ugly realism'. But Zola doubtless had not exaggerated the misery of Claude, a character patterned after the author. He himself, however, judged his book severely.

'It is weak in certain parts,' he wrote Valabrègue, 'and still contains much childishness. Sometimes it lacks vitality; the observer disappears and the poet returns, a poet who has drunk too much milk and eaten too much sugar. The work is not virile, it is the writing of a child who cries and revolts.'

Marius Roux reviewed *La Confession de Claude* for an Aix paper in an article which Zola called 'the best that has been published'. At Zola's special request 'to give publicity to Baille and particularly to Cézanne, in order to please their families', Roux spoke at length about the two native sons to whom the book was dedicated. It is the first article which mentions Cézanne. Roux wrote:

'We are a group of citizens of Aix, all of us old schoolmates, all of us joined in good and genuine friendship. We do not know what the future has in store for us, but meanwhile we are working and struggling. . . . If we are all joined in the bonds of friendship, we are not always united in our conception of the beautiful, the true, and the good. In such an instance, some of us vote for Plato and others for Aristotle; some admire Raphael and others Courbet. M. Zola, who prefers the 'Fileuse' [by Millet] to the 'Virgin of the Chair' [by Raphael], dedicates his book to two devotees of his school.

'M. Cézanne is one of the good students which our Aix school has contributed to Paris. He has left us with the memory of an undaunted worker and a conscientious pupil. There he will establish himself, thanks to his perseverance, as an excellent artist. Although a great admirer of Ribera and Zurbaran, our painter is original and gives his work a style of his own. I have seen him at work in his studio and if I cannot yet predict for him the brilliant success of those he admires, I am sure of one thing, that his work will never be mediocre. Mediocrity is the worst thing in the arts. Better be a mason if that is your profession; but if you are a painter, be a complete one or die in the attempt.

'M. Cézanne will not die in it: he has brought from the school of Aix principles which are too good, he has found here examples which are too excellent, he has too much courage, too much perseverance in his work to fail in reaching his objective. If I were not afraid of being indiscreet, I would give you my opinion of some of his canvases. But his modesty does not permit him to believe that what he produces is adequate, and I do not want to hurt his fine feelings as an artist. I am waiting until he displays his work in broad daylight. That day, I shall not be the only one to speak. He belongs to a school which has the privilege of provoking criticism.'

La Confession de Claude soon attracted the attention of the courts because of its daring language. In a letter to the keeper of the seals, however, the attorney general concluded that the purpose of the book was not immoral. 'What the author intended,' he said, 'was to cause young people to become disgusted with these impure relationships into which they allow themselves to be drawn at the word of poets who have idealized these bohemian love affairs.'

Nevertheless an investigation ensued at the Librairie Hachette, where Zola held the position of chief of propaganda service at an annual salary of 2400 francs. As a result of this incident, Zola resigned and resolved to devote himself entirely to literature.

*   *   *

Cézanne was more fortunate than his friend in not having to earn his own living, although he often was short of funds despite the allowance his father gave him. He made shy attempts to sell pictures but with little success. His life at Aix was calmer than in Paris. He retired to the 'Jas de Bouffan' where he saw no one and worked in complete solitude, painting chiefly portraits. One of his favourite models was 'L'Oncle Dominique' (Pl. 4), a bailiff by profession, whose surname was Aubert and who was the brother of Cézanne's mother. Cézanne's father also posed for him several times, as well as his two young sisters and some friends, including Achille Emperaire, Antony Valabrègue, and Fortuné Marion. He hardly ever did portraits of his mother.

Cézanne obtained permission to decorate the big salon of the 'Jas', and he copied Lancret's 'Dance in the Country' directly onto the wall. This painting reveals a feeling for tones of green, while the shadows still are often painted black. Opposite to this, Cézanne copied Sebastiano del Piombo's 'Christ Descending to Limbo', of which he had found a print in one of his books. In the centre of an alcove at the end of the room, in the place of honour, so to speak, Cézanne painted the portrait of his father in profile, and on the two side panels he represented the four seasons in a style which strangely combines a primitive awkwardness with sophisticated elegance. He signed these panels very conspicuously with the name of Ingres, for no apparent reason. This seems all the more amusing since Cézanne had admired Manet's work precisely for 'the kick it gave the Institute'.

Besides portraits and murals, Cézanne worked between 1863 and 1870 at various group compositions of an unusual character. In these the artist was guided solely by his inspiration, haunted by the grandiose and passionate scenes which his mind and restless imagination constantly conjured up. Possessed by a veritable rage for work, Cézanne now felt no patience to study nature and obstinately pursued the realization of his dreams.

The execution of these paintings, sometimes slow, sometimes impetuous, and their heavy texture bear witness to long and arduous work. Their composition often lacks verisimilitude, and the figures frequently appear out of proportion. The foreground, the middle ground, and the background are not sufficiently distinct from one another to allow any orientation, and instead of being spread out in depth, the composition is often built up as if seen from above. Cézanne finally realized that he was attacking problems too difficult for him and was subsequently satisfied with simpler compositions, dominated by groups in the foreground. If he learned anything from Manet, it was doubtless how to organize space in definite planes. His paintings of this period represent the phases of his struggle to balance the baroque inclination of his fancy and the slowly growing tendency to interpret what he saw.

Sometimes, seeking a kind of prop, Cézanne more or less freely copied reproductions in books and magazines, such as the *Magasin Pittoresque* and the *Musée des Familles*, to which his sisters subscribed, as well as the art volumes of Charles Blanc.

Cézanne's palette shows the influence of Delacroix with his Veronese green, his purple, and his Prussian blue. Already at this early date one can see in Cézanne (in the words of Roger Fry) the gift which never failed him, his sensitivity to colour. It was never possible for him to put a touch of colour on the canvas which was discordant or failed to add to an original chromatic creation.

In his youthful work, in which imaginary scenes predominate, a few portraits afford a contrast, for while his compositions are passionate and full of movement, his likenesses have a certain gravity. In these Cézanne sought after the greatest possible simplicity and liked to represent his models either full face or in profile with a strong tendency towards symmetry. These portraits are sometimes more than life size. They are striking by virtue of the contrasts of vivid colour—Achille Emperaire (Pl. 13) is shown wearing an intense blue dressing gown with a very bright red foulard and violet trousers—and they also have a plasticity which is not apparent in Cézanne's purely imaginative work. It is above all in a portrait of his father seen full face, seated slightly sideways, that a great mastery of the problems of volume and space manifests itself (Pl. 14). These large canvases seem to be the fruit of much less painful toil and of a greater self-confidence than most of Cézanne's other work of this period. The influence of Courbet appears not only in the size and the execution, but also in the approach to the model, yet these portraits are sufficiently individual to show that by now Cézanne only needed experience to develop his amazing gifts.

The technique of Cézanne's paintings of this period is not always the same. Like Courbet, Cézanne often used the palette knife, building up in pigment such portraits as those of 'L'Oncle Dominique', his father reading *L'Événement* (Pl. 14), and a 'Self Portrait' (Pl. 17) which is completely modelled in paint, and in which the high domed forehead, magnificently wild beard, and energetic expression portray him as an inspired creator.

Still experimenting with methods, Cézanne overcame his hesitations by will power and enthusiasm for work. But his isolation at Aix often weighed upon him so that from time to time he felt the need to plunge himself into the stimulating atmosphere of Paris.

VII

ZOLA AS ART CRITIC

1866

CEZANNE spent the winter of 1865 at Aix. 'I often see Paul in the afternoon', Valabrègue informed Zola. 'He is always the best of comrades. He, too, has changed, for he speaks, he who seemed your silent shadow. He expounds theories, builds up doctrines; crime of crimes, he even suffers that one talk politics with him (theoretically, of course) and replies by saying terrible things about the tyrant.'

Once more, Cézanne attended the art school. He also met frequently with Fortuné Marion who introduced him to the German musician, Heinrich Morstatt. The latter used to play for them, and Cézanne was delighted to let his 'nerves vibrate to the noble tones of Richard Wagner,' as he wrote in a letter. This admiration for Wagner was soon to find expression in a painting entitled 'Overture to Tannhäuser' (Pl. 11).

In February 1866, Cézanne returned to Paris where he joined the group of friends that gathered every Thursday evening at Zola's. In cordial though heated debates, Baille, Coste, Pissarro, Solari, Cézanne, and Zola discussed painting, poetry, and criticism. Each spoke of his projects, his dreams, and all were animated by the desire to help each other. When Solari, for instance, had spent all the money from a fellowship in sculpture given by the academy of Aix, Cézanne helped him out. Cézanne was very fond of this friend with his exalted visions who, however, lacked a sense of the demands of life. Remarkably indifferent, serious, absent-minded, always calm, he was a disinterested and timid bohemian.

The atmosphere of the meetings at Zola's is revealed in a letter written by the novelist to Antony Valabrègue, who was still in Aix: 'I do not conceal the fact that I would have preferred to see you among us, fighting like ourselves, daily renewing your attempts, striking to the right, striking to the left, always marching ahead.'

Many of Zola's friends complained to him of hard times. Zola alone was successful. On February 1 he had become book reviewer for the influential newspaper *L'Evénement*. Meanwhile Cézanne was preparing paintings for the Salon, which, as he told Pissarro the preceding year, 'would make the Institute blush with rage and despair'. He was quite sure that his entry would not be accepted but felt a certain pleasure at the prospect of shocking the jury. According to Zola, Cézanne 'now maintained that one should always present something to the jury, if only to put it in the wrong; moreover, he recognized the usefulness of the Salon, the only battlefield on which an artist could reveal himself at one stroke'.

Cézanne's entry had been rejected the year before, though an exceptionally broad-minded jury had accepted even Manet's 'Olympia'. But the public reaction to that painting had been so violent that the jury decided to make no future concessions. Its anger was turned particularly against Manet, whom Cézanne met for the first time in April 1866. A record of their meeting is preserved in a letter from Valabrègue to Marion: 'Cézanne has already written to you about his visit to Manet. But he has not written you that Manet saw his still-lifes at Guillemet's. He found them powerfully treated. Cézanne is very happy about this, though he does not expatiate about his happiness and does not insist on it as is his wont. Manet is going to call on him. Parallel temperaments, they will surely understand one another.' What Cézanne did not know was that Manet actually considered him 'not much more than an interesting colourist'.

Manet's appreciation bolstered Cézanne's morale in the events which followed his two submissions to the Salon in 1866, one of which was a portrait of Valabrègue (Pl. 10). He delivered his entries to the Palais de l'Industrie, where the Salon was held, on the last possible day and at the last minute. They were brought in a wheelbarrow, pushed and pulled by his friends. At their arrival in front of the Palais, Cézanne slowly removed his canvases from the wheelbarrow and showed them to the crowd of idlers at the door.

Cézanne had no illusions; he knew perfectly well that his entries would be rejected—he even wished it. Thus Marion wrote to his friend Morstatt, in March 1866: 'I have just had a letter from my Paris friends: Cézanne hopes to be rejected at the exhibition and the painters of his acquaintance are preparing an ovation in his honour.'

A little later Valabrègue, who in the meantime had arrived in Paris, informed Marion: 'Paul will without doubt be rejected at the exhibition. A philistine in the jury exclaimed on seeing my portrait that it was not only painted with a knife but with a pistol as well. Many discussions have arisen. Daubigny [a member of the jury] said some words in defence of my portrait. He declared that he preferred pictures brimming over with daring to the nullities which appear at every Salon. He didn't succeed in convincing them.'

Marion forwarded Valabrègue's letter to Morstatt, adding:

'Since then I've had more news: the whole realist school has been refused, Cézanne, Guillemet, and the others. The only pictures accepted are Courbet's things—it appears that he is growing weak

—and a "Fife Player" by Manet, one of the youthful glories who decidedly occupies the first rank. . . . [Marion erred here, Manet's canvas was actually rejected.] In reality we triumph and this mass refusal, this vast exile, is in itself a victory. All we have to do is to plan an exhibition of our own and put up a deadly competition against those blear-eyed idiots.

'We are in a fighting period: youth against old age . . . the present, laden with promise of the future, against the past, *that black pirate*. Talk of posterity. Well, we are posterity. And we are told that it is posterity that judges. We trust in the future. Our adversaries can *trust at best in death*. We are confident. All we want is to *produce*. If we work, our success is certain. . . .'

Cézanne shared this point of view and upon learning that his paintings had been rejected along with those of Manet, Renoir, and others, he wrote a strong letter to M. de Nieuwerkerke, Director of Fine Arts, demanding the re-establishment of the Salon des Refusés. As he did not receive an answer, Cézanne wrote again on April 19:

'Sir,
'Recently I had the honour of writing to you concerning the two pictures that the jury has just turned down. Since I have had no reply, I feel compelled to insist on the motives which caused me to apply to you. As you have no doubt received my letter, I need not repeat here the arguments that I thought necessary to submit to you. I shall content myself with saying once more that I cannot accept the unfair judgment of colleagues whom I myself have not commissioned to appraise me. I am therefore writing to you to emphasize my demand. I wish to appeal to the public and show my pictures in spite of their being rejected. My desire does not seem to me extravagant, and if you were to ask all the painters in my position, they would reply without exception that they disown the jury and that they wish to take part in one way or another in an exhibition which should be open as a matter of course to every serious worker.

'Therefore, let the Salon des Refusés be re-established. Even were I to be there alone, I ardently desire the public to know at least that I do not wish to be confused with the gentlemen of the jury any more than they seem to wish to be confused with me.

'I hope, Monsieur, that you will not choose to remain silent. It seems to me that any decent letter deserves a reply.
'Paul Cézanne
'22 Rue Beautreillis'

Cézanne's letter is more than an expression of personal feelings. It no doubt represents the opinion of all those whose entries had received the same treatment and who belonged to the camp of insurgents led by Manet. Probably Zola had a part in this manifesto, for it contains the same impassioned and ironical phrases that reappear in the series of articles on the Salon which Zola was shortly to publish. If Zola helped Cézanne with his letter, the painter also collaborated indirectly in this series, which also demanded the

reopening of a Salon des Refusés. But nothing could induce the Beaux-Arts to change its decision. On the margin of Cézanne's letter was written the draft for the official reply: 'What he asks is impossible; it has been recognized how little suitable the exhibition of the rejected was for the dignity of art, and it will not be re-established.'

Emile Zola availed himself of the opportunity to use his pen on behalf of his painter friends. He obtained permission to review the Salon for *L' Événement* and immediately announced that he intended to attack the jury and to reveal 'great and terrible truths' about it. His friends, especially Guillemet, gave him the inside story on the way the jury got itself elected and how it fulfilled its functions, 'amputating art and only presenting the crowd with the mutilated corpse'. He explained first of all that a 'Salon in our day is not the work of artists, it is the work of a jury.' Indeed the rules of the Salon specify that the jury on awards and commissions shall be elected by artists having previously won awards. But they do not mention the fact that the prize-winning artists, those who elect the judges of their colleagues, were admitted to the Salon without being passed upon by the jury.

On this jury, according to Zola, 'there are the nice fellows who reject and accept with indifference, there are the successful ones who are above the battle, there are the artists of the past who cling to their beliefs, who deny all novel attempts, and finally there are the artists of the present whose little style has its little success and who hold onto this success with their teeth while scolding and threatening any approaching colleague'.*

It was obvious that any artist who blazed his own trail, refusing to follow official aesthetic paths, was doomed to rejection. Zola states that 'the exhibitions were created to give ample publicity to serious workers. All taxpayers contribute and the question of schools and systems should not open the door to some and close it to others. . . . Yet there are men placed between the artists and the public. With their omnipotent authority, they only reveal a third, only a quarter, of the truth'. In order to show better how they judged, Zola gives the example of a painter known as a pupil of Courbet, who had entered paintings under two different names. Those signed with his real name were rejected, whereas those bearing a pseudonym were accepted.

Zola's articles, signed Claude, did not fail to attract public attention. Though he was not the first to attack the Salon jury, he did it with unusual eloquence shot through with irony, and above all he did it in a widely-read paper. Up to now, Zola had only criticized the judges and demanded a new Salon des Refusés. Pressed to give a positive opinion on contemporary art, he did so in the second article of his series.

'We live in times of struggle and fever,' he wrote. 'We have our talents and our geniuses.' Referring to the Salon as a 'mass of

*Zola even mentioned by name several members of the jury, praising Daubigny's attitude, reproaching Corot for cowardice, and saying that Rousseau was severe; as for the others, he refused to acknowledge their right to judge their colleagues. This passage was omitted by Zola when he collected his articles in a pamphlet, Mon Salon (later incorporated in the volume Mes Haines). In a note Zola explained: 'I believe I should excise this part of the article. I have been shown that there is little basis for a number of details of whose veracity I had been previously assured. The general spirit was undoubtedly true; but not knowing where the inaccurate begins, I find it simpler to erase it all and to stick only to my opinions in matters of art.'

mediocrity,' he said that although it contained two thousand pictures, not even ten men were represented there. Zola then proceeded to develop his conception of art, explaining: 'A work of art is a corner of nature seen through a temperament.' This definition was doubtless the fruit of long discussion about art between Zola and Cézanne, though, curiously enough, the painter had not yet found the balance between nature and temperament.

Zola's third article was devoted to Edouard Manet. In it he declared that before guiding the readers of *L'Evénement* through the vast halls of the Palais de l'Industrie, full of nonsense, he wished to visit with them the studio of Manet and speak to them of the only painter he admired. The fact that in a long article he praised the painter whom everyone ridiculed was enough to provoke lively protest. The critic affirmed that 'Manet's place in the Louvre was reserved, like that of Courbet,' and the public took offence at such remarks. It was scandalized that he should start his comments on the Salon by speaking of a rejected painter as though he were a master. M. de Villemessant, editor of *L'Evénement*, received innumerable letters of protest thus:

'Sir,
'When I read your paper this morning, I asked myself whether you were still running it, for I have always noticed that you had consideration for your subscribers. This is not the case today, and I have rarely seen an article in which the author ridicules his readers with such impudence as he who signs himself Claude in your paper.

'I do not know what ties of kinship or amity link this writer with M. Manet, but in truth, it is abusing his public strangely and making a fool of it to declare this bungler to be the foremost painter of the epoch. Moreover it is a bad thing to insult the painters most beloved by the public in order to make of these insults a pedestal for the miserable dauber he would like to consider an artist.

'It seemed to me that you had made it your mission, in creating your various papers, to enlighten your readers while amusing them, and that that is what has made them successful; but a few more articles in the taste of the one to which I refer, and I do not doubt that a good number of your intelligent readers (and, in spite of what M. Claude may think, there are still a few) will dispense with a newspaper that treats them thus as imbeciles and fools. . . .

'It is good to have, as you often say, a rostrum from which all ideas and opinions may be expressed; however, there must be a brake on shamelessness and bad faith.

'I hope, sir, that you do not see in this letter anything but an expression of the sympathy which attaches me to your publications and my desire that they should not degenerate in giving asylum to such senseless works.

'Please accept etc. . . .'

Another reader, signing himself 'bourgeois, though artist,' wrote to M. de Villemessant in the same vein;

'Your M. Claude is exasperating; no theories, no aesthetic knowledge, no reasoned criticism; an enthusiasm in the void and insults, it is too much and too little. . . .

'M. Claude politely calls idiots all those who laugh at M. Manet's paintings. But why is not M. Manet satisfied with being mediocre? Why is he vulgar and grotesque? Why do his dirty figures seem to have emerged from a sack of coal? One looks with pity upon involuntary ugliness; how then is one not to laugh at affected ugliness? . . .
'For mercy's sake, Monsieur le directeur, spare your readers any further mental torture by your M. Claude or the cancellation of subscriptions, which is a reality, will soon follow.'

And a painter, over the signature of A.P., bade the editor of *L' Evénement* 'raise a little the standard of criticism by entrusting it to clean hands'.
M. de Villemessant was obliged to yield to his indignant readers. He and Zola agreed that 'Claude' was to share his task with a more conformist art critic and that each of them would be allowed three articles. Thus Zola, who had expected to write a series of sixteen or eighteen essays, could only add three more to the five already published.
In order to show that he was not the standard-bearer of a school, as he had been reproached for being, Zola had attacked the 'realists' of the Salon on the grounds that nothing except their subject matter aspired to realism. It was not the subject, Zola said, but rather its technique and individual character which determined whether or not a work of art was realistic. He considered Claude Monet's 'Camille' the only 'realist' work in the Salon. Further he declared: 'Any school is displeasing to me, for a school is the very negation of human liberty to create.' To emphasize his independence, Zola, in his sixth article, did not hesitate to reproach Courbet, Millet, and Rousseau for not living up to their own standards. But he began to ask himself whether it were really any use to be disagreeable and to speak his mind frankly when the next day, in the same place, his opposite number was handing around compliments. Zola now no longer had the courage necessary to write the articles he had planned in favour of Daubigny, Corot, and Pissarro, knowing that they would be received with scorn. Moreover, was he doing them any good by praising them in his discredited series? Consequently, instead of writing the two articles to which he was still

entitled, Zola sent only one more to *L'Evénement*, 'Farewell of an Art Critic,' and handed in his resignation.

'Actually I am delighted,' he concluded. 'Imagine a doctor who does not know where the wound is and who, in palpating the body of the patient hears him cry out in terror and anguish. I admit to myself that I found the right place, since it causes pain. It does not matter to me that you do not want to get well. I now know where the wound is.'

Zola had indeed achieved his purpose; he had discovered the sad truth that the more commonplace one is the more one is admired and understood: 'Ah! if art had not become a pomposity and a joke, if there were fewer daubers painting for amusement and vanity, if our painters lived like fighters, like powerful and vigorous men, if they learned their business, if they forgot the Ideal and remembered Nature, if the public were willing to be intelligent and not to hoot at new personalities, we would perhaps see other works hung on the walls of the galleries, works alive and human, full of deep truth and interest.'

Zola immediately reprinted his articles in a pamphlet bearing on the cover and the title page the words: 'That which I seek above all in a picture is a man and not a picture.' This booklet was published in the spring of 1866 and entitled *Mon Salon*. Its long dedication to Cézanne is a symbol of Zola's gratitude for his friend's more or less direct collaboration, for it was in their discussions that most of the ideas were born which Zola later developed. But it is to his childhood friend rather than to the young painter that this dedication is addressed:

'I experience deep joy, my friend, in having a tête-à-tête with you. You cannot imagine how much I have suffered from this quarrel which I have just had with the herd, with the unknown crowd; I felt so misunderstood, I felt such hatred around me, that discouragement often made me drop my pen. Today I can avail myself of the intimate pleasure of one of the good talks we have had together for the past ten years. It is for you alone that I write these few pages, I know you will read them with your heart, and that tomorrow you will love me more affectionately.

'Imagine that we are alone together in some remote place, far from any struggle, and that we are talking like old friends who know each other's very soul and understand each other at a mere glance.

'For ten years we have been speaking of art and literature. We have lived together—do you remember?—and often daybreak caught us still conversing, searching the past, questioning the present, trying to find the truth and to create for ourselves an infallible and complete religion. We shuffled stacks of terrible ideas, we examined and rejected all systems, and after such arduous labour we told ourselves that outside of powerful and individual life there only exists lies and stupidity.

'Happy are they who have memories! I envisage your role in my life as that of the pale young man of whom Musset speaks. You are my whole youth; I find you mixed up with all my joys, with all my sufferings. Our minds, in brotherhood, have developed side by side. Today, at the beginning, we have faith in ourselves because we have penetrated our hearts and flesh.

'We used to live in our shadow, isolated, unsociable, enjoying our thoughts. We felt lost in the midst of the complacent and superficial crowd. In all things we sought men, in every dawn, in every painting or poem we wanted to find an individual emphasis. We asserted that the masters, the geniuses, are creators, each of whom had made a world of his own, and we rejected the disciples, the impotent, those whose trade it is to steal here and there a few scraps of originality.

'Did you know that we were revolutionaries without being aware of it? I have just been able to say aloud what we told each other for ten years. The noise of the quarrel reached you, did it not? And you have witnessed the fine welcome accorded our dear thoughts. Ah! the poor lads who lived healthily in the middle of Provence, in the sun, and who clung to such folly and such bad faith!

'For—you probably did not know this—I am a man of bad faith. The public has already ordered several dozen strait-jackets to take me to Charenton. I only praise my relatives and my friends, I am a fool and evil man, I am a scandalmonger.

'This inspires pity, my friend, and it is very sad. Will it always be the same story? Will we always have to talk like the others or be still? Do you remember our long conversations? We said that the least new truth could not be revealed without provoking anger and protests. And now I, in turn, am being jeered at and insulted.

'It is a good experience, my friend. For nothing in the world would I wish to destroy these pages; they are not much in themselves but they have been, so to speak, my touchstone of public opinion. We now know how unpopular our dear thoughts are.

'Yet, I am pleased to present my ideas a second time. I believe in them, I know that in a few years everyone will agree with me. I am not afraid that they will be thrown in my face later on.

'Emile Zola
'Paris, May 20, 1866'

VIII

PORTRAIT OF CÉZANNE

CÉZANNE, approaching thirty, was tall and thin, 'bearded, with knotty joints and a strong head. A very delicate nose hidden in the moustache, eyes narrow and clear . . . deep in his eyes, great tenderness. His voice was loud.' At this period he wore 'a battered black felt hat and an enormous overcoat, once a delicate maroon, which the rain had streaked green. He was a little stoop-shouldered and had a nervous shudder which was to become habitual. He planted himself in laced boots and his short trousers revealed blue stockings.' Thus Zola depicted him several years later when creating the character of the painter Claude Lantier in *Le Ventre de Paris*, published in 1873. The notes for this novel mention Cézanne by name. Subsequently, when preparing *L'Œuvre*, a novel of which Claude Lantier was the protagonist, Zola dwelt in greater detail upon his recollections of the youthful Cézanne:

'He was wary of women. . . . He never brought girls to his studio; he treated them all like a boy who ignored them, hiding his painful timidity under a rude bluster. . . . "I do not need any women," he said, "—that would disturb me too much, I don't even know what they are good for—I have always been afraid to try".'

Zola wrote and underlined the words 'very important' in the margin of this last note. He also underlined another remark apropos of the grossness of Cézanne's language: 'He swore, used filthy words, wallowed in mud, with the cold rage of a tender and exquisite soul who doubts himself and dreams of being dirty.' Cézanne's mood was very uneven; gay in the morning, unhappy in the evening. Sometimes he called painting 'a dog's profession'; sometimes he said, 'When I paint, it's as though I tickled myself'; sometimes he exclaimed in despair, 'I have never finished, never, never.'

'Paul is wonderful this year,' wrote Marion to Morstatt in the summer of 1866, 'with his scarce and extremely long hair and his revolutionary beard.'

The son of Henri Gasquet, who knew Cézanne toward the end of

47

his life, later wrote: 'Those who saw him at that time described him to me as frightening, full of hallucinations, almost bestial in a kind of suffering divinity. He changed models each week. He was in despair because he could not satisfy himself. He suffered from those combinations of violence and timidity, of humility and pride, of doubts and dogmatic assertions, which shook him all his life. He shut himself up for weeks, not wanting to let a living soul enter his studio, shunning any new acquaintance.'

At such times Zola witnessed 'the outburst of the artist, impotent in the face of substantial and living works of which he dreamed'. 'Every day, a long despairing effort', he noted, adding: 'He destroys about fifteen canvases . . . reproaches himself for the failure of his painting. . . . Never again will he touch a brush.'

In Cézanne's studio there was complete disorder. It was only swept once a month 'for fear that the dust might cover his fresh canvases'. A thousand things were strewn on the floor, and ashes piled up there. The sole big table was always littered with brushes, paints, dirty plates, a spirit lamp, etc. Unframed sketches hung on the wall all the way down to the floor, where they were piled up on a heap of canvases.

Cézanne had very little money, for either his father did not give him a large enough allowance, or else Cézanne did not know how to control his expenses. His mother managed to send him funds from time to time by economizing on household expenses, but in any case he was delighted to accept occasional loans from Zola and Baille, for, as he said in a letter: 'I am still sadder when I have no money.' Cézanne was working very hard. His discouragements no longer made him think of going back into his father's bank, but rather stimulated him to new efforts. Relentlessly he touched up earlier paintings, a method that often obliged him to do the pictures all over again.

Cézanne spent the summer of 1866 with Zola and his mother in Bennecourt near Paris, where they were joined by Baille, Solari, Valabrègue, Chaillan, and Gabrielle. Their carefree life in the country, on the banks of the Seine, at the inn of Mère Gigoux, brought the friends closer together and animated their exchange of views.

'After dinner', Zola reports, 'the group stretched out on two bales of straw which Mère Gigoux had the generosity to provide in a corner of the courtyard. It was the hour of theories, of furious discussions which lasted till midnight and kept the trembling peasants awake. We smoked pipes while contemplating the moon. We called each other "idiot" or "half-wit" for the least difference of opinion.'

What made their debates particularly heated was the fact that the poets defended romanticism while the painters were rabid realists.

'We executed men in the limelight, we were drunk with the hope of overthrowing everything in the future so as to reveal a new art of which we would be the prophets.' Zola formed a plan of writing an essay on the work of art before criticism, but he never carried it out.

Cézanne had brought his canvases and paints along, and Zola informed Numa Coste: 'Cézanne works; he becomes increasingly firm on the original road to which his nature has led him. I have much hope in him. We expect him to be rejected for another ten years. Right now he is trying to do big works, canvases four to five metres in size.'

A refusal by the jury of the Salon had come to have the same meaning as an award in the eyes of the young friends. Among Zola's comrades only Solari succeeded in being accepted. He had just exhibited a more than life-size bust of Zola in the casting of which Zola and Cézanne had helped him (Pl. 20). Cézanne himself was all the less discouraged by the rejections of his pictures, for he believed, as he wrote Pissarro, that 'in following the path of virtue one is always rewarded by men, but not by painting'. Nevertheless, he preferred to find satisfaction in his work.

*　　*　　*

From Bennecourt Cézanne returned to Aix where, as Marion wrote Morstatt, 'we are beginning to attract attention. They bow to us. Some idiot dedicated a poem to Paul Cézanne in the local newspaper. What a bunch of clods!'

This notoriety, added to the sincere admiration of his friends, helped to bolster Cézanne's morale, as did the arrival of Antoine Guillemet who came to Aix in mid-October. After spending a few days at the 'Jas de Bouffan', he rented a small house near the Route d'Italie, not far from where Zola had lived. Guillemet, in a letter to Zola, reported:

'For a month now I have been in Aix, this Athens of the Midi, and I assure you that the time has not passed slowly. Fine weather, beautiful country, people with whom to talk painting and develop theories which are demolished on the morrow have all helped to make my stay in Aix agreeable. In his two letters Paul told you more about me than about himself and I shall do the same thing, that is to say the opposite, and shall tell you a lot about the master. His physique has rather improved, his hair is long, his face reflects health, and his costume makes a sensation on the main street. You may therefore feel reassured on this score. His mind, although always in effervescence, leaves him moments of clarity, and his painting, encouraged by some real commissions, promises to reward his efforts. In a word, "the sky of the future seems at times to be less black". On his return to Paris you will see some pictures which you will like very much, among others an "Overture to Tannhäuser" . . . and a "Portrait of His Father in an Armchair" (Pl. 14) which looks very good. The painting is light in colour and the effect very fine; the father looks like a pope on his throne were it not for *Le Siècle* that he is reading [the elder Cézanne actually is reading *L' Evénement*]. In a word, it goes well, and be sure that we shall soon see very beautiful things.

'The people of Aix continue to get on his nerves; they ask to see his painting only to malign it afterwards. He has found a good way of dealing with them: "*Je vous emmerde*," he tells them and the people who have no temperament flee in horror. In spite or perhaps because of that there is obviously a movement towards him and the time is near, I believe, when he will be offered the directorship of the museum. I greatly hope for this because either I know him little or else we shall be able to see there some pretty successful landscapes done with the palette knife which have no other chance of getting into a museum.

'The cholera, as you know, has left the Midi, but we still have Valabrègue who, with surprising fecundity, daily brings to light one or more corpses (in verse, that goes without saying). He will show you quite a lovely collection on his return to Paris. The verses which you are familiar with as 'The Two Corpses' are now called 'The Eleven Corpses'. . . . A very nice fellow, giving the impression of having swallowed a lightning conductor, making it difficult for him to walk.

'As for young Marion, whom you know by reputation, he is cherishing the hope of being called to a chair of geology. He excavates hard and tries to demonstrate to us that God never existed, and that it is a put-up affair to believe in him. About which we bother little, for it is not painting. . . .'

In Guillemet's letter it is difficult to distinguish between seriousness and irony but it is not impossible that Cézanne's friends really thought for a time that he had a chance of becoming curator of the museum. They seem to have been intoxicated by the sensation their group made in Aix, the poem dedicated to Cézanne, and the writings of Zola. It was at this period that Marion wrote to Zola: 'Paul has been an epidemic germ in Aix. Now all painters, even glassmakers, have begun to impaste!' Cézanne himself was doubtless inspired to paint enormous canvases by the belief that glory was near. But it goes without saying that all these dreams were far from realization and meanwhile discouragement, as usual, followed upon enthusiasm. Thus Cézanne wrote Pissarro: 'I see Guillemet every day. He is going to paint a large picture as soon as possible. . . . I always am working a little, but paints are scarce here and very expensive; and apathy, apathy. Let us hope that the sale will come off. In that event we shall sacrifice a golden calf. I do not want to submit any more [to the Salon in Marseilles], especially as I have no frames and it involves expenses which would be better saved for painting. I say this as regards myself, and *merde* for the jury.'

And Antoine Guillemet added to Cézanne's letter: 'Cézanne has done some beautiful paintings. He is making them light again and I am sure you will be pleased with the three or four canvases he will bring back.'

Guillemet took advantage of his stay in Aix to induce Cézanne's father to increase Paul's allowance. Cézanne's stay with his parents evidently lasted longer than expected, for Zola wrote Valabrègue in December 1866: 'Tell Paul to come back as soon as possible. He will bring some courage into my life. I await him as a saviour. If he is not coming in a few days, ask him to write. Let him be sure to bring me all his sketches to prove to me that I must work.'

IX

NEW ARTICLES BY ZOLA

1867–1868

AT THE beginning of 1867 Cézanne was again in Paris. 'Paul works hard;' Zola wrote to Valabrègue, 'he dreams of immense paintings.'

Preparations for the Salon this time took on especial importance as it was hoped that Zola's violent articles had produced a change of attitude. Moreover, the World's Fair, which was taking place in the same year, attracted a large crowd to Paris. But Zola and his friends were to be disappointed once more. The jury replied to Zola's attacks by new rejections.

In April 1867, *Le Figaro* reprinted an article by Arnold Mortier which had appeared in another paper:

'I have heard of two rejected paintings done by M. Sésame (nothing to do with the *Arabian Nights*), the same man who, in 1863, caused general mirth in the Salon des Refusés—always!—by a canvas depicting two pig's feet in the form of a cross. This time M. Sésame has sent to the exhibition two compositions which, though less queer, are nevertheless just as worthy of exclusion from the Salon. These compositions are entitled: 'The Wine Grog'. One of them depicts a nude man to whom a very dressed-up woman has just brought a wine grog; the other portrays a nude woman and a man dressed as a *lazzarone:* in this one the grog is spilt.'

Zola immediately protested to *Le Figaro* in a letter which was printed on April 12:

'My dear Colleague:

'Be good enough, I beg you, to insert these few lines of correction. They concern one of my childhood friends, a young painter whose strong and individual talent I respect extremely.

'You reprinted a clipping from *L'Europe* dealing with a M. Sésame who was supposed to have exhibited at the Salon des Refusés in 1863 "two pig's feet in the form of a cross" and who, this year, had another canvas rejected, entitled "The Wine Grog".

'I must say that I had some difficulty in recognizing under the mask stuck on his face one of my former schoolmates, M. Paul

Césanne [sic], who has not the slightest pig's foot in his artistic equipment, at least so far. I make this reservation because I do not see why one should not paint pig's feet just as one paints melons and carrots.*

'M. Paul Césanne, in excellent and numerous company, has indeed had two canvases rejected this year: "The Wine Grog", and "Intoxication". M. Arnold Mortier has seen fit to be amused by these pictures and to describe them with flights of imagination which do him great credit. I know all that is just a pleasant joke which one must not worry about. But I have never been able to understand this particular kind of criticism which consists of ridiculing and condemning what one has not even seen. I insist at least on saying that M. Arnold Mortier's descriptions are inaccurate.

'Even you, my dear colleague, add your opinion: you are "convinced that the artist may have put a philosophical idea into his paintings". That is an inappropriate conviction. If you want to find philosophical artists, look for them among the Germans, or even among our pretty French dreamers; but know that the analytical painters, the young school whose cause I have the honour to defend, are satisfied with the great realities of nature.

'Moreover it is up to M. de Nieuwerkerke that the "Wine Grog" and "Intoxication" be exhibited. As you know, a number of painters have just signed a petition demanding the re-opening of the Salon des Refusés. Perhaps some day M. Arnold Mortier will see the canvases which he has so glibly judged and described. Such strange things do happen.

'It is true that M. Paul Césanne will never call himself M. Césame and that, whatever happens, he will never be the creator of "two pig's feet in the form of a cross".

'Your devoted colleague,

'Emile Zola.'

This time, like the preceding year, there was no Salon des Refusés; the newspapers carried an announcement saying that Count Nieuwerkerke had once more refused the appeal addressed to him by the rejected artists. 'Paul has been rejected,' Zola informed Valabrègue, 'Guillemet has been rejected, all have been rejected; the jury, annoyed by my Salon review, has thrown out all those who follow the new path. . . .' And he added: 'I have been obliged to give up the idea of writing a Salon review. It is possible, however, that I may publish a pamphlet on my painter friends.'

Indeed, Zola did publish a series of articles on Manet. But according to Paul Alexis, who had it from Zola himself, Zola also wrote a Salon review for a newspaper called *La Situation* which

---

*In the Salon des Refusés there was, however, a canvas entitled 'Pig's Feet', signed Graham.

belonged to the King of Hanover. This paper can no longer be found and, furthermore, this series was almost immediately stopped because of the reviewer's violence.

His numerous publications on art gave Zola an important place in the group of young painters. His pamphlet with its long and affectionate dedication to Cézanne and his intervention on the latter's behalf in *Le Figaro* were to have a curious result. Until then, to the artists to whom Cézanne had introduced Zola, the writer had been 'the friend of the painter'. Now that Zola had become the champion of the group, it was the painter who was known as 'the friend of the writer'.

A letter from Valabrègue to Zola at the end of April 1867 confirms this state of affairs by alluding to the correction Zola had sent to *Le Figaro:*

'Paul wrote to me recently. Your letter had informed me of his rejection by the jury which I expected, as did you and he. When will Paul not be rejected? On the other hand, I have learned with pleasure of the vigorous way you answered for him. . . . You are destined to torture his enemies. It is impossible to congratulate you too heartily on this fine role. Paul is the child, innocent of life, of whom you are the guardian and guide. You watch over him, he walks by your side, always sure of being defended. An alliance between you to defend him has been signed, an alliance which will even be an offensive one if necessary. You are his thinking soul; his destiny is to make paintings, just as yours is to make his life!'

Without Zola's devoted friendship, Cézanne would surely have felt still more isolated and discouraged, especially as the repeated rejections by the jury affected him much more than he wished to admit and deprived him of the only means of exhibiting his paintings. 'Cézanne will go back to Aix in about ten days', Zola wrote Valabrègue in May 1867. 'He will spend three months in the solitude of the province and will return to Paris in September. He has great need of work and of courage.'

After Cézanne's departure, Marius Roux also went to Aix, and Zola asked him to see Cézanne and speak to him. Zola then received the following report from Roux, which reflects the strange impression that Cézanne made on his friends:

'I promised to write to you immediately upon my arrival in Aix. This would have been too soon for I would not have been able to answer your questions. Even now is too soon. Paul to me is a real sphinx. I went to see him during the first few days of my stay here. I saw him at his house and we talked quite a long time. A few days ago we went to the country together and slept there one night; we had a lot of time to chat.

'Well! All I can tell you about him is that he is in good health.

Nevertheless, I have not forgotten our conversations. I will report them to you verbally and you will translate them. As for me, I am not capable of translating them. You understand what I mean: I have not a deep enough intimacy with Paul to know the exact meaning of his words.

'However (for I can hazard a guess), I believe that he has retained a holy enthusiasm for painting. He is not yet beaten; but without having for Aix the same enthusiasm as for painting, I believe that henceforth he will prefer the life he leads here to that which he leads in Paris. He is vanquished by this Gomard-like [?] existence and he has a devoted respect for the paternal vermicelli.

'Does he deceive himself? And does he believe himself to be beaten by Gomard [?] instead of by Nieuwerkerke? That is what I cannot tell you and what you will decide for yourself when I describe our conversations at greater length.'

It seems, however, that Cézanne was able once again to overcome his deep discouragement and return to work, for at about the same time Marion (Pl. 8) wrote to their friend Morstatt: 'Paul is here, painting, more Paul than ever, but imbued this year with a firm determination to succeed as quickly as possible. Lately he has painted some really beautiful portraits, no longer with the knife, but just as vigorous and much more skillful and pleasing in technique. . . . His watercolours are particularly remarkable, their colouration amazing, and they produce a strange effect of which I did not think watercolours were capable.'

'I wish you could see the canvas he is doing now,' Marion wrote a little later. 'He has taken up again the subject you already know, 'The Overture to Tannhäuser', but in entirely different tones, in very clear colours, and all the figures are very finished. There is a head of a blonde girl, which is both pretty and amazingly powerful, and my profile is a very good likeness; it is carefully done without harshness of colour and that somewhat repellent ferocity. The piano is wonderful, as in the other painting, and the draperies, as always, astonishingly real. Probably it will be refused at the exhibition, but it will certainly be exhibited somewhere; a canvas like this is enough to make a reputation.'

But Cézanne was far from gaining the reputation that Marion hoped for him. An attempt to show a picture at the beginning of that year had proved this, as Valabrègue described to Zola: 'I want to tell you that Marius exhibited a painting of Cézanne's in Marseilles, in a shop window. The result has been a lot of noise. People gathered in the street; the crowd was stupefied. Paul's name was asked, there was some activity on that side and a slight *succès de curiosité*. For the rest, I think that if the painting had been displayed much longer, they would have ended by breaking the window and smashing the canvas.'

Zola, in Paris, was associated more or less exclusively with painters. He wrote Valabrègue that there was not a single writer in his circle with whom he could talk. He was often seen with Manet at the Café Guerbois, in the Batignolles quarter. They met almost daily in this café and spent many evening hours there discussing art with Duranty, Fantin-Latour, Degas, Monet, Burty, and others. The acknowledged leader of what was commonly called *Le groupe des Batignolles* was Manet, who always showed up dressed as a gentleman, with gloves and cane, wearing a top hat.

Cézanne rarely came to the Café Guerbois. He did not like the atmosphere of discussions and theories at these reunions. In spite of his admiration for Manet as an artist, he despised his mannerisms. He himself was not satisfied with expressing in his painting alone his disdain for conventions, but wished to express revolt with his whole being. He was negligent of his clothing and language and took a certain pleasure in shocking those around him.

On arriving at the café, Monet later remembered, Cézanne would give the group a mistrustful look. Then, opening his vest, he would pull up his trousers and ostentatiously re-adjust his red sash, after which he would shake hands all round. But in Manet's presence, he would take off his hat and in a nasal voice say with his smile: 'I do not shake your hand, Monsieur Manet; I have not washed for a week.'

He would sit in a corner, seeming little interested in the remarks being exchanged around him. Sometimes, when he heard an opinion expressed which was too much opposed to his own, he would rise abruptly and instead of answering, take himself off without a word to anyone.

In the spring of 1868 Zola, and with him the Batignolles group, once more impatiently awaited the jury's decision. Solari, who had obtained a great success at the Salon the year before, went to the Palais de l'Industrie to get the latest news on the deliberations. He reported to Zola: 'I met there Pissarro, Guillemet, in short all the Batignolles. They consider Cézanne's painting very good. Since then, I have seen Cézanne who told me that the last is even better.'

Cézanne's entry was rejected again, although the jury showed itself less severe toward his friends. The paintings of Manet, including his 'Portrait of Emile Zola' (Pl. 21), as well as works by Pissarro, Claude Monet, Bazille, and Renoir were accepted. This success doubtless led the management of *L'Evénement Illustré* (which had replaced *L'Evénement* and of which M. de Villemessant was no longer director) to entrust Zola with reviewing the Salon, at the same time reserving for the paper the right to follow up with a series of articles by a more conciliatory author. Zola began his work with the proviso that he could speak of the official school only in generalities, and Zola actually did, in his own words, avoid 'mentioning by name a single one of the painters whose pictures irritate me'.

As a result, this new series of critical articles did not reveal the same belligerent spirit as the first. It was now simply a question of drawing attention to painters like Jongkind, Monet, Renoir, and Pissarro, whose works had otherwise little chance of being noticed. Zola wrote:

'The classical landscape is dead, killed by life and by truth. No one nowadays would dare to say that nature needs to be idealized, that the sky and water are vulgar, and that it is necessary to make horizons harmonious and correct in order to create beautiful works. . . .

'Certain landscape artists of our day have created a nature after the taste of the public, which has a certain appearance of truth and possesses at the same time the sparkling grace of the lie. . . . What I accuse them of is of lacking personality. They have created a conventional nature, cut after the pattern of real nature and one finds that nature indistinctly in all their paintings. Naturalists of talent, on the other hand, are individual interpreters; they translate truths in original language, they remain profoundly truthful and at the same time keep their individuality. They are above all human and mix their humanity with every leaf they paint. That is what will make their work live.

'Our landscape artists leave at dawn, box on back, happy as hunters who love fresh air. They sit down anywhere, at the edge of the wood, or near the water, hardly choosing their themes, finding everywhere a living horizon of human interest so to speak. . . .'

Zola thus gives the impression that all his friends worked outdoors, whereas actually they had hardly begun to do so. Until then, artists had painted landscapes in their studios with the aid of sketches done in the open. Most of the landscapes of Millet, Daubigny, Rousseau, Courbet, and Corot were done in that way. But Corot's sketches from nature, for instance, were obviously, as Zola put it, 'more sincere and striking' than his large studio canvases in dull and dreamy harmonies. Only a last step toward nature remained to be taken—that of painting entirely outdoors. Jongkind was among the first to do watercolours in this fashion; Eugène Boudin and Claude Monet followed his example, and that very year Pissarro, working at Pontoise, near Paris, sent to the Salon a painting of the Hermitage done completely from nature. It was this canvas which prompted Zola to remark: 'A beautiful picture by this artist is the deed of an honest man'.

Zola probably owed his knowledge of outdoor painting to Pissarro, Monet, Boudin, and possibly Renoir, rather than to Cézanne, who did group compositions, nudes, portraits, and still lifes, but rarely landscapes. Theoretically, however, Cézanne was enthusiastic about open-air painting. In 1866 he had told Zola: 'You know, all pictures painted inside, in the studio, will never be as good as the things done in the open air. When outdoor scenes are represented, the contrast between the figures and the ground is astounding and the landscape is magnificent. I see some superb things and I shall have to make up my mind only to do things out-of-doors. . . . I feel sure that all the paintings by the old masters representing outdoor scenes have been done from imagination, for they do not seem to me to have the true and above all original aspect lent by nature.' Obviously again Cézanne's opinions on art were reflected in Zola's writings.

Zola closed his series of articles, in which he had dealt at length with painters he admired, with high praise for an enormous piece of sculpture by Solari, entitled 'Sleeping Negro', and with these general comments on the exhibition: 'Melodrama abounds. Deceived husbands who shoot pistols are much appreciated. There is also a taste for dying persons who marry to the accompaniment of the sobs of the bystanders. Young artists of tomorrow, take these as models. Success lies in lugubrious or terrible subjects. It is useless to know how to paint, to have individuality, and eagerly to seek after truth. . . . That is the highest skill: to tickle the senses and make a show of idealism.'

The publishers of *L'Evénement Illustré* followed up Zola's review with two articles by one Paul Delmas, explaining: 'As our colleague Emile Zola has only dealt with a restricted number of exhibiting artists in a very personal way, *L'Evénement*, while allowing him complete freedom of expression, has reserved for itself the right to supplement his deliberate omissions'.

There follows 'a list of remarkable canvases exhibited this year', chosen from what must have been a 'non-personal' point of view. It begins with Cabanel and Bouguereau, the chiefs of the official school, and goes right on down the line. Thus in his second battle Zola won no further ground for his friends; this may be due to the fact that he had not completely lived up to his own motto: 'It is not enough to speak well of those whom one admires; one must speak ill of those one hates'.

*　　*　　*

It is surprising that Zola, in reviewing the works of his friends, did not discuss Cézanne's canvases. The explanation could of course be that in a report on a Salon there is no place for painters who have not been admitted. But if Cézanne had no place among the exhibitors, he had one—prominent at that—among the rejected. Had Zola so desired, he could have found more than one way to proclaim his admiration for the painter of 'The Wine Grog', whom he had defended against ridicule without, however, any word of real appreciation. Had not Zola written about Manet, though he was not represented at the Salon? Possibly this curious neglect was occasioned by the fact that while Cézanne remained for Zola his most precious childhood friend, the artistic friendship which linked him to Manet was stronger.

It is questionable, of course, whether Zola's preference for Manet was based on purely aesthetic considerations. Zola wanted to be the chronicler of modern life and was interested in an artist whom he presumed to have the same goal. Besides, Manet's work and fame could contribute to the future prestige of his own theories. Deficient in aesthetic appreciation, Zola was unable to understand fully the efforts of either Manet or Cézanne. But, while Cézanne was still caught in his peculiar romanticism, Manet offered a counterpart to Zola's naturalistic theories. It was doubtless because Manet's approach was clearer to him that Zola became the ardent champion of his art.

Some of their common friends, however, already considered Cézanne a very great artist. For instance, when Marion discussed with Morstatt the respective merits of Courbet and Manet in 1867, he wound up by stating: 'Paul is really much stronger than they. He is convinced of being able, by a more skilful execution and perception, to admit details while retaining breadth. Thus he would achieve his aims, and his works would become more complete. I think that the moment of his success is not far off. It is merely a question of producing.'

But a little later Marion complained to his friend:

'Realist painting, my dear fellow, is farther off than ever from official success and it is quite certain that Cézanne has no chance of showing his work in officially sanctioned exhibitions for a long time to come. His name is already too well known; too many revolutionary ideas in art are connected with it; the painters on the jury will not weaken for an instant. And I admire the persistence and nerve with which Paul writes me: "Well! They will be blasted in eternity with even greater persistence." All that considered, he ought to think about finding another and greater means of getting publicity. He has now reached an astonishing perfection of technique. All his exaggerated fierceness had been modulated, and I think it is time that circumstances offer him the means and opportunity to produce a great deal.'

Why did Zola not help Cézanne by giving him the publicity of which Marion speaks? Perhaps a more important reason for this silence is to be found in Zola's mental evolution. The years had blunted his youthful enthusiasm for Cézanne as a painter. His faith in Cézanne's genius remained intact, but he doubted increasingly Cézanne's ability to express this genius. Although he was shocked by the repeated rejections of Cézanne's work, he nevertheless believed that Cézanne had not yet given his best. A letter from Zola to the critic Théodore Duret is significant here. The continuous rejections of Cézanne's work had resulted in exciting Duret's curiosity, and he wrote to his colleague on the *Tribune*:

'My dear Zola,
'I hear of a painter called Cézanne, or something like that, who comes from Aix and whose paintings have been rejected by the jury. I seem to recall that you once spoke to me of a very eccentric painter from Aix. Could that be the one rejected this year?

'If it is, will you please give me his address and a note of introduction so that I may make the acquaintance of the painter and his work.

'Yours,
'Théodore Duret.'

Zola replied:

'I cannot give you the address of the painter of whom you speak. He shuts himself in a great deal; he is going through a period of groping. And, to my mind, he is right not to allow anyone in his studio. Wait until he has found himself.'

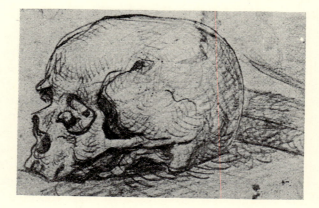

X

CÉZANNE AND ZOLA AT WORK

CÉZANNE spent the summer of 1868 at the 'Jas de Bouffan', where he led such a retired life absorbed in his work that he was even unable to date his letters, and it was 'around the beginning of July' that he wrote to Numa Coste:

'Alexis was good enough to come to see me, having heard from the great Valabrègue of my return from Paris. He even lent me a little review of 1840 by Balzac; he asked me whether you were still painting, etc.—you know, all the things people say when chatting. He promised to come back to see me; I have not seen him for a month. For my part, and especially since receiving your letter, I directed my steps in the evening toward the Cours Mirabeau, which is somewhat contrary to my solitary habits. Impossible to meet him. However, a great desire to fulfil my duty urging me, I shall attempt to descend on his home. But on that day I shall change my shoes and shirt beforehand.

'I have seen Aufan a little, but the others seem to hide themselves and a great vacuum seems to surround one when one has been away for some time. I shall not tell you about him. I don't know whether I am living or simply recollecting, but everything makes me think. I wandered alone over to the dam and to Saint-Antonin. There I slept on a heap of straw at the mill; good wine, good hospitality. I remembered our attempts at climbing [Sainte-Victoire]. Shall we never begin them again? How strange life is, what a diversion, and how difficult it would be at the present time to be once more, the three of us and the dog, where we were only a few years ago.

'I have no amusement, except the family and a few issues of *Le Siècle* where I find unimportant news. Being alone, I hardly ever venture to the café. But deep down I am always hopeful.

'Alexis was kind enough to read me a poem which I found really very good; then he recited by heart a few verses from another one, entitled 'Symphony in A Minor.' I found these few verses more individual, more original, and complimented him on this.'

A second letter to Coste, written 'towards the end of November,' reveals the same ennui. In it Cézanne speaks of his forthcoming return to Paris and of several painters in Aix, especially of his former teacher at the drawing school 'Gibert Pater, bad painter.'

'I was glad to hear from you for it drew me out of the lethargy into which I had fallen. The beautiful expedition to Sainte-Victoire which we were to have made fell through this summer, owing to the heat, and in October, owing to the rain. From that you can judge the softening which is beginning to make itself manifest in the will-power of our little comrades. But that is how it is, it seems one is not always full of vitality; one would say in Latin *semper virens*, "always vigorous," or better, "full of will".'

Besides Alexis, whom Cézanne considered very talented, he again saw a great deal of Fortuné Marion. Cézanne accompanied him on his search for fossils (at the age of twenty-one Marion had just published a treatise on prehistoric man in Provence) and Marion in turn went with Cézanne to the 'motif', being himself an amateur painter.

'Cézanne is planning a picture,' Marion wrote to Morstatt, 'for which he will use some portraits. One of us, in the middle of a landscape, will be speaking while the others listen. I have your photograph and you will be in it. . . . Paul intends to make a gift of the canvas, nicely framed, if it is welcome, to the Marseilles museum, which will thus be forced to display realist painting and our glory.'

What became of this work is not known; perhaps it was never finished. The wild boldness of Cézanne's plans was as usual followed by complete discouragement. As Marion lamented in a letter to Morstatt: 'What a generation of sufferers, my poor old friend Zola, the two of us, and so many others. There are sufferers among us who are just as unhappy with fewer troubles—Cézanne with his living secure and his black despairs of morale and temperament. One must still resign oneself to all that.' And Marion again expresses this resignation in another letter: 'Here it is almost always the same. In the morning I work on geology, evenings I spend at Paul's in the country. . . . We dine. We take a little walk. We don't get drunk. All that is very sad.'

Cézanne returned to Paris at the beginning of 1869. It is about this time that he met a young model, Hortense Fiquet, who was then nineteen. She was born in Saligny in the Jura and had lived in Paris with her mother until the latter's death. Nothing is known of her father except that he was a landowner in the department of Doubs around 1886. Hortense Fiquet was a tall and handsome brunette with large black eyes and a sallow complexion. Cézanne eleven years older than she, fell in love with her and persuaded her to live with him. Thus he was no longer alone, but he kept his affair secret from his parents, or rather from his father. This change in

Cézanne's emotional life does not appear to have influenced either his art or his relationship to his friends.

* * *

At this period Cézanne had a predilection for violent and erotic subjects (fig. 28). His imagination, savage and impulsive, is reflected in his use of colour and movement, whereas Zola's imagination, imbued with romanticism, expressed itself in sobs and lamentations. Zola was disturbed by Cézanne's lack of moderation as revealed in canvases such as one showing a nude negro, lying on a couch, embraced by a fair-skinned girl while in the background appears a maid with a tray (reminiscent of the black servant with the bouquet in *Olympia*), or another in which a naked woman, on a magnificent bed with its curtains wide open, allows herself to be gazed upon by a motley crowd that includes a man with Cézanne's own features.

Later on, in *L'Œuvre*, Zola attempted to explain his friend's eroticism: 'It was a chaste man's passion for the flesh of women, a mad love of nudity desired and never possessed, an impossibility of satisfying himself, of creating as much of this flesh as he dreamed to hold in his frantic arms. Those girls whom he chased out of his studio he adored in his paintings; he caressed or attacked them, in tears of despair at not being able to make them sufficiently beautiful, sufficiently alive.'

An indication of what Zola thought of Cézanne's work at this period may be found in an episode of *Thérèse Raquin*, one of his early novels. The impression produced by the paintings of Laurent, one of the characters of the book, is thus described: 'There were five studies, painted with real energy, thick and solid in appearance, each part standing out in magnificent strokes. . . . Of course these studies were clumsy, but they had a strangeness and character so powerful that they proclaimed a highly developed artistic sense. It might be called painting which had been lived. Laurent's friend had never before seen sketches so full of promise.'

Zola was still awaiting the realization of this promise after so much groping. He was waiting for a work which would reveal strength, will, the man. Meanwhile Zola looked upon Cézanne's works as sketches, especially as the artist himself always expressed dissatisfaction with them as soon as the slightest occasion for self-doubt arose.

With the exception of Pissarro and Marion, most of Cézanne's friends, while optimistic about his future, seem to have been reticent on the subject of his painting. Guillemet, for instance, wrote Zola in July 1869: 'Give me news of Paul. Has he successfully finished his picture? It is time for him to create according to his own conception and I am anxious to see him occupy the position he ought to have. What a strange thing painting is; it is not enough to be intelligent to do it well. Still, in time he will arrive, I am sure. . . .'

Zola's reply must have been discouraging, reflecting his lack of confidence in his friend's art, for Guillemet wrote to him the following month: 'What you tell me about Paul makes me very sad; the good fellow must suffer like a damned soul because of all the attempts at painting into which he throws himself headlong and which only rarely succeed, alas! Where there is good material one cannot despair; as for me, I always expect him to produce beautiful things which will give pleasure to us, his friends who love him, and which will confound the sceptics and detractors.'

Cézanne's work done between 1866 and the war of 1870 bears witness to his many efforts to achieve an individual technique and palette. It includes still lifes, portraits, group compositions, sketches made in museums, landscapes. Cézanne still kept his preference for picturesque subjects which distinguished him from the Batignolles group. Thus, while Monet and Pissarro became landscapists, Cézanne appeared as the heir of Delacroix, at least insofar as subject matter was concerned. Under the influence of Courbet, the others simplified their subjects; Monet painted his 'Camille' and Renoir his 'Lise', but Cézanne painted violent scenes, often of an erotic kind, such as 'The Temptation of Saint Anthony', 'The Orgy', and 'The Judgment of Paris'. Whereas the imagination of Manet and his friends was limited by visual experience, Cézanne, at that time, considered himself a visionary. His imagination was aimed at more than a purely plastic rendering of his impressions. Above all he wished to externalize the agitations of his inner life.

One of his most remarkable paintings of this period was done at Zola's house in the Rue de la Condamine, and Cézanne made his friend a present of it. This painting, 'L'Enlèvement', dated 1867, even though not reaching the twelve or fifteen feet of which the artist had dreamed, measures 35 by 46 inches (Pl. 12). It represents a large green plain done in vivid, comma-like strokes which make it look like troubled water. Against this a nude giant strangely bronzed stands out. In his arms he carries a pale woman with blue-black hair; from her hips falls a dark blue drape. The harmony between her white skin and the bronze of the man, surrounded by the blue material and the green plain, is harsh. In the background, in front of a white cloud, arises a mountain vaguely reminiscent of Sainte-Victoire. At the left two little pink bodies of young girls enliven the composition. Zola was to think of them later on when describing in L'Oeuvre a canvas of Claude Lantier. He no doubt admired this painting for its bright colours, its dramatic composition, the impression of force which it gives, as well as the stubborn individualism which was so typical of the companion of his walks and of his dreams.

It is not surprising to note that during those years Cézanne's paintings are very diverse and often have little in common either in technique or composition. Besides large canvases, there are very small ones; besides scenes done completely from imagination, there are others for which Cézanne made use of studies sketched at the Atelier Suisse; besides paintings executed with verve and virtuosity in large strokes with a brush full of paint that sometimes leaves lumps of colour on the canvas, there are those like 'L'Enlèvement' where he employs small and carefully placed brush strokes. Several still lifes were done with the palette knife, while in others Cézanne applied colour in a way which often conceals the individual strokes, though it provides a rich texture and great plasticity.

Among the portraits of this period is one of Cézanne's fifteen-year-old sister, which is known only through the description Cézanne gave Zola: 'I have just finished a small painting which I believe to be the best I have done. It portrays my sister Rose reading to her doll. It is only a little over three feet; if you like, I will give it to you. . . . My sister is seated in the middle, holding a small book which she is reading. Her doll is on a chair, she is in an armchair. Black background, light head, blue hair-net, blue pina-fore, a dark yellow dress, a bit of still life to the left: a bowl and toys. . . . I shall send it to the Salon.'

At the same time, Cézanne was working outdoors and planned to do a painting of Marion and Valebrègue setting out to paint a landscape (Pl. 5). Guillemet admired the sketch for this canvas which, in Cézanne's own words, 'was done from nature and makes everything else fall flat and seem bad.' Valabrègue, however, thought less highly of this sketch and wrote to Zola in October 1866: 'Paul has written you recently. He has just finished two excellent paintings: one a scene in which music is being played, and the other of his sister looking at her doll. At the present time Marion and I are posing for him. We are arm in arm, and have hideous shapes (Pl. 5). Paul is a horrible painter as regards the poses he gives people in the midst of his riots of colour. Every time he paints one of his friends it seems as though he were revenging himself on him for some hidden injury.'

A little later Valabrègue again tells Zola about Cézanne's paintings: 'Paul made me sit yesterday for the study of a head. Flesh: fire-red with scrapings of white; the painting of a mason (fig. 22). I am coloured so strongly that I am reminded of the statue of the curé of Champfleury when it was coated with crushed blackberries. Fortunately I only posed for it one day. The uncle is more often the model. Every afternoon there appears a portrait of him, while Guillemet belabours it with terrible jokes.'

* * *

Cézanne's 'blond style' upon which Guillemet had commented is found chiefly in his outdoor paintings. But even there he does not yet temper the force of his impression; his brush exaggerates the better to emphasize the wonder of the Midi landscape. 'You are perfectly right,' he wrote Pissarro, 'to talk about grey; it alone reigns in nature but it is frightfully hard to capture.'

Most of the landscapes dating from this period portray the garden of the 'Jas de Bouffan' or the banks of the Arc. Cézanne worked outdoors with a palette that comprised white, blue, green, and black and liked to juxtapose these colours; he would, for example, set off greenish-black foliage against a blue-white sky. As for the grey which reigns in nature, Cézanne still does not appear to have succeeded in 'capturing' it, although he understood that he could only achieve it by the use of colour. He needed several more years and above all the example of Pissarro to uncover the mystery of this grey, which is composed of a number of tones and which he was to render in all its richness by means of a technique of small strokes.

In truth, Cézanne was more vigorous at this time than he was subtle, and the clumsiness of certain of his youthful works was due to an excess of passion which art did not control.

Although from 1866 on, Cézanne became increasingly interested in nature, he was no less interested in still lifes, in which he attained a remarkable density of expression and mastery of technique. His 'Still Life with Black Clock' (Pl. 19), which belonged to Zola, his 'Tin Jug', and others are extremely well composed, having great stability and a monumental calm. They are painted in strong tones and his use of black is very plastic. Of all the varied works of his youth, imaginative scenes, portraits, landscapes, murals, copies, etc., it is in his still lifes that Cézanne reveals most clearly the accuracy of his perception and the richness of his genius as a colourist.

In Paris, where he had little opportunity to work in the open, Cézanne often came to Zola and worked on several portraits of his friend and Alexis reading together (Pl. 22). Zola also sat for Fantin-Latour's group composition which was exhibited at the Salon of 1870 under the title 'L'Atelier des Batignolles'. Thus the novelist saw his portrait at the Salon for the third time: the first, that of an 'unknown young man', was the bust by Solari; the second, of the 'avant-garde critic', was by Manet, and the third shows Zola as an important member of the Batignolles group standing with Monet, Renoir, Bazille, and others around Manet's easel.

*   *   *

At the end of 1869 Zola began working every day at the Bibliothèque Impériale in order to study psychology and history in preparation for a projected work which was to be the history of a whole family—*Les Rougon-Macquart*—in about ten volumes. In his general notes on the progress of this series Zola wrote:

'A central family upon which at least two other families exert an influence. Expansion of this family in the modern world, in all classes. Progress of this family towards refinement in sensation and intelligence. Drama within the family due to hereditary causes. . . . Exhaustion of intelligence on account of the rapidity of the leap to the heights of sensation and of thought. Return to a state of degradation. Influence of the feverish modern environment on the impatient ambitions of the characters. The actual environments—locale and place in society—determine the class of the character (worker, artist, bourgeois—myself and my uncles, Paul and his father).'

The last sentence of these notes reveals that from the time he drew up the outline for the stupendous construction of his Rougon-Macquart novels Zola had Cézanne in mind. At that time Zola may not as yet have had any precise ideas about how to utilize Cézanne as a character but among his friends Cézanne apparently seemed the most obvious for his purposes. Besides, Zola intended to devote one volume of his series to artistic problems, planning to depict the 'intense psychological processes of an artist's temperament and the terrible tragedy of an intelligence which consumes itself'.

Cézanne's father provided several traits for the character of François Mouret in *La Conquête de Plassans*, as revealed by Zola's notes: 'Take the type of person that Cézanne's father is, mocking, republican, bourgeois, cold, meticulous, stingy; picture of his home: he refused to give his wife luxury, etc. Moreover, he talks a lot, depends on his fortune, and doesn't care what others do or think. . . .'

Zola's notes for his novels constitute a kind of written soliloquy. In them he indicates what must be done and what must be avoided, and so it is possible to follow the development of his thoughts in detail. 'It is absolutely necessary to note this,' Zola wrote before beginning *Les Rougon-Macquart*. 'I do not deny the greatness of the modern trend, I do not deny that we may progress more or less toward liberty and justice. Only my belief is that men will always be men, good or bad animals, according to circumstances.'

In his series of novels Zola made use of his memories of Aix, which he calls 'Plassans'. In these memories Paul Cézanne was the inseparable companion; thinking of Aix, thinking of his youth, meant for Zola also to think of Cézanne.

The first volume of *Les Rougon-Macquart*, entitled *La Fortune des Rougon*, began to appear in serial form in the newspaper *Le Siècle* in the summer of 1870. Its publication was interrupted by the Franco-Prussian War.

XI

THE WAR

1870–1871

WHEN ZOLA was married in Paris on 31 May 1870, Cézanne was one of his witnesses. At that time Cézanne was living at 53 Rue Notre-Dame-des-Champs. Nothing in his life had changed. 'I have been rejected as in the past,' he wrote to a friend in Aix, 'but I am none the worse for it.' And he added: 'It is unnecessary to tell you that I am still painting.' Cézanne did not mean to give up his painting during the war and remained in the Midi for its duration.

The war scattered the little group of the Café Guerbois. Zola, who was near-sighted, was not accepted in the National Guard and went with his wife and mother to Marseilles where, with Marius Roux, he attempted unsuccessfully to publish a newspaper. Monet went to England where he met Pissarro, whom the invasion had forced to flee. Manet was an officer in Paris, Bazille had enlisted, and Renoir was called up and stationed part of the time in Bordeaux, part of the time in the Pyrénées.

Cézanne does not seem to have been included, at the beginning at least, in any class of mobilization. He left the 'Jas de Bouffan' to meet Hortense Fiquet in L'Estaque and to live with her there without his parents' knowledge. Zola went to stay with him for a while before leaving for Bordeaux, where he arrived in December. In January 1871, he received a letter from Marius Roux:

'Concerning the mobilization of the Guard, I have two pieces of news for you, one unpleasant, and the other astonishing.

'The unpleasant news is that Paul C. . . is being looked for and I am very much afraid he will not escape being found if, as his mother says, he is still in L'Estaque. Paul, who at first did not foresee what was going to happen, was seen in Aix a good deal. He even went there quite often and remained one, two, or three days and sometimes more. It is also said that he got drunk in the company of gentlemen of his acquaintance. He must have—it is even certain—given his address, since the gentlemen in question (who must be jealous of him for not earning his livelihood) hastened to denounce him and to give all information necessary for finding him.

'These same gentlemen (here is the astonishing news) to whom Paul said that he was living in L'Estaque with you—not knowing that since then you were able to leave that hole and not knowing whether you were married or a bachelor—also gave your name as a defaulter. On the evening of 2 January my father took me aside and told me:

' "I have just heard a conscript who said this: 'There are four of us, including Corporal So-and-so, who have been ordered to Marseilles to bring back defaulters".' He gave the names.

' "Among them"—my father told me—"I remembered those of Paul Cézanne and Zola!"

' " 'Those two'—added the conscript—'are in hiding in Saint-Henri [a village near L'Estaque].' "

'I told my father to lend a deaf ear and to take no part in any conversation of this kind. I got busy and the next morning hurried to the town hall. There I have complete freedom and was shown the list of evaders. Your name was not on it. I told Ferand, who is a reliable man and devoted to me, what was being said. He replied: "They must have mentioned Zola only because of Cézanne who is being diligently sought for; but if your friend's name was given, it must have been before information was acquired, since Zola does not come from Aix and is married! . . ."

'At the town hall, nothing official, and among the crowd which bandies Cézanne's name about, I have never heard yours.'

Evidently the police went to the 'Jas de Bouffan', where Madame Cézanne told them to search the place freely, that her son had left two or three days before, and that she would notify them when she knew where he was.

It is doubtful that Cézanne was hunted in L'Estaque itself, for then it would have been almost impossible not to find him. He did not conceal his presence in the little village by the Mediterranean, thirty kilometres from Aix, where he worked in the open air, painting the rocks, the hills, the village, and the sea (Pl. 24). Roux's information notwithstanding, Cézanne does not seem to have been worried. It is certain that he took no part whatsoever in the war and, later on, when asked about the life he had led during that period, he replied that he had been in L'Estaque, dividing his time between landscape painting and work in his studio.

Thus Cézanne remained far from the fever which shook his country, far from the battlefield, and far from his friends, most of whom did not even know where he was, though supposing him to be somewhere in the Midi. He also stayed away from Aix, where, since the proclamation of the Third Republic, things had happened which could not have left him indifferent. When, on Sunday, 4 September 1870, toward ten o'clock in the evening, a telegram arrived from Paris, announcing the Republic, the republicans of Aix went *en masse* to the town hall where they proclaimed the fall of the local government and of the municipal council established by the last elections. The mayor and an assistant, who had rushed to the scene, were obliged to withdraw in the midst of uproar and confusion. Then the republicans met in the council hall and a provisional municipal body was chosen by popular acclaim.

The democratic list, defeated at the previous election, furnished the necessary names for the new council. But among the new members of the municipal council thus elected were also some who had not figured on that list, among them Baille, who was with the Paris observatory; Victor Leydet, merchant (another schoolmate); Valabrègue, writer; and Louis-Auguste Cézanne, banker. One Alexis, pharmacist, became provisional mayor.

After the election, the bust of Napoleon III and his portrait were destroyed. The painting was torn to shreds; the cast-iron bust was knocked off its pedestal, kicked out of the room, and finally thrown in the fountain.

The Republic was officially proclaimed at ten o'clock the following morning on the steps of the Palace of Justice, and on 11 September was posted an appeal to the population of Aix, signed by the entire municipal council: 'Let us arise, citizens, and march as one man! The Municipal Council of Aix calls you to the defence of your country; it assumes the responsibility of providing for the needs of the families of all those who will volunteer to bear arms to save France and gain respect for our glorious and pure Republic.'

In spite of the seriousness of the situation, Marius Roux couldn't help writing to Zola: 'I am bored stiff here. I watch the revolution pass. In the gang are our admirable friends, Baille and Valabrègue. They amuse me tremendously. Can you see those slackers from Paris who come here to stick their noses into the local government and vote resistance. Let us march like one man say their proclamations. March! They are a fine pair.'

The new municipal council took its duties seriously and, in one of its first sessions, formed committees. Louis-Auguste Cézanne, then seventy-two years old, was chosen member of the committee on finance; Baille was put on the committee of public works; and Valabrègue and Leydet were put on the one dealing with miscellaneous issues. Baille and Valabrègue also took part in the census for the organization of the National Guard, and they may well have prevented too thorough a search for Cézanne.

The painter's father was usually absent from the meetings of the municipal council, possibly because of a reluctance to commit himself on current issues. Elected without having been a candidate, he probably owed this honour to his financial ability, which also put him on the committee on finance. It does not seem as though his political convictions had caused his nominations since his shunning of the meetings 'without known reason' (as recorded in the minutes) would be even more incomprehensible. While he kept away from the council, the latter honoured his son by nominating him member of the committee on the art school and the museum. But Cézanne took as little interest in civic affairs as his father, who was not even candidate for the municipal council which replaced the provisional one in the spring of 1871. When the arts committee was dissolved at about the same time, Cézanne lost the opportunity to influence the policy of the museum, an opportunity of which he had failed to avail himself.

'As soon as the municipal elections are over,' the local press announced, 'the elections for the Constituent Assembly will take place. Among the republican candidates from the Bouches-du-Rhône will probably be one of our local citizens, M. Emile Zola.'

Nothing came of this, although Zola had aspired at one time to become sous-préfet of Aix. Indeed, he had abandoned his literary activity for the duration of the war and had devoted himself to politics. In Bordeaux he became parliamentary correspondent for *La Cloche*, and his writings here during the period were the only products of his pen with the exception of numerous letters to his friends. He received a reply to one of these from Manet under the date Paris, 9 February 1871:

'I am very glad to have good news from you. You have not wasted your time. Recently we have suffered a great deal in Paris. Only yesterday I heard of the death of poor Bazille. I am overcome—alas, we have seen many people die here in many ways. At one time your house was lived in by a family of refugees. Only the ground floor; all the furniture was moved upstairs. I think no damage was done to your things. I am leaving soon to join my wife and my mother in Oloron in the Basses-Pyrénées. I am anxious to see them again. I shall pass through Bordeaux and will perhaps come to see you. I shall tell you then what cannot be put on paper.'.

At the beginning of March, Zola wrote to Paul Alexis from Bordeaux that he had not heard from Cézanne, whom he imagined to be somewhere in the country near Aix. A few weeks later Alexis, who had seen Zola in Paris in the meantime, wrote to him from L'Estaque: 'No Cézanne. I had a long talk with M. Giraud, called Longus [owner of the house Cézanne rented in L'Estaque]. The two birds flew away—a month ago! The nest is empty and locked. "They went to Lyons," M. Longus told me, "to wait until Paris stops smoking." I am surprised that for a month we have not seen him in Paris. I hope that when you receive this letter you will know more about him than I do.'

To this Zola replied:

'What you tell me about Cézanne's flight to Lyons is an old wives' tale. Our friend merely wanted to throw M. Giraud off the scent. He went into hiding in Marseilles or in some valley. And I hope to know his whereabouts as soon as possible, for I am worried.

'Just imagine—I wrote to him the day after you left. My letter, which was sent to L'Estaque, must have miscarried, which is not a great loss; but I am afraid lest by an unforeseen chain of circumstances it may have fallen into Cézanne's father's hands. It contains some particulars compromising to the son. You follow the reasoning, do you not?

'I would like to find Paul to have him claim this letter. Therefore I count on you for the following errand: one of these mornings you will go to the "Jas de Bouffan" where you will give the impression of seeking news of Cézanne. You will manage to talk to the mother for a moment privately and will ask her for her son's exact address. . . .'

Alexis apparently had no difficulty in tracing Cézanne, who then wrote to Zola. The latter replied immediately, on 4 July 1871.

'My dear Paul,
'I was very glad to get your letter, as I was beginning to be worried about you. Four months have elapsed since we have heard from one another. I wrote to you to L'Estaque around the middle of last month. Then I found out that you had left there and that my letter might be lost. I was having great difficulty finding you when you helped me out.

'You ask for my news. Here is my story in a few words. I wrote to you shortly before leaving Bordeaux and promised to write you another letter as soon as I returned to Paris. I arrived in Paris 14 March. Four days later the Commune was established, the postal services were suspended, and I no longer thought of getting in touch with you. For two months I lived in the furnace, night and day, with cannon and, towards the end, shells whistling over my head, in my garden. Finally, on 10 May I was threatened with seizure as a hostage. I fled, with the help of a Prussian passport, and went to Bonnières to spend the worst days. Today I am staying quietly at the Batignolles, as though I were waking up from a bad dream. My pavilion is the same, my garden has not budged; not a single piece of furniture or plant has suffered and I could even believe that the two sieges were bad jokes invented to frighten children.

'What makes these bad memories more fleeting for me is that I have not stopped work for a moment. Since leaving Marseilles I have been earning my living very well. . . . I am telling you this so that you may not pity my lot. I have never been more hopeful or desirous of working. Paris is being reborn. As I have often told you, our reign has begun!'

XII

L'ESTAQUE AND AUVERS

1871 – 1874

CÉZANNE's first paintings done in L'Estaque have much in common with his previous work. They show the same dramatic emphasis and exuberance, the same violent colour contrasts. Though black predominates, there are strong reds and warm ochres which enhance the power of his style.

Still imbued with the ardour that produced 'L'Enlèvement' and 'The Temptation of Saint Anthony', Cézanne dramatized what he saw. Trees, rocks, and houses became manifestations of his passionate temperament. Abandoning imaginary scenes more and more, Cézanne felt inspired by the mangificent bay of Marseilles, surrounded by mountains, by the roofs of villages and the belfries and tall chimneys which rose toward the cloudless sky, by the pines on the green hills, and by the reflection of little rocky islands in the water.

The scenery around L'Estaque is extremely beautiful. Zola described it in one of his novels:

'A village just outside of Marseilles, in the centre of an alley of rocks which close the bay. . . . The country is superb. The arms of rock stretch out on either side of the gulf, while the islands, extending in width, seem to bar the horizon, and the sea is but a vast basin, a lake of brilliant blue when the weather is fine. At the foot of the mountains the houses of Marseilles are seen on different levels of the low hills; when the air is clear one can see, from L'Estaque, the grey Joliette breakwater and the thin masts of the vessels in the port. Behind this may be seen, high on a hill, surrounded by trees, the white chapel of Notre-Dame de la Garde. The coastline becomes rounded near Marseilles and is scooped out in wide indentations before reaching L'Estaque; it is bordered with factories that sometimes let out high plumes of smoke. When the sun falls perpendicularly to the horizon, the sea, almost black, seems to sleep between the two promontories of rocks whose whiteness is relieved by yellow and brown. The pines dot the red earth with green. It is a vast panorama, a corner of the Orient rising up in the blinding vibration of the day.

'But L'Estaque does not only offer an outlet to the sea. The village, its back against the mountains, is traversed by roads which disappear in the midst of a chaos of jagged rocks. . . . Nothing equals the wild majesty of these gorges hollowed out between the hills, narrow paths twisting at the bottom of an abyss, arid slopes covered with pines and with walls the colour of rust and blood. Sometimes the defiles widen, a thin field of olive trees occupies the hollow of a valley, a hidden house shows its painted façade with closed shutters. Then, again, paths full of brambles, impenetrable thickets, piles of stones, dried-up streams, all the surprises of a walk in the desert. High up, above the black border of the pines, is placed the endless band of the blue silk of the sky.

'And there is also the narrow coast between the rocks and the sea, the red earth where the tile-works, the big industry of the district, have excavated large holes to extract clay. . . . One would think one were walking on roads made of plaster, for one sinks in ankle deep; and, at the slightest gust of wind, great clouds of dust powder the hedges. . . .

'When this dried out country gets thoroughly wet, it takes on colours . . . of great violence: the red earth bleeds, the pines have an emerald reflection, the rocks are bright with the whiteness of fresh laundry.'

*　　*　　*

Only a small number of the pictures which Cézanne painted in L'Estaque are known, but these suffice to show his artistic development, which drew him from the expression of his visions to the study of nature. Continuing in this vein, Cézanne was later to say that art can develop only from contact with nature, a contact which he began to seek only at the age of thirty. The ardour which produced his first landscapes was succeeded by the sensitivity of his eye which made him perceive differences of tone. In order to develop his individuality more freely, Cézanne needed technical advice, which he was able to get from his friends who had returned to Paris as soon as the war was over.

The gatherings at the Café Guerbois were resumed, though less frequently than formerly, and soon the meeting place was changed to the Café de la Nouvelle-Athènes. The calm which followed the change of government filled the group with new hope. In Paris Cézanne found not only Zola and Pissarro, but also Valabrègue, Roux, and Solari. The latter had married before the war and supported his wife and child in any way he could, sometimes by 'turning out saints at sixty centimes an hour while waiting for something better'. Cézanne lived for six months in the same house as Solari, 5 Rue de Chevreuse, but in December 1871 he moved to the

Rue de Jussieu, opposite the Halle aux Vins (Pl. 25). There, on 4 January 1872, Hortense Fiquet gave birth to a boy who was registered by his father under the name Paul Cézanne. Soon after, the little family left Paris.

Ever since he himself had settled outside Paris, a few years before the war, Pissarro had tried untiringly to persuade his friends to abandon the city and join him in the country. Convinced of the advantages of outdoor painting, Cézanne now went with Hortense and his child to join Pissarro in Pontoise. There he would be able to benefit from the advice of his friend, almost ten years older than he. Pissarro was always anxious to help others profit from his experience. This generous attitude explains the role he played among his friends: no one would advise, help, encourage as he could, and though his criticism was just, it was tempered by indulgence. It is not surprising, then, that a small group of painters gathered in Pontoise around Pissarro, a group of which Cézanne now became a member.

In September 1872 Pissarro proudly informed Guillemet: 'Béliard is still with us. He is doing very serious work at Pontoise. . . . Guillaumin has just spent several days at our house; he paints in the daytime and in the evening works at his ditch-digging.* What courage! Our friend, Cézanne, raises our expectations, and I have seen and have at home a painting of remarkable vigour and power. If, as I hope, he stays some time in Auvers, where he is going to live, he will astonish a lot of the artists who were too hasty in condemning him.'

*   *   *

Not far from Pontoise, at Auvers-sur-Oise, where Daubigny lived, Dr Gachet, an habitué of the meetings of the Batignolles group, had just bought for his ailing wife a large and lonely house on a hillside overlooking the entire valley (Pl. 38). He usually spent three days a week there with her and their two children. Pissarro and Cézanne, as well as Guillaumin, who joined them, saw a lot of the doctor ·He particularly urged them to do etchings—he himself being an enthusiastic engraver—and put at their disposal his plates and the press that he had installed in his house.

At the beginning of 1873, Cézanne left Pontoise for Auvers where he took up residence near Dr Gachet. Auvers was little more than a village of thatched cottages on unpaved country lanes, in contrast to Pontoise, which was more a town, though with a certain rural character. In Auvers Cézanne could work at ease without being watched by curious spectators (whom he loathed), whether he

---

*At that time, Guillaumin was employed by the Department of Bridges and Highways and painted only in his spare time.

painted on the road that led to Gachet's house (Pl. 26) or out in the fields. And he did so with untiring effort. It is said that Daubigny, who once had recommended Cézanne's 'Portrait of Valabrègue' for admission by the jury, one day watched the painter at work and could not restrain his enthusiasm. 'I've just seen on the banks of the Oise an extraordinary piece of work,' he told a friend. 'It is by a young and unknown man, a certain Cézanne.'

Cézanne's two years in Pontoise and Auvers were crucial ones in his artistic development. He profited greatly from his more or less direct collaboration with Pissarro, for the latter clarified his palette and produced a change in his technique. Although he no longer made use only of dark colours, Cézanne at first continued to paint with dramatic strokes, but soon, following his friend's example, he employed special knives about two fingers wide, very long, flat, and supple, to paint large masses of colour. With these knives he built up the colour, sketching in the features of his motif rather summarily; by means of accentuated shadows and a few sharp tones of red and yellow-green, he tried to give his landscapes a certain plasticity. The better to assimilate Pissarro's palette and technique, Cézanne faithfully copied a large 'View of Louveciennes', painted by his friend. He gradually abandoned dark colours, with the exception of black, and did away with heavy and earthy tones.

'We are perhaps all derived from Pissarro,' Cézanne later said. 'Already in '65 he had eliminated black, bitumen, sienna, and ochres. This is a fact. "Only paint with the three primary colours and their immediate derivatives," he told me. . . .'

Cézanne took this advice. The winter, with its snow which he had not known in the Midi, introduced to him tones of light grey, and he continued to brighten his palette by painting winter scenes. Twenty years later, Pissarro explained to his son that while they had often set up their easels side by side, it was certain that each kept the one thing that counts, his 'sensation'.

Pissarro was happy to see Cézanne gain control of his ebullient temperament in intimate contact with nature, but he was too modest to insist on the part he himself played in this decisive period of Cézanne's evolution. When Zola and Béliard were surprised by the similarity of some of their works, Pissarro pointed out that it was wrong to think 'that artists are the sole inventors of their styles and that to resemble someone else is to be unoriginal'. Conscious of the give-and-take between artists who work together, Pissarro later acknowledged having been influenced by Cézanne, even while influencing him (Pls. 35, 36).

Thus the advice which Pissarro gave to his friend was by no means intended to prevent him from realizing his own sensations. On the contrary, Pissarro incessantly repeated that one should have no master but nature, who was always to be consulted. He was satisfied with giving Cézanne certain practical advice, the fruit of his experience, telling him, for example, that it was not necessary to insist on linear form, since form could be achieved by other means, namely colour.

But now that Cézanne had replaced his dark palette with a bright one, he needed to develop this new palette so that it might attain the richness of colour he admired so much in Delacroix. And he depended on nature for that richness which he sought for the expression of his sensations. He remembered Pissarro's remark that museums ought to be burned, that 'we must portray what we see and forget what appeared before our time'.

Consequently, Cézanne studied effects of light and air and tried to convey them through colour; he learned that objects have no specific colour of their own, but reflect each other, and that air intervenes between eye and object. Cézanne not only made these observations on nature but also expressed them in his still lifes. The first of these, painted in Auvers, still reveal some of Manet's influence and are in sombre tones: dull yellows and reds against absolutely black backgrounds. Cézanne painted them in Dr Gachet's studio and chose as subjects glasses, bottles, knives, and other not very colourful objects. He also painted a plaster medallion by Solari, a portrait in profile of the sculptor, and some tapestries which he had brought with him. But Cézanne soon tired of the limited range of whitish browns and the greys which predominate in these compositions and began to paint the flowers which Madame Gachet picked for him in her garden. These little canvases have remarkably clear and vibrant colours: blues, reds, and yellows of extraordinary intensity which bear witness to the pleasure he felt in rendering such richness of tone. However, the realization was still difficult and painful. Cézanne now went even further in his scruples to be truthful than he had once gone in his independence of nature. He no longer dared to work with sweeping brush strokes, but instead covered his canvases with heavy layers of colour through the use of small patches and spots of paint. His extreme effort to render every nuance observed led him to proceed patiently and as if he were building up a mosaic. Thus he worked slowly, and one day when he was painting some distance away from Pissarro in the outskirts of Auvers, a peasant told Pissarro, 'Well, sir, you have an assistant over there who isn't doing a stroke of work!'

When he was questioned later concerning his reasons for abandoning the impetuosity which characterized his first period in favour of the technique of separate touches in his work at Auvers, Cézanne replied: 'I cannot convey my sensation immediately; so I put colour on again, and I keep putting it on as best I can. But when I begin, I always try to paint sweepingly, like Manet, by giving form with the brush.'

As a result, Cézanne's paintings have amazing colour-relief, for on the first layer of paint are placed innumerable small daubs which give tremendous richness of tone: the skies are not only blue, but also pale green, blue-grey, bright violet, brown, and pink. The straw roofs have a comparable range of colour, the tree trunks and foliage are touched with violet, the contours of objects are done in yellow, maroon, and blue. Cézanne observed that there are no lines in nature, no shadows without colour. He was later to remark: 'Pure drawing is an abstraction. Line and modelling do not count; drawing and outline are not distinct, since everything in nature has colour. . . . By the very fact of painting, one draws. The accuracy of tone gives simultaneously the light and shape of the object, and the more harmonious the colour, the more the drawing becomes precise. . . .'

In his attempt to achieve this accuracy of tone, Cézanne had difficulty in finishing a picture, for he was always anxious to add more touches of paint. When his friend, Dr Gachet, decided that a painting had nothing more to gain, but, on the contrary, a lot to lose, he would say: 'Come on, Cézanne, leave that picture alone, it's finished. Don't touch it.' And Cézanne obeyed, grumbling. The doctor bought a number of paintings from him, as well as from Pissarro and Guillaumin, thus acquiring a truly remarkable collection. It was on the advice of Dr Gachet and Pissarro that the grocer in Pontoise accepted some paintings from Cézanne in payment of his bills.

To please their friend, both Pissarro and Cézanne made a few etchings, the only ones Cézanne ever did, among them a portrait sketch of Guillaumin. He also drew a portrait of Dr Gachet etching and a profile of Pissarro as well (Pl. 33). The latter, in turn, did several portraits of Cézanne: on copper, in pencil, and in oils (Pls. 31, 32, 34).

In spite of his intense work from nature during this period, Cézanne was still haunted by the idea of composing agitated scenes. He painted a 'Temptation of Saint Anthony' and an astonishing 'Modern Olympia' which is perhaps the strangest work produced by him in Auvers (Pl. 53). In this painting he himself appears, seen from behind, gazing upon a woman who is half crouching, half lying on an enormous divan while a negress removes her last veil. This is a less refined and more female 'Olympia' than Manet's, presented in an atmosphere less cold and reserved, and surrounded by fireworks of colour. A huge bouquet picked in a dream-meadow illuminates the scene.

Pissarro must have praised this painting for Théodore Duret wrote to him: 'If it were possible, I would be glad to see some of Cézanne's work in your home, for in painting I look more than ever for sheep with five legs.' Pissarro immediately replied: 'If it is five-legged sheep that you are seeking, Cézanne can satisfy you, for he has made some studies which are very strange and seen in a unique manner.'

Cézanne was working feverishly. Oil paintings, watercolours, drawings, etchings, and even pastels, the latter probably at the behest of Guillaumin, served him as means of expression. He had no wish to leave the friends who had been so helpful to him, and he tried to explain to his parents why he dreaded going back to Aix:

'You ask me in your last letter why I have not yet returned to Aix. Apropos of this I have told you that it gives me more pleasure than I can express to be with you, but once in Aix, I am no longer free. When I want to return to Paris it is always a struggle for me, and although your opposition to my return is not adamant, I am very much shaken emotionally by your resistance. I fervently wish that my freedom of action were not hampered, and, if that were the case, I would be all the happier to hasten my return.

'. . . I will be very glad to work in the Midi which offers my painting so much . . . and I believe that in the Midi I can pursue the studies that I wish to undertake.'

* * *

A feeling of confidence and optimism ran high among the Batignolles friends, most of whom worked in the outskirts of Paris but saw each other from time to time. They realized the necessity of sticking together and holding on, the more so as it became obvious that in progressing in their work they abandoned more and more the standards of the Salon. Among the dealers, only Paul Durand-Ruel, whom Monet and Pissarro had met in London, supported their efforts.

'We are beginning to make ourselves a niche,' Pissarro wrote Duret. 'We are contested by some masters, but mustn't we expect these differences of view, when we have succeeded as intruders in setting up our little banner in the midst of the fray? Durand-Ruel is steadfast; we hope to advance without worrying about opinions.'

As they were anxious to show the public the results of their studies, and as they felt increasing confidence, the friends presently decided to hold a joint exhibition of their work.

XIII

FIRST EXHIBITIONS

1874–1877

THE *Société Anonyme des Artistes, Peintres, Sculpteurs, Graveurs* opened its first exhibition on 15 April, 1874. It lasted for one month and was located in Nadar's studios, Boulevard des Capucines. No longer willing to submit their works to a jury which they considered incapable of appreciating them, the Batignolles group decided to ignore the Salon with its medals and official encouragements. At their own expense, risk, and peril, they now addressed themselves to the public, who was to judge them, criticize them, or support them. 'This procedure is not without daring,' the press admitted. 'It bears witness to much good faith.' Thirty artists are listed in the catalogue of the exhibition, among them Boudin, Cézanne, Degas, Guillaumin, Monet, Berthe Morisot, Pissarro, Renoir, and Sisley. Several artists objected to including Cézanne, fearing public opposition, but Pissarro insisted that he participate in their common showing.

Two of the most important members of the Batignolles group did not join their friends. One was Manet, who was now being accepted more or less regularly at the official Salon and who did not want to risk his chances of achieving success there. And Zola failed to draw the attention of the public to his friends' work or to foster understanding of it. Certainly, understanding on the part of the public was conspicuously lacking, and the exhibition provoked the same reaction as Manet's painting at the Salon des Refusés. The public came to laugh. In *L'Œuvre* Zola later transcribed the atmosphere of an art gallery resounding with the laughter of curiosity-seekers: 'These laughs were no longer smothered by the handkerchiefs of the ladies, and the men distended their bellies the better to give vent to them. It was the contagious mirth of a crowd which had come for entertainment, was becoming excited by degrees, exploded apropos of nothing, and was enlivened as much by beautiful things as by execrable ones. . . . They nudged each other, they doubled up . . . every canvas had its appreciation, people called each other over to point out a good one, witty remarks were constantly being passed from mouth to mouth . . . the round and

25. *Cézanne: The Halle aux Vins in Paris, 1872. Formerly Coll. Camille Pissarro*

26. *Cézanne: The Vieille Route at Auvers, 1872–3*

27. *Cézanne: Self Portrait, c.1880*

28. *Photograph of Paul Cézanne, c.1871*

30. *Cézanne (seated) and Pissarro (standing at right)*
in Pissarro's garden in Pontoise, c.1873

29. *Photograph of Paul Cézanne on his way to work,*
near Auvers, 1873

32. *Pissarro: Portrait of Paul Cézanne, 1874*

31. *Pissarro: Portrait of Paul Cézanne, 1874*

34. *Pissarro: Portrait of Paul Cézanne, c.*1873

33. *Cézanne: Portrait of Camille Pissarro, c.*1873

35. *Pissarro: The Hermitage at Pontoise,* 1875

36. *Cézanne: The Hermitage at Pontoise, c.*1875

37. *Cézanne: View of Médan, c. 1880. Formerly Coll. Paul Gauguin*

38. *Cézanne: View of Auvers (with Dr Gachet's house at left), c.1874*

40. *Renoir: Portrait of Victor Chocquet, c.*1875

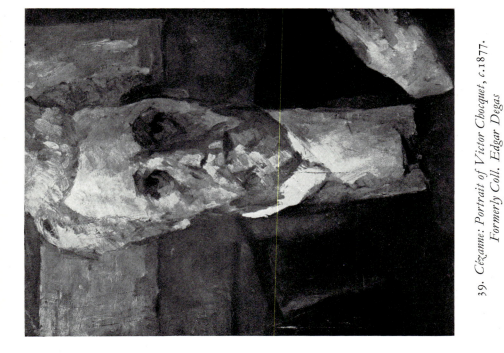

39. *Cézanne: Portrait of Victor Chocquet, c.*1877.
Formerly Coll. Edgar Degas

41. *Cézanne: Self Portrait, c.1875*

42. *Photograph of Paul Cézanne, c.1875*

43. *Cézanne: Melting Snow in Fontainebleau, c.*1880. *Formerly Coll. Claude Monet*

44. *Photograph used by Cézanne for his 'Melting Snow in Fontainebleau',*
recently discovered among the artist's papers

45. *Cézanne: The Farmhouse at the Jas de Bouffan, c.*1885

47. *Photograph of Paul Cézanne*, 1889

46. *Cézanne: Self Portrait, c.*1877

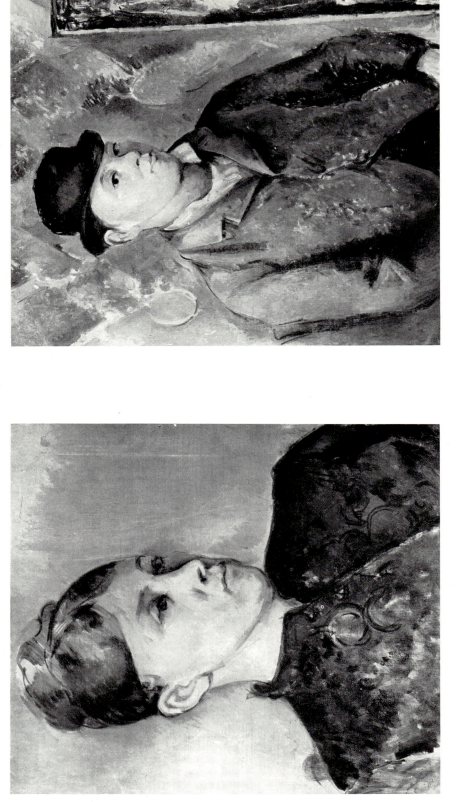

49. *Cézanne: Portrait of the Artist's Son, c.1890*

48. *Cézanne: Portrait of Madame Cézanne, c.1885*

50. *Cézanne: The Arc Valley and Mount Sainte-Victoire, c.1887*

51. *Photograph of the same subject*

52. *Renoir: Portrait of Paul Cézanne,* 1880

53. *Cézanne: A Modern Olympia, c.1873. Shown at the first Impressionist Exhibition, 1874*

54. *Cézanne: Still Life, c.1877. Formerly Coll. Victor Chocquet*

stupid mouth of the ignorant who criticize painting, expressing the sum total of asininity, of absurd commentary, of bad and stupid ridicule, that an original work can evoke from bourgeois imbecility.'

'The conscience of the public was indignant,' one critic stated. 'This was awful, stupid, dirty; this painting had no common sense.' Consequently the so-called serious critics refused to pay any attention to the show. If they mentioned it at all, it was by making fun of an honest effort. 'Shall we speak of M. Cézanne?' the reviewer for *Le Rappel* asked. 'Of all known juries, none ever imagined, even in a dream, the possibility of accepting any work by this painter, who used to present himself at the Salon carrying his canvases on his back like Jesus his cross. A too exclusive love for yellow has up to now compromised the future of M. Cézanne.'

One of the paintings exhibited which aroused the particular mirth of public and reviewers was Cézanne's 'Modern Olympia' (Pl. 53). A lady who signed her articles 'Marc de Montifaud' commented: 'On Sunday the public saw fit to sneer at a fantastic figure which is revealed under an opium sky to a drug addict. This apparition of a little pink and nude flesh which is being pushed, in the empyrean cloud, by a kind of demon or incubus, like a voluptuous vision, this corner of artificial paradise, has suffocated the most courageous, and M. Cézanne merely gives the impression of being a sort of madman who paints in *delirium tremens*.'

If the critics did not express themselves as violently on the other exhibitors, it can hardly be said that they were flattering. A current joke was to say that these painters proceeded by loading a pistol with several tubes of colour and firing it at a canvas. All they had to do was sign the work.

Taking issue with a painting by Monet, entitled 'Impression', the critic for the widely read *Charivari* mockingly called the group of painters 'Impressionist', a name which immediately caught on and was finally—almost in defiance—accepted by the artists themselves. However, the understanding and sympathy the painters had hoped for did not materialize. Though people thronged to their exhibition, they came only to poke fun. From Pontoise, in early May, Pissarro wrote Duret:

'Our exhibition is going well. It is a success. The critics are devouring us and accuse us of not studying; I am returning to my studies—that is more worthwhile than reading. One learns nothing from them.'

When the exhibition closed, Cézanne suddenly left for Aix without even taking leave of his friend Pissarro. No sooner was he back in Aix and had started to paint again, than his former teacher, the painter Gibert, curator of the Aix museum, 'impelled by a curiosity aroused by the Paris newspapers,' asked to see his canvases. This is the report Cézanne gave Pissarro of the interview:

'... To my assertion that on seeing my productions he would not have a very accurate idea of the progress of evil and that he ought to see the works of the great Parisian criminals, he replied: "I am well able to conceive of the dangers run by painting when I see your assaults." Whereupon he came over and when I told him, for instance, that you replaced modelling by the study of tones and was trying to explain this to him by reference to nature, he closed his eyes and turned his back. But he said he understood, and we parted well satisfied with each other. Yet he is a decent fellow who urged me to persevere, because patience is the mother of genius, etc.'

In spite of the resounding failure of the exhibition, Cézanne does not seem to have lost courage. He felt himself on the right track and had few illusions about the value of such attempts. In the autumn, back in Paris, he wrote a letter to his mother which reveals for the first time optimism and self-confidence:

'Pissarro has not been in Paris for about a month and a half; he is in Brittany, but I know that he thinks well of me, who think well of myself. I begin to find myself superior to those around me, and you know that the good opinion I have of myself has only been reached after mature consideration. I must always work, but not to achieve a final polish, which is for the admiration of imbeciles. And this thing which is commonly so appreciated is only the accomplishment of artisan's skill and makes every work resulting from it inartistic and vulgar. I must strive after completion only for the pleasure of giving added truth and learning. And believe me, there always comes a time when one arrives, and one has much more fervent and devoted admirers than those who are only flattered by vain appearances.

'This time is very bad for sales; all the bourgeois look sulky at parting with their sous. But that will end. . . .'

* * *

Ten months after their first exhibition, Monet, Renoir, and Sisley, in need of money to live, arranged for a sale to be held at the Hôtel Drouot. This auction brought them very little money and, despite a few favourable comments in the press, the jeers of the crowd predominated. The sale, however, resulted in acquainting the artists with an understanding collector, Victor Chocquet, who became especially interested in the work of Renoir (Pl. 40). He commissioned him to paint a portrait of Madame Chocquet, and Renoir soon took him to a modest paint dealer, père Tanguy, whom Pissarro had recommended to Cézanne and who had agreed to provide Cézanne with paints and canvases, taking some paintings in exchange. Tanguy was thus the first to handle Cézanne's work.

Chocquet was immediately taken by the pictures which Tanguy showed him and though he feared his wife's opposition, could not resist purchasing one. A little later, the collector met Cézanne through Renoir and a fast friendship soon united them.

A modest chief supervisor in the customs administration, Chocquet had the spirit of the true collector, preferring to make his discoveries for himself, taking as his guide only his own taste and pleasure, never thinking of speculation, and wholly uninterested in what others did or thought. Although his resources were limited, he had lovingly brought together through the years an extremely rich collection of works by Delacroix. Cézanne, who shared Chocquet's admiration for the master, liked to say: 'Delacroix acted as intermediary between you and me,' and it is reported that both men had tears in their eyes when, together, they looked at the Delacroix watercolours owned by Chocquet.

To his collection of Delacroix, Chocquet soon added works by the impressionists. In the catalogue of the second exhibition of the group, held in 1876, he is listed as a lender of canvases by Renoir, Monet, and Pissarro. This second show was organized, like the first, one month before the opening of the Salon. It took place at the Durand-Ruel Galleries and presented more or less the same artists with the exception of Cézanne, who was in Aix and had again submitted to the Salon. The show received once more considerable commentary. Besides the numerous derogatory reviews, this time there were also a few which took sides with the painters. Duret defended them, and Degas' friend, the novelist Duranty, affirmed that the little group's contribution to art 'consists in having recognized that bright light discolours tones, that the sun, reflected by objects, tends, through brightness, to give them this luminous unity which welds its seven prismatic rays into a single colourless brightness, which is light.'

Duret and Duranty were joined, when the third exhibition was organized by the impressionists in 1877, by a new critic and friend introduced by Renoir, Georges Rivière. Through his zeal in the defence of the new painting, Rivière took the place left vacant since Zola had abandoned art criticism.

*   *   *

The exhibition of 1877 was held in April in an apartment rented by the artists in the Rue Le Peletier. According to Rivière, the hanging was in charge of Renoir, Monet, Pissarro, and their friend Caillebotte, who gave Cézanne the most prominent position in the main room. Monet showed no less than thirty paintings, Cézanne seventeen, among them a 'Portrait of Chocquet'. Georges Rivière, who issued a little paper for the duration of the exhibition, *L'Impres-*

sionniste, stated in it that what distinguished the impressionists from other painters was the treatment of a subject in terms of colours and not of the subject itself. He published several articles in strong praise of his friends and began with Cézanne. Rivière wrote:

'The artist who has been the most attacked, the most mistreated by the press and the public for the past fifteen years, is M. Cézanne. There is no outrageous epithet which has not been attached to his name; his works have had a success in ridicule and continue to have it. A newspaper called the portrait of a man exhibited this year, 'Billoir en chocolat' [this was Chocquet's portrait. Billoir was a famous murderer]. These laughs and outcries stem from a bad faith which they do not even attempt to dissimulate. They come to M. Cézanne's works in order to laugh their heads off. For my part, I do not know of any painting less laughable than this. . . .

'M. Cézanne is, in his works, a Greek of the great period; his canvases have the calm and heroic serenity of the paintings and terra-cottas of antiquity, and the ignorant who laugh at the "Bathers", for example, impress me like barbarians criticizing the Parthenon.

'M. Cézanne is a painter and a great painter. Those who have never held a brush or pencil claim that he does not know how to draw, and they have criticized him for imperfections which are actually a refinement obtained through tremendous knowledge. . . .

'His beautiful still lifes, so exact in the relationship of tones, have a solemn quality of truth. In all his paintings the artist produces emotion because he himself experiences in the face of nature a violent emotion which his craftsmanship transmits to the canvas.'

But Georges Rivière was still one of the few to recognize Cézanne's 'knowledge and greatness'. The public continued to be amused by his work, the chief object of ridicule being his portrait of Victor Chocquet. The collector, who spent all his time at the exhibition, was untiring in his efforts to convince the visitors of Cézanne's mastery. 'He was worth seeing,' Duret later wrote. 'He became a sort of apostle. One after another he took the visitors that he knew or approached others to try and make them share his admirations and his pleasure. It was an ungrateful role. . . . He got nothing but smiles or mockery. M. Chocquet was not discouraged. I remember having seen him try thus to persuade well-known critics and hostile artists who had come simply to run the show down. This gave Chocquet a reputation and whenever he appeared people liked to attack him on his favourite subject. He was always ready. He always had the right word when it was a question of his painter friends. He was particularly indefatigable on the subject of Cézanne whom he placed on the very highest level. . . . Many were amused at Chocquet's enthusiasm which they considered something like a gentle insanity. . . .'

Cézanne painted several portraits of this friend and benefactor; the one he exhibited in 1877 attracted the crowd because of its strange and striking colours. It is a very clear and calm painting; the blue-green reflections in the hair, some blue touches in the beard, red and yellow tones of the skin, greenish parts around the beard and mouth—all this was disconcerting to the public. Despite Chocquet's patience in explaining to the laughing visitors that these were reflections cast by light upon objects, and that the everlasting pink of the skin shown in official portraits were done only to a blind convention, he did not succeed in convincing them. The portrait of Chocquet caused the critic of *Le Charivari* to advise his readers not to linger before Cézanne's painting if they were visiting the exhibition with a pregnant woman, as this might give the infant yellow fever before its birth. The critic for *Le Petit Parisien* summed up the reaction of the majority of the public with less cynicism when he stated that Cézanne's impression of nature was not the same as that of other people. On the whole, the reviewers were less severe than previously, and O'Squarre wrote in *Le Courrier de France*; 'The lion of criticism has become gentler. The wild beast has drawn in its claws and one might think that the hostility which the impressionists met at their debut was only the clumsy and somewhat savage expression of a profound stupefaction.'

However, the beast had by no means lost its claws, and Rivière remarked that 'in France the fear of ridicule is so great that one mistrusts and laughs at everything original'. Indeed, Paul Mantz, influential art critic of *Le Temps*, published the following thoughts on the impressionists: '. . . They have closed eyes, a heavy hand, and superb contempt for technique. There is no need to concern oneself with these chimerical minds who imagine that their casualness will be taken for grace and their impotence for candour. . . . No matter what they do, the prognosis for the future remains reassuring. One need not fear that ignorance will ever again become a virtue.'

Even those who were beginning to be indulgent toward Renoir, Monet, or Berthe Morisot had no respect for Cézanne's work, and when Arsène Houssaye, editor of *L'Artiste*, asked Rivière for an article on impressionism, he requested him not to mention either Pissarro or Cézanne, in order not to shock the readers of his magazine.

Apparently Cézanne was deeply disappointed by this new setback, for he decided to 'work in silence' and not to exhibit with his friends again. This decision was partly reached because of his doubts, because of his tendency never to be satisfied with results and always to attempt improvements, but it may also have been induced by his conviction that critics and public could not be entirely mistaken in their judgment. He accepted certain objections concerning his 'lack of draftsmanship' and his 'immoderate use of colour,' since he felt himself still far from the goal to be attained. He also feared that the noisy ridicule which greeted his paintings might damage the reputation as a serious artist which he coveted. For, if Cézanne no longer exhibited with his friends, each year he continued to send a submission to the official Salon, although he always received a letter of rejection which, as he wrote Pissarro, he found 'neither new nor surprising'. The opportunity to show his work to the public, offered to him by his friends in their exhibitions held annually from 1879 to 1882 and again in 1886, was thus repudiated by Cézanne; he still hoped to be accepted by the jury.

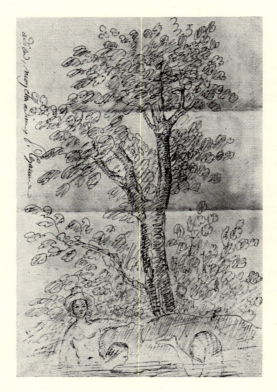

XIV

CÉZANNE AND HIS FAMILY

AFTER the closing of the impressionist exhibition of 1877, Cézanne continued to paint in the outskirts of Paris. He worked with Pissarro in a vegetable garden at Pontoise; he stayed briefly in Auvers; he went to Chantilly, to Fontainebleau; he set up his easel on the banks of the Seine and the Marne. 'If this is of interest to you,' Duranty wrote Zola, 'Cézanne appeared a short while ago at the little Café on the Place Pigalle in one of his costumes of olden times: blue jacket, vest of white linen covered with the strokes of brushes and other instruments, battered old hat. He made quite an impression!'

Zola was spending the summer with his wife and old mother in L'Estaque, to relive a phase of his past and to write his novel, *Une Page d'Amour*. 'The country is superb,' he said in a letter to a friend. 'You would perhaps find it arid and desolate, but I was brought up among these rocks and bare wastelands, which is why I am moved to tears when I see it. The mere odour of the pines evokes my whole youth.'

Cézanne took advantage of Zola's stay in L'Estaque to ask him to give messages to his mother who, as usual, had rented a small house in the village. The painter did not want to write to his mother directly, knowing that his father opened all her letters.

'I would like you to let my mother know,' he wrote Zola, 'that I do not want anything, as I expect to spend the winter in Marseilles. If in December she wishes to find me a very small two-room apartment in Marseilles, inexpensive, but in a district where not too many murders take place, I would be very pleased. She could have a bed put in it and whatever else is needed for sleeping, and two chairs from her house in L'Estaque, in order to avoid unnecessary expense.

'I go to the park of Issy here every day to make some studies. And I am not too dissatisfied, but it appears that profound desolation reigns in the impressionist camp. Gold is not exactly flowing into their pockets and the pictures are rotting on the spot. We are living in very troubled times and I do not know when unhappy painting will regain a little of its lustre. . . . With the exception of two or three painters, I see absolutely no one.'

A few days later Cézanne wrote to Zola countermanding his message to his mother and saying that he expected to visit Aix in December or early January.

Cézanne went to live in L'Estaque at the beginning of 1878 in order to 'savour the most perfect tranquillity', but no sooner had he taken up residence there than the misunderstanding between him and his father became painfully manifest.

Cézanne the banker had all the qualities and faults of the self-made man. Strong-willed and direct in pursuit of his aims, he was exasperated by the everlasting hesitations and the apathy of his son. As he was intelligent and observant, he knew Paul's faults, but on the other hand, his uncultivated and unimaginative mind was incapable of grasping his son's intellectual needs and artistic aspirations. Although he was very rich, M. Cézanne gave Paul little money, rather from resentment than avarice, for he was appalled that a man of forty should be unable to earn his living. He continued to treat his son as a child and even opened his mail. Thus, one day he read a letter from Chocquet addressed to the painter, in which Chocquet mentioned 'Madame Cézanne' and 'little Paul'. Embarrassed and against all evidence, the son denied his liaison and the existence of his child. This made his father so furious that he decided to reduce his allowance from two hundred francs to one hundred a month, on the ground that this was sufficient for a bachelor. Consequently, Cézanne's financial straits were such that he was obliged to write to Zola begging him to find him any sort of job so that he might support his family. Zola, who had just obtained his first great success with the novel, *L'Assommoir*, persuaded his friend not to provoke a complete rupture with his father and generously offered financial help for as long as would be necessary. Cézanne accepted gladly, especially as his boy was ill and living with his mother in Marseilles, while Cézanne himself was with his parents in Aix. He asked that the money be sent directly to Hortense; he took every precaution against giving his father definite proof of his liaison, whereas the latter tried by every means to catch him.

'I stole away on Tuesday, a week ago,' Cézanne wrote Zola on 4 April 1878, 'to go to see the boy; he is better, and I had to return to Aix on foot as there was a mistake in the time-table, and I had to be back for dinner.' Cézanne was an hour late to dinner, although Aix is about eighteen miles from Marseilles.

The situation was very difficult for Cézanne; it was aggravated by the fact that the owner of his Paris apartment forwarded mail to the 'Jas de Bouffan', where the banker promptly opened it. In this way Cézanne's father learned that his son had left the key to his apartment with a shoemaker who had let a few relatives stay there during the World's Fair of 1878. The banker concluded that his son was 'hiding women in Paris'. 'It's beginning to resemble a vaudeville,' wrote the painter bitterly to Zola.

Cézanne's father, who knew already from others that Paul had a child and who had every intention of 'ridding' him of his dependents, now went so far as to have him followed. Thus one day, meeting the painter Villevieille, a friend of his son's, the banker said to him out of a clear blue sky:

'You know, I'm a grandfather!'

'What do you mean? Paul isn't married!'

'He was seen coming out of a shop with a rocking horse and other toys. You are not going to tell me that they were for himself.'

'So much the better,' was Villevieille's only reply. 'It's about time you found out.'

And according to a letter Numa Coste sent Zola, the father knew that 'Paul has a brat. He said to somebody who questioned him: "It seems that I have some grandchildren in Paris; I'll have to go and see them some day".'

But the silent struggle between father and son went on.

In November 1878 Hortense had to go to Paris for several weeks and Cézanne stayed in L'Estaque with his child, fearing momentarily a visit from his father. He was so tired of all the quarrels that he was ready to renounce his rights to any future inheritance on condition that his father settle on him two or three thousand francs more per year. 'My good family,' he wrote to Zola, 'which is very worthy, to be sure, is perhaps a bit tight-fisted to an unfortunate painter, who has never been able to do anything; it is a light failing and doubtless easily excusable in the provinces.' Toward the year's end, however, everything must have been straightened out. Cézanne was no longer obliged to accept money from Zola, having succeeded in obtaining an adequate allowance from his father, doubtless at his mother's behest.

Little is known of Madame Cézanne, and there are no letters of hers extant. Her son painted her seldom. She was probably just as shy as Paul, and this may have prevented her from posing. Yet, Cézanne did make one drawing of her at about this time, while she was asleep in her armchair. If he inherited certain morbid character traits from his mother, it was perhaps to her that he also owed his genius. She was very intelligent, with a subtle and impulsive mind and a lively imagination. Dark and tall, with a big frame and a thin face, she resembled her son. Paul was her favourite child and, far from trying to dissuade him, she even encouraged his painting, full of confidence in her son's talent. Her husband showed a preference for their daughter, Marie, because of her calmness, which was in such contrast with Paul's turbulence.

Cézanne found in his mother a confidante and ally; they seemed always to have been in complete agreement of ideas and feelings. Not only had she secretly helped him out when he was short of money, but she apparently also knew about his liaison from the beginning. She visited her grandchild on the sly and loved him dearly, the more so because she was a grandmother for the first time. It was quite natural that she should have attempted to win over her husband. Due to her insistence, no doubt, the banker eventually consented to his son's marriage. It may even be that the marriage came about only because Cézanne's family pushed him to take this step. His pious sister, Marie, for instance, is known to have told him over and over again: 'Marry her, why don't you marry her.'

If Cézanne finally agreed to marry Hortense Fiquet at a time when he was no longer in love with her, it was doubtless to legitimize his son, whom he adored, and to put an end to the equivocal situation. In any case, on 28 April 1886, Paul Cézanne and Hortense Fiquet were married at Aix in the presence of the painter's parents, who both signed the marriage register at the town hall. The witnesses to the religious ceremony which took place the following morning at the church of Saint-Jean-Baptiste were his sister Marie, and Maxime Conil, the husband of his sister Rose. A few months after this marriage, Cézanne's father died on 23 October 1886, at the age of eighty-eight. After his death the painter constantly expressed his admiration for him and said: 'My father was a man of genius; he left me an income of twenty-five thousand francs.'

Four years before his marriage, Paul Cézanne had thought of making his will because, being of an anxious disposition, he thought himself destined to die young. But he made fun of his own fears, and wrote to Zola: 'I am thin and can do nothing for you. As I shall be the first to go, I shall arrange with the All-Highest to reserve a good place for you.'

In November 1882 Cézanne wrote to Zola asking his advice concerning his will. His father, who had retired from the bank after the war of 1870, had placed his fortune in the name of his children in order to avoid inheritance taxes. Feared by his children for his authoritarian temper, Louis-Auguste Cézanne knew that he could trust them not to touch the fortune which, though legally theirs, he continued to administer. While not using this money, Paul Cézanne was entitled to bequeath it to whomever he wished, and he decided to leave half of it to his mother, and half to his son. He asked Zola to keep a copy of his will for him and sent it to him from L'Estaque in May 1883 after having consulted a lawyer in Marseilles. This will must have been revised after Cézanne's marriage.

*   *   *

Cézanne's marriage produced no change in his existence for, after his father's death, he continued to live with his mother and his sister Marie. His wife—using her delicate health as an excuse—spent most of her time in Paris with their son. She did not like the Midi although she loved to travel. Cézanne said of her: 'My wife likes only Switzerland and lemonade.' From time to time she visited Aix, but she and her husband did not get along very well. Cézanne's old mother tried to mediate in their quarrels, and though not extremely fond of her daughter-in-law, did her best to be agreeable. Hortense's only contribution to her husband's life as an artist was in posing for him repeatedly and that without moving or talking. Cézanne rarely painted any other woman, and it must have entailed considerable sacrifice on the part of his lively and talkative wife to lend herself to the endless sittings he inflicted on her. When she occasionally attempted to participate in the discussions on art which Cézanne had with his friends, her husband would say to her in a quiet, reproachful voice: 'Hortense, be still, my dear, you are only talking nonsense.'

A long letter from Alexis to Zola, written in Aix on 13 February

1891, gives a good picture of Cézanne's marital life. Alexis tells that by cutting her allowance in half, the painter succeeded in bringing his wife and son to Aix:

'Yesterday evening, Thursday, at seven o'clock, Paul left us to meet them at the station . . . and the furniture, brought back from Paris for four hundred francs, is arriving too. Paul expects to settle the whole business in a place he rented on the Rue de la Monnaie, where he is going to pay them an allowance. . . .

'Nevertheless, he himself does not intend to leave his mother and his older sister with whom he is living in the outskirts [doubtless the "Jas de Bouffan"] and where he feels very well, definitely preferring this life to that woman. Now, if—as he hopes—the Ball [the nickname of Hortense Fiquet] and the little one take root here, nothing will prevent him from spending six months in Paris every now and then. "Long live the bright sun and freedom!" he cries.

'Besides, he has no financial troubles. Thanks to the author of his days whom he now venerates . . . he has enough to live. He has divided his income into twelve monthly shares, and each of them is sub-divided into three: for the Ball, for the bullet, and for himself. Only the Ball, not very delicate as it seems, shows a constant tendency to infringe on his personal fraction. Today, braced by his mother and sister, who can't stand the lady in question, he feels strong enough to resist.'

Since the share of Hortense Cézanne and her son was about sixteen thousand francs a year, the painter had thus provided generously for his wife, and could believe that he owed her nothing more. Although indifferent as a husband, he was a tender and indulgent father. Cézanne not only loved his son, but forgave him in advance for any pranks. 'Whatever mischief you may get into,' he told him, 'I shall never forget that I am your father.'

The very qualities Cézanne had been unable to appreciate in his father, common sense, balance, and self-assurance, he now admired in his own son. 'Life is fearful,' was one of Cézanne's habitual remarks. Finding himself 'weak', as he put it, in the face of the realities of life, he instinctively sought a prop. His mother and Zola fulfilled this function for many years. After the former's death he leaned upon his son, who remained his adviser and confidant throughout his life, taking care of money matters and the sale of pictures. That Cézanne was well aware of his incapacity to direct his own life is revealed by a letter which he wrote to Chocquet in 1886, the year of his marriage: 'I should have wished to possess the intellectual equilibrium that characterizes you and permits you to achieve without fail the desired end. . . . Chance has not favoured me with an equal self-assurance; it is the only regret I have about things of this earth.'

Little by little, this lack of 'intellectual equilibrium', his fear of life and doubtless also of death, as well as the influence of his mother and sister, made of Cézanne, who had been inveterately anti-clerical, a church-going Catholic. 'It is fear!' he explained to Paul Alexis in 1891. 'I feel that I have only a few days left on earth —and then what? I believe I shall survive and do not want to risk roasting *in eternum*.'

Cézanne went to mass, which, however, he mockingly referred to as taking his 'slice of the Middle Ages'. He hated priests and was afraid of getting into their 'clutches', and this aversion even extended to religion, which he called 'moral hygiene'. Sometimes he fell asleep during services, and one day, irritated by an organist who played off-key, he wrote to his son: 'I think that to be a Catholic one must be devoid of all sense of justice, but have a good eye for one's interests.' Nor did Cézanne's faith prevent him from speaking ill of priests, whom he often called filthy, and it also failed to eliminate his swearing. Curses were for him a way of relieving his rages and when he had trouble with his painting he would sometimes sing to a tune of the vespers: 'Nom de Dieu de nom de Dieu de nom de Dieu. . . .'

But in spite of all his sallies and jeers, it seems certain that Cézanne did find in religion the support which he sought. 'Once we have attained a certain age,' he was to write his young niece, 'we find no other support and consolation than in religion.'

Some people have attributed Cézanne's assiduity at mass to the influence of his sister Marie, as well as to his desire not to offend his neighbours in Aix. Yet it is a fact that the painter attended religious services regularly, even when away from his home town. Provincial environment and family beliefs thus eventually shaped a part of Cézanne's individuality, confining it within the limits of its rigid customs and prejudices, while his artistic individuality continued to develop and broaden his whole life long.

XV

CÉZANNE AT ZOLA'S IN MÉDAN

THE SUCCESS of *L'Assommoir* in 1878 made it possible for Zola to buy a summer house, surrounded by a garden on the Seine, at Médan, near Paris. There he worked, saw his friends, and lived in the open air. Cézanne was delighted to hear the news. 'I congratulate you on your purchase,' he immediately wrote Zola, 'and with your consent I shall take advantage of it to get to know the country better. If life is not impossible for me either at La Roche-Guyon or at Bennecourt, or a little here and a little there, I shall try and spend a year or two there, as I did at Auvers.'

Cézanne did not carry out this plan, but he often spent weeks in the outskirts of Paris and paid numerous visits to Zola at Médan. Zola soon enlarged his property and added new buildings which made it possible for him to entertain his guests more comfortably. He enjoyed gathering his friends around him, and there was always room for a new arrival. Cézanne, Numa Coste, Antoine Guillemet, and all the other comrades were always welcome for a night, a couple of days, or as long as they chose.

At the end of September 1879 Cézanne was expected at Médan. He accepted the invitation with all the more joy since, as he put it, at that season 'the country is really astonishing. There seems to be greater silence. These are feelings I cannot express; it is better to experience them.'

The following year, before going to Médan for a week, Cézanne wrote Zola from Paris: 'The moment I will not be in your way, please write to me and I shall be very happy to go to Médan. And if you are not alarmed at the length of time that I risk taking, I shall make so bold as to bring a small canvas with me and paint a motif always providing that you see no objection.'

While at Médan, Cézanne worked on the banks of the Seine or on a little green island belonging to Zola, only a stone's throw from his house. Cézanne made use of Zola's boat, called 'Nana', and from this island painted a view of Médan, dominated by the château with its dormer windows (Pl. 37).

The bank agent, Paul Gauguin, who owned this painting,

possibly acquired at *père* Tanguy's, had a story to tell about it, a story he may have heard from Pissarro or from Cézanne himself:

'Cézanne paints a glittering landscape with an ultramarine background, and heavy greens and ochres of silken lustre; the trees are in a straight line, and through the entwining branches may be seen the house of his friend Zola [it is actually the château of Médan; Zola's house was off to the right] with its vermilion shutters made orange by the chromes which sparkle on the limewash of the walls. Crackling Veronese greens indicate the superb foliage of the garden, and the grave contrasting note of the violaceous nettles in the foreground orchestrates the simple poem.

'The pretentious and shocked passer-by looks at what he thinks is a lamentable daub by an amateur and, a smiling teacher, says to Cézanne: "You are painting."

' "Certainly, but so little. . . ."

' "Oh! I can see that. Here, I am a former pupil of Corot, and if you will allow me, with a few deft touches I will straighten all this out for you. Values, values—that is all that counts."

'And the vandal impudently puts some stupid strokes on the glittering canvas. Dirty greys cover the Oriental silks.

'Cézanne exclaims: "Monsieur, you are fortunate and when you paint a portrait you probably put highlights on the tip of the nose, as on the rung of a chair."

'Cézanne takes up his palette and scratches out with his knife all the mess made by the gentleman.

'After a silence he lets out a terrific fart and turning to the gentleman he says: 'What a relief".'

Gauguin has, of course, to take responsibility for this episode, yet all those who knew Cézanne were agreed that he could upon occasion be extremely vulgar. There are even reports that he behaved thus with Zola's guests, but the repeated invitations which Zola extended to him seem to negate this. Cézanne's vulgarity, as Zola remarked, was a mask for his lack of ease and his timidity. More often, however, when he was troubled, the painter reacted with outbursts of rage and sudden flights. For example, one day when he was painting a portrait of Madame Zola, whom he had asked to pose in the garden, standing beside a table and serving tea, Antoine Guillemet interrupted him; whereupon Cézanne broke his brushes, tore holes in the canvas and left, in one of his usual rages.

'No news of Paul,' Zola subsequently wrote to Guillemet. 'He must have run like a hare.' But this kind of incident never prevented Cézanne from starting another canvas, nor did this one stop him from returning to Médan to shake Zola's hand, to chat with him and to inquire whether he shared his opinion about 'painting as a medium for the expression of sensations'.

Cézanne spent the spring of 1881 in Pontoise where he often saw Pissarro, as well as the landscape painter Vignon and Paul Gauguin, who, accompanied by his wife, had come to spend his vacation with Pissarro. The latter was then advising Gauguin in his first attempts at painting. They had long discussions together about theoretical and practical questions, and after Gauguin had returned to his banking business in Paris, he asked of Pissarro:

'Has Monsieur Cézanne found the exact *formula* for a work acceptable to everyone? If he discovers the prescription for compressing the intense expression of all his sensations into a single and unique procedure, try to make him talk in his sleep by giving him one of those mysterious homeopathic drugs and come immediately to Paris to share it with us.'

It must have been this innocent remark, doubtless quoted by Pissarro, which made Cézanne suspicious of Gauguin. He later went so far as to accuse Gauguin of wanting to steal his 'little sensation'.—'Never mention Gauguin to Cézanne!' Monet used to warn. 'I can still hear him shout with his southern accent: "That Gauguin, I'll wring his neck!" '

It was during his stay at Pontoise that Cézanne received an invitation from Zola which he again accepted eagerly. Yet, it is difficult to imagine Cézanne in Zola's house, always full of visitors and cluttered with tasteless bric-à-brac that surprised even the novelist's most fervent admirers. Indeed, Zola lived in pretentious and sumptuous surroundings. The enormous rooms were hung with antique tapestries and received a checkered light through stained-glass windows. In this setting Zola entertained Cézanne, who was accustomed to studios without luxury and to a life of extreme simplicity. If Cézanne was able to stand at Zola's an environment which certainly could not have pleased him, this proves that he was much less eccentric than generally supposed and that his simplicity was not naiveté.

Nowhere was Cézanne welcomed with so much affection as in Médan, and this hospitable atmosphere put him at his ease. In Zola's house he was not the painter ridiculed by the critics, but a friend of the master, and his canvases, of which the novelist owned about a dozen, were hung in the hall. Others decorated Zola's Paris home, along with works by Manet, Monet, and Pissarro. Zola was indifferent to the opinion of those among his guests who could barely conceal their astonishment at finding in his house such paintings 'without great originality, without real value', as one of them remarked.

III. CARD PLAYERS, 1890-2

It is true that Cézanne fled from the company of those who disturbed his work, evaded those who wanted to get him 'in their clutches', was irritated and troubled by people who talked too much, but in this he reacted like any creative person who needs solitude to find himself, and who fears society because he feels misunderstood. Yet it took very little to put Cézanne at his ease. What made him difficult to get along with was a special attitude produced by a mixture of mistrust and confidence, but with his old friends who knew how to handle him, the painter even enjoyed being sociable.

What Cézanne found at Médan was a 'moral support' which he deeply appreciated. It was not only the novelist, however, who made his visits agreeable; in Zola's house Cézanne met his 'compatriot', as he called Paul Alexis, as well as Numa Coste and such writers and critics as Théodore Duret and J.-K. Huysmans. He was grateful to Zola for introducing him to 'these very remarkable people'.

When Zola had guests for whom Cézanne did not care, he was always free to go off and paint the many admirable motifs in the surroundings. On one occasion, in the autumn of 1882, Cézanne spent no less than five weeks at Zola's house.

Thus Cézanne was unquestionably happy in Médan. He found there, if not the esteem to which he was entitled as painter, at least a sincere affection from the bottom of Zola's heart for the oldest and best friend of his youth.

XVI

CRITICISM AND CARICATURES

1880–1881

AT THE Salon of 1880 the paintings were arranged in a new way. They were no longer hung in alphabetical order but were divided into four separate categories: the artists *hors concours*, the artists exempt from being passed by the jury, those not exempt, and, lastly, foreign exhibitors. The drawbacks of this system were soon apparent. For one thing, the large space reserved for artists *hors concours* emphasized the banality of their works; for another, the visitors could not find the canvases they were looking for. 'Where the devil have they hidden your paintings?' asked Zola of Numa Coste, who continued to paint as an amateur and send to the Salon. 'I spent two hours in the Palais de l'Industrie without being able to find them.'

Discouraged by the failure of their successive group exhibitions, Monet and Renoir had decided that year to submit again to the Salon jury. Their works were hung so badly that they addressed a letter of protest to the Minister. They begged Cézanne to forward their letter to Zola. 'This is what I am requested to ask you to do,' Cézanne commented. 'It is to publish this letter in *Le Voltaire*, preceded or followed by a few words on the previous activity of the group. These few words should aim at showing up the importance of the impressionists and the real interest which they aroused.'

Ready to oblige, Zola wrote a series of four long articles on *Le Naturalisme au Salon* in which he referred to the demand of his friends and dwelled at length on impressionism. In these articles he mentioned Cézanne's name for the first time in years.

Although the tone of his articles is friendly, they reveal some of the ideas which were beginning to separate Zola from his painter friends. Zola wondered whether they had acted wisely in ceasing to exhibit their work at the official Salon only to return there as Monet and Renoir were now doing. Manet, who had continued to exhibit at the Salon, had finally been accepted by the public, whereas the others had lost ground through their private exhibitions.

'Of course,' Zola wrote, 'there was a great uproar. The impressionist exhibitions were the talk of the town; they were lampooned,

98

they were laughed at and insulted, but visitors came in droves. Unfortunately that was only noise, the noise of Paris, which is gone with the wind.' Yet, as Zola stated, while the impressionists were being ridiculed, the new art which they proclaimed crept in at the Salon. Their efforts had not been in vain, for there was a slow evolution towards modern subjects and bright painting. 'They shoot us,' Degas remarked bitterly, 'but they pick our pockets'.

'It is,' wrote Zola, 'a rising tide of irresistible modernism which is gradually carrying away the Ecole des Beaux-Arts, the Institute, all the precepts and conventions. . . . It is impressionism corrected, tempered, put within range of the masses. . . .'

In view of this unexpected result, Zola asked himself whether his friends' abstention from the official exhibitions had not left the road to success open to unscrupulous imitators. Zola thought their group shows too easy and too dangerous a means of trying to gain recognition and that the greatest courage lies in 'staying in the breach, no matter what the circumstances'. He was convinced that 'it is enough to paint great pictures; even if they are rejected for ten years, badly hung for another ten years, they always end by gaining the recognition they deserve. So much the worse for the weak who fall to the ground, crushed by the strong! . . .'

But in spite of his objections to their private exhibitions, Zola wanted to help the impressionists and to put an end to the gossip circulating about them: 'They are called practical jokers, charlatans who mock the public and make a lot of noise about their work, whereas on the contrary, they are serious and sincere observers. People seem to ignore that most of these fighters are poor, working themselves to death, struggling with misery and fatigue. Strange practical jokers, these martyrs to their beliefs!'

However, Zola could not hide from himself the fact that these martyrs had not yet produced the great works for which he had so long been waiting. Convinced that impressionism or, as he preferred to call it, naturalism, was the art of the future, he asked himself why his friends had not obtained the success they deserved. Since his own work, since naturalism in literature, was beginning to be accepted, it could not be either naturalism itself or the public which prevented the victory of their common cause. Therefore Zola ended by blaming his friends for not having lived up to their promise, for not having created what they owed to their era. And he concluded:

'The real misfortune is that no artist of this group has achieved powerfully and definitely the new formula which, scattered through their works, they all offer. The formula is there, endlessly diffused; but in no place, among any of them, is it to be found applied by a master. They are all forerunners. The man of genius has not arisen.

We can see what they intend and find them right, but we seek in vain the masterpiece that is to lay down the formula and make heads bow before it. This is why the battle of the impressionists has not yet ended; they remain inferior to what they undertake; they stammer without being able to find the word.'

Thus Zola was disappointed in his hope, which he had expressed so proudly fourteen years earlier, in the preface of *Mes Haines*: 'The hour is palpitating, full of anxiety: One awaits those who will strike hardest and most accurately, whose fists will be powerful enough to close the others' mouths, and at the bottom of each new fighter's heart may be found a vague hope of being this dictator, this tyrant of tomorrow. . . . Let the blind repudiate our efforts, let them see in our struggles the convulsions of agony, though these struggles are the first stammerings of birth. . . .'

These stammerings still had not become words, it seemed to Zola, and he resigned himself to the fact. Since the impressionists 'showed themselves incomplete, illogical, exaggerated, impotent.' they would have to remain merely avant-garde of a cause which, sooner or later, was destined to conquer, instead of being themselves the leaders of an irresistible movement.

The impression made by these articles upon Zola's friends is summed up in a letter from Manet to Théodore Duret. Although Manet was not immediately concerned, he severely criticized Zola's articles; but in a second letter, he asked Duret to destroy the first one, explaining: '. . . It seems that I am in the wrong, but I had not judged Zola's article from a personal standpoint and I thought it contained too much eclecticism. We have so much need of being defended that a little radicalism would have done no harm, it seems to me. . . .'

Cézanne, however, did not look at the matter in the same way. On two occasions he thanked Zola on behalf of himself and his colleagues. His attitude may be explained by the fact that he did not believe he had much in common with the impressionists and shared Zola's opinion of them. This opinion he echoed later in speaking of 'the impressionist gang which lacks a leader and ideas'. As for Zola's remark concerning himself, here again he agreed with his friend. 'M. Paul Cézanne,' Zola had written, 'has the temperament of a great painter who still struggles with problems of technique, and remains closest to Courbet and Delacroix.' Actually Cézanne always did maintain that he was still seeking, that nature presented the greatest difficulties, and that he was far from being satisfied with his results.

But Cézanne was the only one of Zola's painter friends to approve of his ideas. Though they were surprised and worried by Zola's defection, the impressionists nevertheless continued to approach him when they needed a spokesman. In forwarding to Zola the requests of his comrades, Cézanne felt he ought to excuse himself, and wrote in one instance:

'. . . I shall not add that whatever answer you consider proper to give to this request must have no influence on your friendly feelings for me, nor on the good relations that you have been kind enough to preserve between us. For I am liable more than once to have to make requests which could annoy you. I merely act as an intermediary and nothing more.'

*   *   *

Cézanne was no longer very close to the impressionists at this period. His decision not to show with them any more, his frequent absences from Paris and his lack of interest in the meetings at the Café de la Nouvelle-Athènes separated him from his comrades. 'Fearful of seeing new faces,' as Monet described him, Cézanne avoided those gatherings, where, to talk with a few friends, he had to put up with other people who were indifferent to him. He accompanied Zola only once to the salon of Madame Charpentier, who entertained the élite of the literary and political worlds. He rarely went to the house of Nina de Villard where he had met Léon Dierx, Frank Lamy, de Marrast, Ernest d'Hervilly, Villiers de l'Isle-Adam, and others. He visited the Café de la Nouvelle-Athènes, where he could see Zola, Alexis, and Manet, so seldom that most of the younger habitués knew of him only by hearsay. When he appeared there, he did so in his picturesque working clothes, which created quite a sensation and which led Duranty to comment: 'Those are dangerous demonstrations.'

This flouting of conventions was indeed 'dangerous' in the sense that it encouraged all sorts of rumours which began to circulate concerning the painter. For instance, George Moore, who frequented the Café in 1879, wrote in his *Reminiscences:*

'I do not remember ever to have seen Cézanne at the Nouvelle-Athènes; he was too rough, too savage a creature, and appeared in Paris only rarely. We used to hear about him—he used to be met on the outskirts of Paris wandering about the hillsides in jack-boots. As no one took the least interest in his pictures, he left them in the fields. . . . It would be untrue to say that he had no talent, but whereas the intention of Manet and of Monet and of Degas was always to paint, the intention of Cézanne was, I am afraid, never very clear to himself. His work may be described as the anarchy of painting, as art in delirium.'

It is easy to see how Cézanne became a legendary figure. Those who neither knew the painter nor his work were of course incapable of understanding the conscientious efforts and painful vehemence with which he pursued his aims. It was difficult, indeed, for anyone to form an accurate opinion of Cézanne when all that was popularly known about him, besides the rumours which circulated, was that he was Zola's friend, that he had exhibited queer work, and that he was violent, timid, and proud. To the incredible words and deeds that were reported was added, in 1881, a rather heavy-handed caricature of Cézanne by Duranty, published after the author's death. The principal character of a story, the painter Maillobert, was partly based on Cézanne. Reporting a visit to Maillobert's studio, Duranty had written:

'When I was about to knock, I heard a parrot's voice within. I knocked. "Come in," someone shouted in an extraordinary accent.

'No sooner had I entered than I exclaimed to myself, "I am visiting a madman!"

'I was completely confused by the environment and the individual. . . . The painter, bald, with a huge beard . . . looking at once both young and old, was himself like the symbolic divinity of his studio—indescribable and sordid. He made me a deep bow, accompanied by a smile which I could not define, sly and idiotic.

'At the same time my eyes were assailed by so many enormous canvases hung everywhere, and of such terrible colours, that I was petrified.

' "Ah! Ah!" said Maillobert in a nasal, drawling, and exaggerated accent of Marseilles, "Monsieur is a connoisseur of painting? Here are the little scraps from my palette!" he added, pointing to his most enormous canvases.

'At this moment the parrot cried out: "Maillobert is a great painter. . . ."

' "That is my art critic," the painter said to me with a disturbing smile. . . .

'Then, when he saw me looking curiously at a number of large pharmacist's pots bearing the abbreviated Latin inscriptions Jusqui., Aqu., Still., Ferrug., Rib., Sufl., Cup., Maillobert said:

' "This is my paintbox. I show the others that with drugs I can do real painting whereas they, with their beautiful colours, only make drugs!"

'. . . My eyes fastened on a very tall picture representing a coalman and a baker clinking glasses in front of a nude woman over whose head was written "Cooperation." When I say a coalman and a baker, it is because Maillobert explained to me that such were these naked people, the one slashed with white, the other with brown. The three figures were giants, twice normal size, done against an entirely black background by means of wide, jerky strokes in which vermilion, Prussian blue, and silver-white clashed furiously; huge eyes with a shining dot in each stood out on their heads. Nevertheless an arm here, a lip there, or a knee were treated with a certain power.

' "It is the expression of civilization," Maillobert told me, "we must satisfy the philosophers who are always barking at our heels."

'A series of portraits then attracted me, portraits without faces, for the heads were a mass of spots in which no feature could be seen; but on each frame a name was inscribed, often as strange as the painting: Cabladours, Ispara, Valadéguy, Apollin, all disciples of this master.*

' "Maillobert is a great painter," cried the parrot who seemed instinctively to know the right moment to intervene.

' "He is right," the painter said with animation.

'At this time two of his friends arrived, bearded, black, dirty.

' "Might he be the head of the school of chimney sweeps?" I thought.

'They contemplated the works of the master as though seeing them for the first time.

' "How bold! What energy!" they exclaimed. "Compared to this, Courbet and Manet produce only chaff."

'Maillobert smiled, expansive.

'He dipped a spoon in one of the pharmacist's pots and drew out a regular trowelful of green which he applied to a canvas on which a few lines indicated a landscape. He turned the spoon around and, with an effort, one could see a meadow in what he had just smeared on. I then observed that on his canvases the colour was about half an inch thick and formed valleys and hills in relief. Apparently Maillobert believed that a pound of green was greener than an ounce of the same colour.'

Thus the picture of Cézanne continued to be distorted. His few friends could not deny everything, and he himself did not make the slightest effort to correct this kind of criticism. Since he had ceased to exhibit, his paintings, hidden in his studio, could not bear public witness to his sincerity, to his hard and painstaking work. Thus, when J.-K. Huysmans published his book on modern art in 1883, he did not give Cézanne the importance which, according to Pissarro, was due him. Indeed, Pissarro reproached the author in a letter, asking: 'Why is it that you do not say a word about Cézanne whom all of us recognize as one of the most astounding and curious temperaments of our time and who has had a very great influence on modern art?'

Huysmans immediately replied. His explanation once more reflects the current misconceptions about Cézanne. 'Let's see,'

*One recognizes a take-off on the names of *Valabrègue*, and of *Achille Emperaire* whose name actually is inscribed in large letters on his portrait by Cézanne.

Huysmans wrote to Pissarro: 'I find Cézanne's personality congenial, for I know through Zola of his efforts, his vexations, his defeats when he tries to create a work! Yes, he has temperament, he is an artist, but in sum, with the exception of some still lifes, the rest is, to my mind, not likely to live. It is interesting, curious, suggestive in ideas, but certainly he is an eye case, which I understand he himself realizes. . . . In my humble opinion, the Cézannes typify the impressionists who didn't quite bring it off. You know that after so many years of struggle it is no longer a question of more or less manifest or visible intentions, but of works which are real childbirth, which are not monsters, odd cases for a Dupuytren museum of painting [Dupuytren was the founder of a medical] museum of anatomy].'

Huysmans's letter illustrates the opinions on Cézanne held by Zola's entourage in Médan. Yet the views of this group were rather diversified. Zola, for example, while agreeing with Huysmans's criticism of Monet to the effect that Monet worked too rapidly and was satisfied with rough drafts, did not agree with him concerning Courbet, whom Zola admired, and Degas, whom he did not like. Zola wrote Huysmans: 'As years go by, the more I detach myself from points of view which are simply odd, the more love I feel for the great and prolific creators who produce a world.'

'And the more I turn away from the impressionists,' he might have added.

XVII

CÉZANNE IN PROVENCE

1881 – 1885

AFTER spending the summer of 1881 in the Ile-de-France, where he stayed with Pissarro in Pontoise, but worked, as he told Zola, 'without much vigour,' Cézanne paid a visit to Médan and then went south in the autumn. He returned to Paris in February 1882 for a period of six months and spent five weeks in Médan. In October he was again in Aix, where he settled down for the next three years to the calm existence in Provence.

Life in Aix could hardly have been interesting, to judge from Alexis's letters to Zola, written when family matters forced him to go there. 'It seems to me that I am at the bottom of a well!' Alexis complained. 'Neither air nor sun, intellectually speaking. Ouf! . . . here no one talks about literature or, if they do talk about it, it is enough to make your hair stand on end. A year here will make me stupid or insane.'

If Cézanne did not find the provincial atmosphere suffocating, it was because he seldom saw anyone and rarely left the 'Jas de Bouffan'. Hortense Fiquet and his son had probably remained in Paris, for Cézanne does not mention them in his letters, and he had lost touch with his friends during his frequent absences from the Midi. The pupils of his former schoolmate, Villevieille, who now taught drawing at the Academy in Aix, made fun in the street of Cézanne's tangled hair which surrounded his bald dome, and this decided him to have his hair cut. 'It may be too long,' he confessed. Fortuné Marion had become professor of science in Marseilles, but Cézanne could not make up his mind to visit him there as he suspected him of 'not being sincere about art'. Cézanne could not reach an understanding with the old 'Sieur Gibert' either, for, as he wrote to Zola: 'These people see correctly, but they have the eyes of professors,' regretting that it was only technical questions which interested them in art. However, Cézanne did not dislike his life of solitude in Aix, for it enabled him to work. Furthermore, he did not care for the pleasures of cities.

'Marseilles is France's oil capital,' he wrote Zola, 'just as Paris is the butter capital. You have no idea of the presumptuousness of this fierce population; they have but one instinct, that of money. It is said that they earn a lot, but they are very ugly. Communications efface the most salient features of the types from an external point of view. In a few centuries it will be quite senseless to be alive, everything will be so flattened out. But the bit that remains is still very dear to the heart and to the eye.'

At this period Cézanne used to visit Marseilles quite often, nevertheless, to see the painter Monticelli, with whom he had become very friendly. He liked to arrive unannounced, to chat and to watch Monticelli work. On one occasion they took off together, their packs on their backs, to spend a month roaming about the country between Aix and Marseilles.

It may have been on Monticelli's behalf that Cézanne asked M. Chocquet by letter 'how to go about sending a painting to the administration of the Beaux-Arts in order to submit it to the approbation of the Salon jury'. He explained carefully that he was asking this question 'to help out one of my compatriots. . . . It is not for me.'

Cézanne himself continued each year to submit works to the jury. When he did not deliver his canvases personally to the Palais de l'Industrie, he apparently asked *père* Tanguy to do it for him. Cézanne's paintings were regularly rejected, an experience he called 'undergoing the dry guillotine'. Suffering from public indifference, in Aix as well as in Paris, Cézanne ardently desired to be accepted by the Salon, if only to impress the people of his home town. He wished to show them in his obstinacy that he could obtain admission to the official exhibitions. Although he chose canvases which seemed least likely to be rejected, he never made any concessions to official art. He thought that in following his own path and in succeeding to satisfy himself he would at the same time succeed in satisfying the demands of the jury. Thus, upon learning of a new rejection, he had once exclaimed: 'I can quite understand that it could not be accepted because of my starting-point, which is too far removed from the aim to be attained, that is to say, the rendering of nature.'

In 1879 Antoine Guillemet, now a member of the jury, had done his best to have a painting by Cézanne accepted, but 'alas, without bringing any change in the attitude of those hard-hearted judges'. It was only in 1882 that Guillemet managed to have a canvas of Cézanne's 'accepted' by using his prerogative as a member of the jury to exhibit the work of one of his students. Cézanne, who had sent in a 'Portrait of Monsieur L. A.' is thus listed in the catalogue as a 'pupil of Antoine Guillemet'. But his portrait did not attract public attention, and a critic, taking the 'pupil of Antoine Guillemet' for a novice, wrote: 'Monsieur L. A. is painted with wide brush-strokes. The shadow of the eye-socket and that of the right cheek as well as the quality of the light-tones presage a future colourist.'

However, the prerogative which had opened the back door of the Salon to Cézanne, was remanded that same year, and Guillemet thus was no longer able to use his position on his friend's behalf.

* * *

Goaded by his endless difficulties with the jury, Cézanne continued his 'research in painting'. In the beginning of 1882 he worked again at L'Estaque. It was there that Auguste Renoir met him in February and was immediately taken in with the charm of the landscape. 'As it is very beautiful here,' Renoir wrote from L'Estaque to his dealer Durand-Ruel, 'I am staying another fortnight. It would really be a pity to leave this lovely country without bringing back something. And the weather! The spring with a gentle sun and no wind, which is rare in Marseilles. Moreover, I ran into Cézanne and we are going to work together.'

But Renoir was stricken with pneumonia a few days later. On 2 March he wrote to Chocquet: 'I have just been ill and am convalescing. I cannot tell you how nice Cézanne has been to me. He wanted to bring me his entire house. We are going to have a farewell dinner with his mother at his home; he is going back to Paris and I am obliged to stay somewhere in the South. . . . At lunch Madame Cézanne made me eat a ragout of cod; this is, I think, the ambrosia of the gods. One should eat this and die. . . .'

Cézanne returned to Paris in the spring of 1882, and again the following spring when, on 4 May 1883, he attended Manet's funeral together with Renoir, Pissarro, Durand-Ruel, Clemenceau, Puvis de Chavannes, etc. Among the pall-bearers were Zola, Degas, Monet, Fantin-Latour and Duret. Manet's friend, Antonin Proust, made a short and moving speech at the grave.

A few days later, Cézanne returned to the Midi and settled in L'Estaque for the rest of the year. 'I have rented a little house and garden at L'Estaque,' he wrote Zola, 'just above the station and at the foot of the hill where behind me rise the rocks and the pines. I am still busy painting, I have some beautiful viewpoints here, but they do not quite make motifs. Nevertheless, climbing the hills at sunset, one has a glorious view of Marseilles in the distance and the islands (Pl. 59), the whole giving a most decorative effect when bathed in the evening light.'

In December 1883, Monet and Renoir, coming from Genoa, went to see Cézanne in L'Estaque, but apart from these infrequent visits and his walks with Monticelli, Cézanne lived in complete solitude. Only the letters and reading matter sent him by Zola withdrew him from his isolation. He asked Zola to enliven 'the long sequence of identical days' and wrote him: 'When you can, if you want to tell me about the state of affairs in art and literature you will give me much pleasure. Thus I shall be still farther removed from the Provinces and nearer to Paris.'

The situation in the world of art was of particular concern to Cézanne, inasmuch as he was trying to leave impressionism behind him. He felt that the moment of impressionism was passing. The group of artists who had banded together to combat two terrible enemies, the past (classicism and romanticism) and the present (academicism) began to disperse. Cézanne was no longer the only one to abstain from the group shows; Monet, Renoir, and Sisley did not contribute regularly. Although their artistic convictions had united all the impressionists, each one of them had kept his own personal temperament, vision, and style. After their common exhibitions, each had confined himself in his work to develop his personality and his understanding of nature. With de Maupassant, they felt: 'What childishness to believe in reality since each one of us carries his own in his thought and organs. . . . The great artists are those who impose on humanity their own personal vision.'

In seeking his own individuality, Cézanne endeavoured to react against the danger which he felt was inherent in Monet's complete dissolution of mass and elimination of local colour. This did not prevent him from saying admiringly of Monet: 'He is nothing but an eye, yet what an eye!' However, Cézanne felt that observation was not enough, that thought was essential. As he later remarked: 'There are two things in the painter: the eye and the brain. The two must co-operate; one must work for the development of both, but as a painter: of the eye through the outlook on nature, of the brain through the logic of organized sensations which provide the means of expression.'

The difference between the impressionistic sensation, which is rapid, ephemeral, and fleeting, and that of Cézanne is that his sensations result logically in the full knowledge of the subject in the classical sense. Cézanne often said that he wished 'to become classical again through nature, that is to say, through sensation'. And classicism, as he understood it, meant to 'revive Poussin in the contact with nature'. Nature was the essential element, the source of art, but 'one must not reproduce it, one must interpret it. By means of what? By means of plastic equivalents and colour.'

'As you say,' Cézanne wrote from L'Estaque to Zola, 'there are some very beautiful views here. The difficulty is to reproduce them; it is not exactly what I am achieving. I began to perceive nature rather late, though this does not prevent it being full of interest to me.'

A letter to Pissarro reveals the strong emotion aroused in

Cézanne by the view of the beautiful bay of L'Estaque: 'It is like a playing card. Red roofs on the blue sea. The sun is so terrifying that it seems as though the objects are silhouetted, not only in black and white, but in blue, red, brown, and violet. I may be mistaken, but it seems to me to be the very opposite of modelling.'

In this light, which appears to emphasize the contours of objects, to flatten them while at the same time giving them a gentle and precise relief, Cézanne attempted to oppose to the transformation of masses into coloured spots the precision of planes that he perceived. He used contrasting colours to create space and proceeded with a slow thoughtfulness that tried to capture the general character of a landscape beyond its momentary aspect. Cézanne painted many views of the village of L'Estaque, with its roofs, factories, and belfries, often as seen through the pines which grow tenaciously on the rocky slopes (Pl. 59). In the background there is always the sea and a little sky. It is an extraordinary landscape, whose main forms combine the cubes of the houses and the irregular shapes of the trees with the huge plane of the multi-coloured water, the pre-dominant blue of which is intensified by the rays of the sun.

'Art is changing terribly in its outer form,' he wrote Zola in somewhat cryptic style, 'and is assuming all too strongly a poor, miserable aspect while at the same time the ignorance of harmony is being revealed more and more in the discordance of the colouring and, what is even worse, in the deadness of the tone. After groaning, let us cry, "Long live the sun, which gives us such beautiful light".'

*　　*　　*

At the beginning of 1885 Cézanne's lonely contemplation of nature was interrupted by a violent love affair with a woman about whom little is known except that Cézanne met her in Aix. On the back of a drawing the painter wrote the draft of a love letter which breaks off at the bottom of the page without entirely revealing the secret of this strange episode:

'I saw you and you permitted me to embrace you; from that moment on a profound emotion has not ceased tormenting me. You must excuse the liberty that a friend, tortured by anxiety, takes in writing to you. I do not know how to excuse this liberty, which you may think a great one, but could I have borne the burden that oppresses me? Is it not better to give expression to a sentiment rather than to conceal it?

'Why, I asked myself, should I suppress the cause of my agony? Is it not a relief to suffering to give it expression? And if physical pain can find some assuagement in the cries of the unfortunate, is it not natural, Madame, that spiritual sadness seek the consolation afforded by confessing it to a beloved being?

'I realize that this daring and premature letter may seem indiscreet to you, and that it has to commend me to you only the goodness of. . . .'

Stirred, confused, tormented, the prey of a sudden and irresistible passion, Cézanne asked Zola to act as intermediary for the correspondence that had to be hidden: I would like you to do me a favour, which is, I think, tiny, but vast for me. It would be to receive some letters for me and to forward them by mail to the address I shall send you later. I am either mad or very sensible. *Trahit sua quemque voluptas.** I am appealing to you and I implore your absolution. Happy are the sages.'

The following month Cézanne, Hortense Fiquet, and their son were staying with Renoir at La Roche-Guyon not far from Paris. Cézanne immediately begged Zola: 'If you should receive a letter from Aix, be good enough to address it to General Delivery and to send me a line and let me know by making a cross in a corner of your letter.'

But in his agitation and confusion Cézanne forgot to collect his post. Life at La Roche-Guyon became difficult for him, 'due to fortuitous circumstances'. He was restless, and after spending about a month at Renoir's where he began a landscape which he never finished (Pl. 57), he suddenly left for Villennes near Médan but found no lodging and so proceeded to Vernon. Zola could not put him up at Médan for two weeks.

'I am at Vernon,' he informed Zola. 'I cannot find what I want in the conditions in which I now am. I have decided to leave for Aix as soon as possible. I shall go by Médan to shake your hand.' And a few days later, on 19 July, he wrote again: 'I would have liked to go on with my painting, but I was in a state of very great perplexity. For, as I must go south, I concluded that the sooner the better. On the other hand, perhaps it would be better if I waited a little. I am in a state of indecision. Perhaps I will get out of it?'

Apparently Cézanne, not wanting to stay in Vernon, passed briefly through Médan where Zola may have read him a few chapters of the novel he was working on, *L'Œuvre*. Cézanne finally returned to the 'Jas de Bouffan'. He was to remain there for two or three years without revisiting the Ile-de-France.

What happened at Aix, after his return, is not known, but it is unlikely that Cézanne saw there the woman who had aroused him so deeply. In a letter to Zola of 20 August he speaks of the 'pebbles under my feet which are like mountains'. And a few days later he specifies: 'As for me, the most complete isolation, the brothel in

* 'Each one is carried away by his own desire.'

town, or anything else, but nothing more. I pay, the word is ugly, but I need rest, and at this price I get it. . . . If my family were only indifferent, everything would have been for the best.'

Perhaps it was in order to escape his family as well as the memories of his romance that Cézanne went off every morning to the neighbouring town of Gardanne, only returning late in the evening to the 'Jas de Bouffan'. Soon, to avoid these daily trips of about six miles each way, Cézanne rented a small apartment in Gardanne and moved there with Hortense Fiquet and young Paul, now thirteen years old, who was sent to the local school.

'I am beginning to paint,' Cézanne informs Zola toward the end of August, 'because I am almost without troubles.' Everything seems forgotten. He had taken up his brushes again and in his canvases of Gardanne there is not the least reflection of mental turmoil. It was from Gardanne that Cézanne wrote to Victor Chocquet: 'The country here, which has never found an interpreter worthy of the richness it harbours, contains many treasures to be gathered.'

* * *

Gardanne is a picturesque little town nestling against a small hill crowned by a steepled church which gives the landscape the shape of a pyramid (Pl. 55). Cézanne frequently painted the still life of roofs and square houses, interspersed with a few trees. The slopes in the background are studded with the squat towers of three old mills. In the outskirts of Gardanne Cézanne found admirable motifs composed of slightly undulating planes stretching to the Mont de Cengle, a foothill of Mount Sainte-Victoire. The mountain is seen here as an elongated and jagged plateau; its heavy mass bars the horizon. Its colours vary from a full grey to a limpid blue, passing through shades of pink and pale grey. Cézanne painted several views of this harmonious landscape which reveal the purity of its form and richness of its colours; the red of the earth, the yellow of the houses, the green of the trees, and the blue of the sky, create an atmosphere of admirable serenity.

At about this time, that is, around 1885, Cézanne's brother-in-law, Maxime Conil, bought an estate called Bellevue south-west of Aix (Pl. 61). It is situated on a hill that dominates the entire wide valley of the Arc to the distant wall of Sainte-Victoire. Cézanne often went there to paint and in several pictures represented the house, the farmyard, and the pigeon-tower of Bellevue (Pl. 68). One of his favourite motifs was the view from the edge of a little wood on the summit of the hill, between Bellevue and the neighbouring estate of Montbriant. Thence he overlooked the valley extending all the way to the truncated cone of Mount Sainte-Victoire. This landscape, composed of wide planes, large masses, and sharp lines, such as the railway in the foreground and the viaduct farther back with its light arches, this landscape in which the masses seem to absorb the details, might explain why Cézanne loved, as he said, 'the conformation of my country.' He preferred it to the landscapes of the north because there he did not find such closed panoramas and his eye could not take in such views without being brought up short or losing itself in the distance. Moreover there was the difference of colour and light; here on this hill of Bellevue a landscape spread itself at his feet, rich and firm, harmonious in its lines, soaked in the southern sun.

It was on these motifs that the painter endeavoured to develop his sensibility further, to discover the laws of perspective and colour which enabled him to reproduce his sensations, to remain faithful to nature, and to translate all its richness and space on a piece of canvas.

'I try to render perspective through colour alone,' Cézanne later explained. And he added with emphasis: 'I proceed very slowly, for nature reveals herself to me in very complex form and constant progress must be made. One must see one's model correctly and experience it in the right way and furthermore express oneself with distinction and strength.'

'I believe,' he said on another occasion, 'that I am daily closer to achieving it, albeit painfully, for if the strong feeling for nature—which I assuredly have—is the necessary basis for all conception of art upon which depend the greatness and beauty of all future work, the knowledge of the means of expressing our emotion is no less essential and is only to be acquired through very long experience.'

As Cézanne developed his art, he detached himself increasingly from the impressionist conceptions. He did not seek to capture the impression and vibrant atmosphere of a landscape but rather to portray its forms and colours, its planes and light. He did not approve of Monet's attempts to render the same subject at different times of the day, to show the different forms and colours produced by the varying intensity of the sun. Nor did he approve of the efforts of 'the humble and colossal' Pissarro, as he called him admiringly, who was then being attracted by the divisionism of Georges Seurat and painted his pictures in the pointillist technique. Regretfully Cézanne remarked: 'If he had continued to paint as he did in 1870, he would have been the strongest of all.' He now criticized Manet severely for having been 'poor in feeling for colour'. As for Renoir, Cézanne did not like his landscape technique, which he called 'cottony' (Pls. 65, 67). Altogether he had the impression that his friends experimented too much, that they did not look behind the colourful exterior for the actual structure of things, and it is doubtless for this reason that he assumed the task of 'making out of impressionism something solid and durable like the art of museums'.

IV. STILL LIFE WITH TEAPOT (*Watercolour*), 1895–1900

XVIII

ZOLA'S *L'ŒUVRE*

1885 – 1886

SINCE back in 1868, when Zola began his work on *Les Rougon-Macquart*, he had decided to devote a novel of this series to the story of an artist member of that family, called Claude Lantier. When Paul Alexis published in 1882 a book on Zola, who himself furnished all documents and details, he was able to announce the literary plans of his friend. Giving specific information about Zola's projects, Alexis mentioned a 'work for which the documentation will be less difficult: the novel he plans to write on art. Here he need only recall what he saw in our circle and experienced himself. His chief character is all ready: this painter, captivated by the modern ideal of beauty, who appears briefly in *Le Ventre de Paris* [1873] is Claude Lantier of whom he says in the family tree of the Rougon-Macquarts: "Claude Lantier, born in 1842—mixture, blending; predominating mental and physical characteristics from his mother (Gervaise in *L'Assommoir*); the inheritance of a neurosis turning into genius. Painter."

'Zola's purpose is to describe in this novel his years in Provence. . . . I know that in Claude Lantier he plans to study the terrible psychology of artistic impotence. Around the central man of genius, the sublime dreamer whose production is paralyzed by an infirmity, other artists will gravitate, painters, sculptors, musicians, men of letters, a whole band of ambitious young men who have also come to conquer Paris: some of them failures, others more or less successful; all of them cases of the sickness of art, varieties of the great contemporary neurosis. Of course Zola, in this work, will be obliged to use his friends, to assemble their most typical traits. If I find myself included in it and even if I am not flattered, I promise not to bring suit against him.'

These last lines indicate clearly that Zola by no means hid from his friends his intention of giving this project more or less the character of a *roman à clef*. Zola's notes for this novel, *L'Œuvre*, are a further proof, since he constantly uses the proper names of his friends, instead of the invented ones which they were to bear in the book.

In Zola's work this novel is unique, for no other contains such detailed use of personal memories, nor lends itself better to a study of the people who surrounded the author in his youth. A long time before beginning *L'Œuvre*, Zola had written in the *Nouveaux Contes à Ninon* that 'memory is today the only joy in which my heart finds rest'. In going back to his youth, Zola sought a moment of respite after so many novels which had required careful research into surroundings unfamiliar to him. After *L'Assommoir*, *Nana* and *Germinal*, he now had merely to gather his recollections of Cézanne, Baille, Coste, Valabrègue, Manet, and so many others. 'Before making the outline,' he wrote in his notes, 'I must make a list of memories.' The outline itself comprises only a few sentences:

> *Passion, good nature, gaiety.*
> *Genesis of the work of art, nature embraced and never conquered.*
> *Struggle of the woman against the work, the childbirth of the work against the childbirth of real flesh.*
> *A whole group of artists.*

Proceeding with his list of memories, Zola jots down:

'My youth at school and in the fields—Baille, Cézanne—All the memories of school, comrades, professor, quarantine, we three friends.—Out of doors, hunting, swimming, walking, reading, the families of my friends.

'In Paris. New friends. School. Arrival of Baille and of Cézanne. Our Thursday reunions.—Paris to conquer, walks.

'The museums.

'The various lodgings—Chaillan—the cafés; Solari and his marriage.

'Manet's duel [with Duranty]. The studios of Cézanne. The stays at Bennecourt.—The Thursday reunions continue.'

Of himself, Cézanne, and Baille, Zola remarks: 'No cafés, no women, an outdoor life which saved them from provincial stupidity.' And several times in his notes occurs the phrase: 'I would like gay characters.'

It must be noted, however, that if the author's youthful companions were used in *L'Œuvre* and furnished physical as well as character traits, not one of them is directly portrayed. Far from copying faithfully the personalities of his various friends, Zola mixed their characteristics in such a way that each figure in his book shows peculiarities of more than one of them. Thus, Claude Lantier is not only Paul Cézanne as he was in *Le Ventre de Paris*, but also has some of Manet's traits, especially in his role as leader of the group, and in his paintings may be found details of works by Cézanne, Manet, Monet, and others. Furthermore he bears the Christian name used by Zola himself when he published his *Confession de*

Claude and again when he signed his first Salon reviews in *L'Événe-ment*. Some of Zola's own blood flows in the veins of Claude Lantier.

As Zola had to adapt the characters in his novel to the social background of *Les Rougon-Macquart*, Claude Lantier is not, like Cézanne, the son of a rich provincial banker but comes from a working-class family, that of Gervaise and Auguste Lantier, in *L'Assommoir*. Zola intended studying in this artist 'a curious effect of heredity, which transmits genius to the son of illiterate parents'.

But Claude Lantier's artistic training is that of Cézanne, for Zola notes: 'Musée de Plassans [Aix], Atelier Suisse, a master who tells Claude he will never accomplish anything, the Louvre. . . .' Claude, very uncompromising, accepts only Delacroix and Courbet.

Cézanne's first name constantly escapes from Zola's pen when he is writing about Claude Lantier:

'Not to forget Paul's despair; he always thought he was discovering painting. Complete discouragement, once ready to give up everything: then a masterpiece, nothing but a sketch, quickly done and which rescues him from his extreme discouragement.—The question is to know what makes him powerless to satisfy himself: he himself, primarily, his physiognomy, his breeding, his eye trouble; but I would like our modern art to play a role, our fever to want to do everything, our impatience in shaking traditions, in a word, our lack of equilibrium. What satisfies G. [Guillemet?] does not satisfy him; he goes further ahead and spoils everything. It is incomplete genius, without full realization: he lacks very little, he is a bit hither-and-yon due to his physical make-up; and I add that he has produced some absolutely marvellous things, a Manet, a dramatized Cézanne, nearer to Cézanne.'

Another time Zola ascribes to this unbalanced artist some of his own traits:

'In Claude Lantier I wish to paint the artist's struggle against nature, the creative effort in the work of art, effort of blood and tears to give one's flesh, to create life: always wrestling with the truth and always beaten, the battle with the angel. In short, I shall relate my intimate life as creative artist, this perpetual and painful childbirth; but I shall enlarge the subject and dramatize it through Claude who is never satisfied, who is tormented by his inability to give birth to his own genius and who, at the end, kills himself before his unfulfilled work.—He will not be an impotent artist, but a creator with too great an ambition who wants to put all nature on a single canvas and who dies in the attempt. I shall have him produce some superb things, fragmentary, unknown, and possibly ridiculed. Then I shall give him a dream of immense pages of modern decoration, of frescoes epitomizing the whole epoch, and it is there he will destroy himself.'

Zola gives Claude Lantier a friend, Sandoz, a writer who 'is only there,' Zola says, 'to give my ideas on art—my character, my ideas.' Sandoz is above all the portrait of the author and appears 'either to complement Claude or to be contrasted with him'. And Zola specifies:

'It will be best to consider me only as a theorist, to leave me in the background, without giving any details concerning my production. Claude's schoolmate, doing work of my own, scoffed at, humiliated, successful toward the end; only less absolute; yielding to my nature, and producing, whereas Claude stumbles. . . . I shall only furnish ideas, with the fatigue, the pallor of work, without details; whereas the whole battle of production will be on Claude. Myself, always respectful of his efforts. . . . Myself, born in Paris, but a student at Plassans where I was a schoolmate of Claude and the architect (Baille), both born there. We met Valabrègue not at school but in a little pension; Alexis joins them from there, younger . . .'

Claude Lantier and Pierre Sandoz, the painter and the writer, are the two principal characters in the novel. They represent 'two young creators, full of their future, plunging into the literary and artistic current'. They stand out against the background of the Salon des Refusés, the first impressionist exhibitions, and the battle fought by the painters around Manet.

'The question of the impressionists' Zola underlined. 'I shall take for Claude some theories of the impressionists, the *plein-air*, the decomposition of light, all this new painting which require a genius to be fulfilled. . . . Claude will rise up against their too hasty work, the painting done in two hours, the sketch which satisfies them, the hasty sales of Monet. . . .' Claude Lantier 'is at bottom a romantic, a builder. Thence the struggle; he wants to embrace nature which eludes him.'

Zola records the whole period of the Salon des Refusés and his discussions with Cézanne after their first visit to the exhibition. His own Salon reviews Zola ascribes in the novel to Jory, a 'poet fallen into contemporary journalism'. These articles create a furore, although they do no more than repeat 'the theories accepted by the group'. But Jory is also 'an Alexis dramatized and made evil, a great rake'.

Valabrègue is transposed into a painter who 'with great and naïve ambitions, sinks to little insignificant paintings', and the sculptor Mahoudeau is based on Solari, whose natural strength had to be diminished 'since strength belongs to Claude'. He has 'no primary education, only instincts'.

Baille, under the name of Dubuche, is at first 'architect at the Ecole des Beaux-Arts, very staid, cold, duty, good student,' and later 'an employee not caring about art, who makes a rich marriage'.

Victor Chocquet appears as Monsieur Hue who had chosen Claude Lantier's 'crudest works which he hung next to his paintings by Delacroix, prophesying for them equal fame'.

Christine Hallegrin, the friend, model, and wife of Claude Lantier, is the only woman who plays an important part in this story of artists. From all that is known about her, it appears that Zola had Hortense Fiquet in mind when he described this eighteen-year-old girl at the beginning of the novel, at the time she meets Claude: 'A tall, supple, and slim girl, still a little thin in body, but exquisitely pure, young, and virginal. Already rather full-breasted, with a slim waist. . . . A brunette with black hair and black eyes. The upper part of the face very gentle, with great tenderness. Long eyelids, pure and tender forehead, small and delicate nose. When her eyes laugh, exquisite tenderness. But the lower part of the face is passionate, the jaw is a little prominent, too strong. . . .'

To the notes on the various characters Zola added an outline for the novel, dealing with the march of events, and containing memoranda by Zola himself or by his friends. Antoine Guillemet reported on the functioning of the Salon jury of which he was a member; Francis Jourdain furnished information about architecture, and Béliard about music and musicians. There are also notes on art dealers, including Durand-Ruel and Petit, and on collectors, supplied by Guillemet. Zola once more studied the public, the artists, and the paintings at the Salon and took detailed notes. He also dwelt at length upon the different aspects of Paris, the bridges and quais, views of the Cité, Montmartre, the Place de la Concorde, the cemetery, etc., to which he added some photographs to refresh his memory.

One document which does not appear among Zola's notes but which deserves mention has to do with the suicide of Claude Lantier in front of his large canvas. In writing this final episode Zola must have recalled his visit in 1866 to the studio of a young artist who had just committed suicide after being rejected by the Salon jury. Indeed, Zola's famous articles in *L'Evénement* were preceded by a short notice entitled *Un Suicide*, in which Zola described this visit to the sad and empty studio and announced his attack upon the jury. Thus even Claude Lantier's death, although the logical result of the sequence of events, belongs to the author's memories of his youth.

Sometimes Zola's memories were so little changed that his intimates could easily recognize them. Guillemet, for example, on reading serials of *L'Œuvre* in the newspaper *Le Gil Blas*, wrote Zola on 1 February 1886: '. . . I came across a scene at Bennecourt which is so masterfully described, so moving, so true that I relived there a little of my—of our—youth; and the small stream of Jenfosse and the islands and all that returned to my memory—and I was deliciously moved. It is so good to become a little younger.'

Yet in this dramatized story of artistic effort, the historian finds few authentic data on the epoch of which the author as well as his characters were both witnesses and actors. Whatever data Zola does provide are to be found in his notes, rather than in the finished work, precisely because there appear the names of those who served as models. In the novel itself Zola's personages present an agglomerate of traits which prevents their being identified with any one of the author's friends.

Of course the line of demarcation between actual circumstances and those invented by Zola could never be clearly drawn, and this gave rise to misinterpretations. The public, having been prepared by Paul Alexis to find in L'Œuvre portraits of Zola's friends, tried to guess the originals. As it was known that Zola had been closely associated with the group of the Café Guerbois and the Nouvelle-Athènes, his readers expected the novel to offer a romanticized history of impressionism and the impressionists. This certainly was not Zola's intention. The public, nevertheless, insisted on seeing in Claude Lantier an impotent impressionist on the verge of madness. And this unsuccessful painter Zola had made head of the new school in art. The only member of the group who was then well known to the public and who was considered the leader of the impressionists was Zola's friend, Edouard Manet, who had just died. Even those, like Vincent van Gogh, who were close to the impressionists, did not hesitate to take the protagonist of the novel for a portrait of Manet.

Because Cézanne was unknown, no one thought that he could have been the model for Claude Lantier. A few years later only, through literary indiscretions, doubtless originating in Médan, it was hinted 'that in his novel, L'Œuvre, Emile Zola imparted to one of his chief characters the moral traits and artistic ideas of Cézanne'.

The surprising fact, however, and one which escaped most readers, is that Claude Lantier actually has few traits in common with Cézanne, Manet, or any other impressionist. He belongs to no school, for he really is not even a painter; he is the son of a novelist and never quite escapes the influence of his father, Zola. The author doubtless did not intend Claude Lantier to be a true impressionist; he wanted to create an artist belonging to no specific group and carrying on all alone his struggle for innovation. But, as he planned the Rougon-Macquart series as a vast picture of the Second Empire, Zola did not hesitate to make Claude Lantier the exponent of 'some of the impressionist theories', as he had written in his notes. However, he did not succeed in having Claude Lantier do a single impressionist painting, 'some absolutely marvellous things', as was his intention. The works of Claude Lantier are actually literary works because he lacks the impressionist eye. That Claude Lantier was a 'failure' was without a doubt a necessity imposed by the general story of *Les Rougon-Macquart*, but his being a painter imbued with literary spirit and even with academic tradition was an involuntary distortion on Zola's part.

*　　*　　*

George Moore, friend of Manet and Degas, offers in his *Reminiscences of the Impressionist Painters* some interesting information concerning Zola's own conception of Claude Lantier:

'One evening, after a large dinner party given in honour of the publication of *L'Œuvre*, when most of the guests had gone and the company consisted of *les intimes de la maison*, a discussion arose as to whether Claude Lantier was or was not a man of talent. Madame Charpentier, by dint of much provocative asseveration that he was undistinguished by even any shred of the talent which made Manet a painter for painters, forced Emile Zola to take up the cudgels and defend his hero. Seeing that all were siding with Madame Charpentier, Zola plunged like a bull into the thick of the fray, and did not hesitate to affirm that he had gifted Claude Lantier with infinitely larger qualities than those which nature had bestowed upon Edouard Manet. This statement was received in mute anger by those present, all of whom had been personal friends and warm admirers of Manet's genius, and cared little to hear any word of disparagement spoken of their dead friend. It must be observed that Emile Zola intended no disparagement of Manet, but he was concerned to defend the theory of his book—namely that no painter working in the modern movement had achieved a result equivalent to that which had been achieved by at least three of four writers working in the same movement, inspired by the same ideas, animated by the same aestheticism. And, in reply to one who was anxiously urging Degas' claim to the highest consideration, he said: "I cannot accept a man who shuts himself up all his life to draw a ballet-girl as ranking co-equal in dignity and power with Flaubert, Daudet, or Goncourt".'

The way in which Zola confused the subject with its interpretation (judging the subject by its 'dignity' and forgetting even to mention the painter's creative effort) clearly reveals his literary approach to art. Zola's ideas were obviously in complete opposition to the very basis of the impressionist movement. His painter friends were both aroused and pained by his conceptions; Zola's novel not only offended them because of its distortions but also because it reiterated Zola's pronouncements of 1880 in *Le Voltaire* concerning the impressionists:

'They all keep to rough drafts, hasty impressions, and not one of them seems to have the power to be the awaited master. Is it not irritating to see this new recording of light, this passion for truth carried to the point of scientific analysis, this evolution which began with such originality and is delayed and falls into the hands of the clever and is not completed because the essential man has not been born? . . .'

The disappointment with the novel was general among Zola's painter friends, and Renoir commented: 'What a fine book he could have written, not only as an historical record of a very original movement in art, but also as a "human document", . . . if, in *L'Œuvre* he had taken the trouble simply to relate what he had seen and heard in our reunions and our studios; for here he actually happened to have lived the life of his models. But, fundamentally, Zola did not give a hoot about portraying his friends as they really were, that is to say, to their advantage. . . .'

Pissarro did not think otherwise. 'I dined with the impressionists,' he wrote his son Lucien in March 1886. 'I had a long talk with Huysmans; he is very conversant with the new art and is anxious to break a lance for us. We talked about *L'Œuvre*. . . . It seems that he had a quarrel with Zola, who is very worried.' And Pissarro reports than Antoine Guillemet's enthusiasm had vanished once he had read the entire book.

Indeed, Antoine Guillemet, one of Zola's most fervent admirers, could not refrain from voicing some criticism, and tactfully called the novel 'a work of creation rather than of observation,' so as not to be obliged to call it badly observed. He wrote Zola:

'A very gripping but a very depressing book, all in all. Everyone in it is discouraged, works badly, thinks badly. People endowed with genius or failures all end by doing poor work; you yourself, at the end of the book, are completely frustrated and depressed; it is pessimism, since the word is fashionable.

'Reality is not so sad, fortunately. When I began to paint I had the pleasure and the honour of knowing the wonderful pleiad of modern geniuses: Daumier, Millet, Courbet, Daubigny, and Corot, the most human and pure of them all. All of them died after producing their best work and all their lives they progressed. You yourself, whose friend I am proud to be, do you not always progress and is not *Germinal* one of your finest works? In your latest book I find only sadness or impotence. . . .

'As for the friends who occupy your Thursdays, do you think

they end as badly—I mean to say as courageously? Alas, no. Our good Paul is putting on weight in the beautiful sunshine of the South, and Solari is scratching his gods; neither one considers hanging himself—very fortunately.

'Let us hope, by God, that the little gang, as Madame Zola calls it, does not try to recognize themselves in your uninteresting heroes, for they are evil into the bargain.'

Guillemet's fears concerning the 'little gang' were only too justified. Degas alone did not excite himself; his hatred for writers merely made him remark scornfully, at Berthe Morisot's, that he thought Zola had only written *L'Œuvre* to prove the superiority of the writer over the painter, an opinion which is consistent with the arguments used by Zola at Madame Charpentier's. Degas doubtless thought it beneath him to discuss such a point of view, but Monet took a different attitude, not only seeing the causes, but also fearing the results. As soon as he had finished the novel, Monet asked Pissarro: 'Have you read Zola's book? I am very much afraid it will do us a great deal of harm.' But Pissarro was more calm and did not see things in this light.

'I am half through with Zola's book,' he answered. 'No! That is not it. It is a romantic book; I do not know the ending, it doesn't matter, that is not it!—Claude is not carefully studied; Sandoz is done better, one can see that he understood him.—As far as doing us harm is concerned, I don't think so. It is not a successful novel for the author of *L'Assommoir* and *Germinal*, that is all.'

Yet, Monet not only considered *L'Œuvre* an unsuccessful novel, he foresaw the confusion it would create in the public mind and felt he ought to speak to Zola directly of his fears. Realizing that Zola was chiefly guilty of clumsiness and a lack of understanding, Monet wrote him from Giverny on 5 April 1886:

'My dear Zola,
'You were good enough to send me *L'Œuvre*. I am very grateful to you for it. I have always enjoyed reading your books, and this one was doubly interesting to me because it raises questions about art for which we have been fighting so long. I have just read it and I am worried and upset, I admit.

'You were purposely careful to have none of your characters resemble any one of us, but, in spite of that, I am afraid lest our enemies amongst the public and the press identify Manet or ourselves with failures, which is not what you have in mind, I cannot believe it.

'Forgive me for telling you this. It is not a criticism; I have read *L'Œuvre* with great pleasure, finding memories on every page. Moreover you are aware of my fanatical admiration for your talent.

No; but I have been struggling for a long time and I am afraid that, just as we are about to meet with success, our enemies may make use of your book to overwhelm us.

'Excuse this long letter. Remember me to Madame Zola, and thank you again.

'Devotedly yours,
'Claude Monet'

Zola's reply is not known. We do know, however, his answer to a young student who, several years later, asked him for the real names of his characters in *L'Œuvre*. '. . . What good would it be to give you names?' Zola wrote. 'They are those of failures whom you would hardly know, I think.'

XIX

THE BREAK WITH ZOLA

CÉZANNE was closer to Zola than anyone else. He could not be taken in by any disguise or any trick. When, in *Le Ventre de Paris*, Zola had used him for the minor figure of Claude Lantier, Cézanne had doubtless been amused to recognize himself. Now he found his portrait enlarged and retouched in the first chapters of *L'Œuvre* and, according to Joachim Gasquet, he was profoundly touched. Cézanne described these chapters as being of an authenticity hardly transposed and intimately moving to him, bringing back the most beautiful hours of his youth. Later, when the story branches off, with the character of Lantier threatened by madness, Cézanne understood, as he told Gasquet, that this was necessitated by the plot, that he himself had completely gone from Zola's mind, that—after all—Zola had not written his memoirs but a novel, and one which was part of an immense, carefully planned whole.

Cézanne fully realized the duality of Zola's hero: Paul Cézanne and Claude Lantier at the same time. He was too intelligent not to discern the characteristics which Claude Lantier inherited from the Rougon-Macquarts and realized that they must fatally and logically lead to madness and suicide. On the other hand, Cézanne understood Zola too well, and himself well enough not to experience a painful shock at the description of Sandoz's thoughts on looking at a painting by Lantier:

' . . . He recalled their efforts, their certainty of glory, the splendid unlimited hunger, their talk of swallowing Paris in one gulp. At this period how often had he envisaged Claude as the great man whose unbridled genius would far outstrip the talents of others! Great canvases were dreamed of which would shatter the Louvre; a continuing struggle, ten hours of work a day, the entire gift of his being. And then, twenty years of this passion result in this, this poor thing! . . . So many hopes, tortures, a life made up in the hard labour of childbirth, and then that, and then that, my God!'

Here Cézanne understood that he himself, rather than Claude Lantier, was the object of Sandoz-Zola's bitter regrets. It was he, his struggles, his dreams of immense paintings, all his efforts, his hopes and discouragements that his friend was evoking. And it was of him that Zola thought when he spoke of the fraternity of artists which united Sandoz with Claude Lantier and which increased when Sandoz, as the novelist said, 'saw Claude lose his footing, drown in the heroic folly of art. At first he had been amazed for he had believed in his friend even more than in himself; he had always considered himself second since college, had placed Claude very high among the masters who revolutionize a school. Later he had been seized with a painful compassion for this failure of genius, with a bitter and heart-rending pity for this frightful torment of impotence. Did one ever know in art where madness began? All failures moved him to tears. . . . He quivered with charity, with the need of burying piously, in the extravagance of their dreams, these victims of their work.'

Rough in aspect and manners, Cézanne had a subtle mind. Step by step he had followed the decline in Zola's enthusiasm, once so overflowing, for the genius of the painter; first the silence about him in Zola's articles, then the reticence in his praise, which seemed addressed to the personal friend rather than the artist, and finally the advice Zola gave him. All this showed Cézanne what was going on in Zola's mind. It was he, Cézanne, the failure, the 'abortive genius', as Zola was to say later; it was he as much as Claude Lantier.

Cézanne was deeply hurt, both in his pride and in his friendship for Zola. Hiding immense pride under a modest exterior, Cézanne had, in spite of his moments of doubt and discouragement, a high opinion of his own talent, and his faith in his genius was absolute. His pride did not permit him to show his wound, to allow anyone to guess how much he felt himself hit through the figure of Claude Lantier. Shut up within himself, he knew how to keep the secret of his acts and his thoughts and when, by chance, a secret escaped his vigilance, Cézanne could obstinately deny it against all evidence. Wishing at any price to hide the truth, he could maintain that *L'Œuvre* had nothing to do with his break with Zola, just as he had refused to admit to his father that he had a mistress and a child.

It has often been maintained that Cézanne got along better with Zola while Zola was poor and that Cézanne disliked the pretentious environment of Médan. In spite of the affection with which he was treated by Zola and his wife, Cézanne may not have felt quite at his ease in these surroundings, so agitated and luxurious for his taste. But do not his repeated visits to Médan show that the painter forgave Zola his way of life, just as the novelist forgave his friend the uncouthness of his dress and manners? Moreover, what importance could their differences of taste have precisely at that time when Cézanne had retired to the Midi, and how could these differences have stopped an almost brotherly correspondence which had lasted for thirty years?

It is true, however, that all kinds of irritations must have prepared the ground for the break. The two friends had quarrelled several times: after Cézanne's first trip to Paris when a certain coldness caused an interruption in their correspondence, and then after the war of 1870 when Achille Emperaire, staying with Cézanne in Paris informed some friends in Aix: 'I found him completely deserted. He no longer has a single intelligent or affectionate friend. Zola, Solari, and the others, there is no question of them.'

These two quarrels were probably followed by others, and doubtless all ended in the same way, by reconciliation and a return of affection. But it seems certain that it was not such a temporary misunderstanding that separated the two friends for good. It is in *L'Œuvre* that one must seek the cause of this break. For, in acknowledging receipt of the book, Cézanne wrote from Gardanne on 4 April 1886:

'My dear Emile,

'I have just received *L'Œuvre* which you were good enough to send me. I thank the author of *Les Rougon-Macquart* for this kind token of remembrance and ask him to permit me to clasp his hand while thinking of bygone years.

'Ever yours under the impulse of past times.

'Paul Cézanne.'

Previously, Cézanne had always acknowledged receipt of Zola's books promptly, even if he had only read a few pages, and each time he had expressed his interest or anticipation of pleasure in reading them. In this letter, however, Cézanne does not mention the contents of the book, and it seems that the phrase, 'I have just received' is there to excuse him from discussing it. Yet Cézanne may have heard the first chapters from Zola himself, and it is difficult to admit that he should not have read the rest, since *L'Œuvre* had first appeared in serial form in *Le Gil Blas*, the more so as this *roman à clef* excited the curiosity of all those who had anything to do with the impressionists. Besides, in February 1886 Cézanne had been at a literary evening with Pissarro where Zola's new novel was judged 'absolutely bad' by some young poets. Thus, if Cézanne did not say a word about the novel itself in his letter to Zola, it seems obvious that he did not want to do so.

When thanking Zola for a new book, Cézanne had always written with simplicity and affection, as between friends, but this time he asks the permission to clasp the hand of the author of *Les Rougon-Macquart* while thinking of bygone years, and it is also 'under the impulse of past times' that he signs his letter. Everything is for the past—for the present nothing, not a sign of interest, not a word of friendship.

The formal tone of this letter contrasts with that of the other letters, and its spirit of sadness and regret makes it seem like a letter of farewell, which in fact it was, for it marks the end of the correspondence between Cézanne and Zola.

The two friends never saw each other again. It does not seem, either, that Zola ever tried to renew his relations with Cézanne; like all the other friends of the painter, he thus conformed with Cézanne's desire to be left alone. But if the friendship between Zola and Cézanne was broken off, the ties which had united them for more than a quarter of a century were never completely cut. Unlike so many broken friendships, this one did not end in bitterness and recrimination; neither one ever bore any grudge or manifested any animosity.

When in 1891 Paul Alexis, one of Zola's closest friends, spent some time in Aix, Cézanne saw him frequently and showered him with canvases, although Alexis was near-sighted and had little taste for art. Might one not see in Cézanne's cordiality and generosity here a gesture of friendship and affection that was not meant for Alexis alone? Doubtless the latter spoke to him at length of Zola, just as he sent a detailed report to Médan on everything Cézanne did, thought, and said.

As for Zola, he retained his affection for his old friend. His face lit up when anyone spoke of Cézanne, and when he himself mentioned the name or evoked their youth, it was with an obvious pleasure mingled with emotion. His daughter remembered with what joy he once showed her some of Cézanne's paintings when visiting Paul Alexis. However, when Gustave Coquiot interviewed him around 1896, Zola expressed himself somewhat unkindly about Cézanne:

'Ah, yes, Cézanne. How I regret not having been able to push him. In my Claude Lantier I have drawn a likeness of him that is actually too mild, for if I had wanted to tell all . . . !

'Ah, my dear Cézanne does not think enough of public opinion. He despises too much the most elementary things: hygiene, dress, language. And even all that, dress, self respect, not very much, after all, if my dear, great Cézanne had only had genius. You may imagine how much it cost me to be obliged to abandon him! . . . Yes, to start out together in the same faith, in the same enthusiasm, and arrive alone, attain glory alone, it is a great pain that weighs you down. Yet it seems to me, in spite of all, that in *L'Œuvre* I have noted with the most attentive scruples all the efforts of my dear Cézanne. But what would you? There were those successive failures; good starts and then sudden stops; a brain which no longer thought, a hand that fell, powerless. Never anything carried through to the end with magnificent tenacity and force. All in all, no realization whatever!'

If the general idea of this interview is correct, the actual wording seems reported rather too freely, for the undertone of false modesty and the philistine reproaches sound unlike Zola. However, there is no doubt that the novelist considered Cézanne a failure. He went even further; he now began to detach himself publicly from the efforts of all his former painter friends.

*   *   *

In May 1896 Zola took up once more the role of art critic, in a review of the official Salon that appeared in *Le Figaro*. It was this new article which revealed to the full extent the abyss that separated him from the impressionists:

'Suddenly the Salon of thirty years ago came back to me, these last few days when I visited the Salon. And what a heart-throb. I was twenty-six, I had just come to *Le Figaro*, which was still called *L'Evénement*. . . . I was then intoxicated with youth, with truth and the intensity of art, drunk with the need of asserting my beliefs with knock-down blows. And I wrote that Salon review of 1866, *Mon Salon*, as I called it with provocative conceit, in which I acclaimed Edouard Manet's talent, and the first articles of which produced such a violent storm, a storm which was to continue around me and which has not stopped for thirty years.

'Yes, thirty years have passed and I have somewhat lost interest in painting. I had grown up virtually in the same cradle as Paul Cézanne; one is only now beginning to discover the touches of genius in this abortive great painter. I mixed with a group of young artists, Fantin, Renoir, Guillemet, and others whom life has dispersed and strewn on different stages of success. And in the same way I continued along my path, separating myself from the studios of my friends, taking my passion elsewhere. I think I have written nothing about painting for thirty years. . . . What a shock I felt in my breast when this whole past was resurrected for me by the thought that I was writing for *Le Figaro* again and that it would be interesting to talk about painting once more after a silence of almost a third of a century!

'Let us assume that I slept for thirty years. Yesterday I was still pounding with Cézanne the hard pavement of Paris in the fever of conquering it. Yesterday I went to the Salon of 1866 with Manet, Monet, and Pissarro, whose paintings had been summarily rejected. And after a long night I awaken and go to the Salon. . . . O amazement! O unexpected and astounding wonder of life! O harvest whose seeds I saw and which astonishes me as though it were the most wild and unforeseen thing. What strikes me first is the clear, dominating tone. Everything is by Manet, Monet, Pissarro! Formerly when one of their canvases was hung in a room, it made a hole of light among the others. . . . It was the window open to nature, the famous open air which came in. And nowadays there is only open air, everyone followed my friends after having insulted them and me. Well, so much the better! Conversions are always pleasing.

'What doubles my astonishment is the fervour of the converts, the abuse of the clear tone which makes certain works look like laundry discoloured by extensive washing. New religions, when admixed with fashion, are terrible in that they exceed the bounds of common sense. And when I see this diluted, whitewashed Salon with its chalky insipidity, I almost begin to long for the black, bituminous Salon of yore. It was too black, but this one is too white. Life is more varied, warmer and more flexible. And I who fought so violently for the open air and light tones, am little by little exasperated by this continuous procession of bloodless pictures, with dreamlike pallor, a premeditated green-sickness aggravated by fashion, and I long for the artist of boldness and darkness!

'But where my surprise turns to anger is in observing the insanity to which the theory of reflected light has led, in thirty years. Another of the victories won by us, the precursors! We maintained, very accurately, that the illumination of objects and figures is not simple; that under trees, for instance, nude flesh becomes green; that there is thus a continuous interchange of reflections which must be taken into account if one wishes to imbue a work with lifelike light. Light ceaselessly decomposes, breaks up and scatters. . . . But as soon as it is dwelt upon, as soon as reason begins to play a role in it, caricature quickly results. And these are really disconcerting works, these multi-coloured women, these violet landscapes and orange houses which are being given us with scientific explanations that they are like that as the result of a certain reflection or decomposition of the solar spectrum. Oh! The ladies who have one blue cheek in the moonlight and the other one vermilion under a lampshade! Oh! The horizons with blue trees, red water, and green skies! It is dreadful, dreadful, dreadful!

'. . . These bright canvases, these open windows of impressionism, how well I know them—they are by Manet and because of them I was almost killed when I was young! These studies of reflection, this flesh with leaf-green tones, this water in which all prismatic colours dance, how well I know them, they are by Monet, and I defended them and was called insane! These decompositions of light, these horizons with blue trees, how well I know them, they are by Pissarro, and newspapers were once closed to me because I dared to say that such effects were found in nature.

'And those are the canvases which were formerly rejected violently at each Salon; nowadays they are exaggerated, have become dreadful and countless! The seeds which I saw sown in the ground have sprouted, have borne fruit of a monstrous kind. I recoil in fright! Never have I been more aware of the danger of formulas, the pitiful end of schools when the founders have done their work and the masters have gone. Every movement becomes exaggerated, becomes a mere process and a lie as soon as it is taken up by fashion. There is no truth which is good in the beginning, for which theoretically one would shed one's blood, which does not become, through imitation, the worst of errors, the tare which must be ruthlessly mowed down.

'I awaken and shudder. What! Was it really for this that I fought? For this bright painting, these spots, these reflections, this decomposition of light? Lord! Was I mad? But it is very ugly, I find it repulsive! Ah! The futility of discussions, of formulas and schools. And when I left the Salon of this year I asked myself whether the task I had once performed was a bad one.

'No, I did my duty, I fought the good fight, I was twenty-six, I was with the young and the brave. That which I defended I would defend again, for it was the daring of the moment, the flag which had to be planted on enemy territory. We were right only because we represented enthusiasm and faith. The truth we established, however little, is accepted today. And if the road which was opened up has become trite, this is because we widened it in order that the art of a period might pass over it.'

This article was called by Gustave Geffroy, Monet's intimate friend, 'a kind of flourish of the trumpets of victory played like a funeral march'. Some have seen in Zola's outcry: 'Was it really for this that I fought?' a disowning of the old battles, but it is rather an avowal of his own incomprehension. Having once fought for something new which was the butt of ridicule, now, the battle won, Zola is left undecided, unsure of the position he should take. His heart and temperament had been with the innovators, but later on his reason had alienated him from an art which he did not understand and which seemed to him to be careless and casual.

Zola's article created great bitterness among his former friends. Instead of sharing their satisfaction, instead of rejoicing in the slow and steadily growing influence of their work, he affirmed that already their movement was turning into a lie. Not satisfied with dropping his support of Monet, Renoir, and Pissarro, who were about to win recognition, Zola expressed his disillusionment and attacked the only one of their group who was still struggling, calling him an 'abortive genius'.

* * *

Two years after the publication of this article, however, when Joachim Gasquet visited Zola, the novelist spoke of Cézanne with 'the most affectionate admiration'. He always felt for Cézanne, 'in spite of his sulkiness, all the friendship of a big fraternal heart.'

'And I even,' Zola told Gasquet, 'begin better to understand his painting, which I have always liked but which for a long time I did not understand, for I thought it exaggerated, whereas actually it is unbelievably sincere and truthful.'

Yet Zola made no attempt to renew his friendship with Cézanne. When he went to Aix to stay for a few days with Numa Coste in 1896, the very year his article in *Le Figaro* was published, Zola did not get in touch with Cézanne. He apparently thought that after the years of separation a meeting might be painful, and that it was better to forget than to patch up a friendship which seemed fated to be broken.

Back in Paris, Zola wrote a few words to Numa Coste: 'My short stay in Aix already seems like a dream, but a charming dream, in which I relived a little of my youth, and in which I saw you again, my dear friend, you who were part of that youth.'

Cézanne, who also, and how much more, had been part of that youth, received a terrible shock when he learned that Zola had been in Aix, that they had been in the same town without seeing each other. His pain was profound and bitter, for he saw in this gesture of Zola's the sign that there were no more ties between them. It was obvious that Cézanne was still extremely fond of Zola. This became evident during the famous Dreyfus scandal. Though Cézanne did not believe in the innocence of the captain and did not approve of Zola's role in the affair, he judged him with an indulgence rather surprising in a man with so unrestrained a temper. Questioned about Zola in 1898, Cézanne merely laughed and commented: 'They took him in.' Monet and Pissarro, however, forgot their grievances against the novelist and joined him in his fight for justice.

In 1899, at the height of the Dreyfus scandal, Cézanne had lunch in Paris with Maurice Le Blond and Joachim Gasquet. They tried to persuade him to accompany them to Zola's, where they were expected that afternoon. Cézanne replied evasively, but when, on leaving the table, they attempted to take Cézanne by the arm and make him go with them, he gave such screams of fright that they were obliged to let him go. Cézanne must have felt instinctively that that an impromptu visit before strangers in an effort to repair the break would be unworthy of the friendship that had been theirs. Perhaps Cézanne was also afraid of showing his emotions, he who often had difficulty holding back his tears.

When, on a September morning in 1902, Cézanne learned from his gardener that Zola had died, asphyxiated by fumes from a defective chimney, he was shattered. He burst into tears and locked himself up in his studio for the rest of the day, alone with his grief. Death immediately effaced all real or imaginary grievances. Now, before his eyes, Cézanne saw his whole life from their childhood to the break, and always he found at his side the untiringly good and devoted friend, the support in difficult days, the enthusiast who in his youthful dreams had conceived fame only as shared with him. It was a part of himself that had ceased to be.

XX

SEARCH FOR PEACE

1890–1899

'ISOLATION is what I am worthy of. Thus, at least, no one gets me in his clutches.' This was to become Cézanne's guiding thought, although he emerged from his retreat from time to time. It was a retreat without stability and quiet. In Aix he largely lost touch with the outer world, except when, in 1889, Renoir with his wife and son reciprocated Cézanne's visit to La Roche-Guyon. After staying briefly at the 'Jas de Bouffan', Renoir rented Montbriant from Cézanne's brother-in-law, Maxime Conil, and spent several months there. The two friends occasionally painted together in the Arc valley or put up their easels in front of the picturesque pigeon tower of Bellevue (Pls. 65, 66, 67, 68). But it seems that Renoir's stay in Aix did not end on a harmonious note. Indeed, Cézanne became increasingly irritable and the diabetes from which he began to suffer around 1890 accentuated his occasional outbursts.

Like all recluses, Cézanne sometimes enjoyed talking. Overflowing with confidence, he then grew very expansive and exuberant. 'It does me good,' he would say. 'I am happy to loosen up.' It was at such a moment that Paul Alexis found the painter in 1891 and received his confidences.

'. . . This town is dreary, desolate, and paralyzing,' Alexis wrote to Zola. 'Coste, the only one that I see fairly often, isn't much fun every day. . . . Fortunately, Cézanne, to whom I found my way back some time ago, puts some spirit and life into my daily round. He at least is vibrant, expansive, and alive. He is furious at the Ball, who, to make up for a stay of a year in Paris, last summer inflicted upon him five months of Switzerland and of table d'hôte . . . where he found little sympathy except from a Prussian. After Switzerland, the Ball, escorted by her bourgeois son, made off again to Paris, but by cutting her allowance in half she has been brought back to Aix. . . .

'During the day Cézanne paints at the "Jas de Bouffan" where a workman serves as his model and where one of these days I shall go to see what he is doing.—Finally, to complete his portrait, converted, he believes and practises.'

Zola apparently had asked all his friends for news of Cézanne, and Numa Coste wrote to him at about the same time:

'How to explain that a rapacious and tough banker could produce a being like our poor friend Cézanne, whom I have seen recently? He is well and physically solid, but he has become timid and primitive and younger than ever. He lives at the "Jas de Bouffan" with his mother, who, for that matter, is on bad terms with the Ball, who in turn does not get on with her sister-in-law, nor they among themselves. So that Paul lives on one side, his wife on the other. And it is one of the most touching things I know to see this good fellow retain his childlike naiveté, forget the disappointments of the struggle, and obstinately continue, resigned and suffering, the pursuit of a work which he cannot produce.'

* * *

The condescension with which Zola and his friends treated Cézanne contrasts sharply with the ever-rising esteem expressed by his painter friends. In 1894 Cézanne went to spend some time in Giverny, where he stayed at the inn, but saw Monet frequently. Monet introduced him to Clemenceau, Rodin, Octave Mirbeau, and Gustave Geffroy. Cézanne was deeply touched by the cordial manner in which he was treated; an affectionate handshake by Rodin in Monet's garden, for example, almost moved him to tears. According to Geffroy, for whom Cézanne showed a special liking, the painter was at that moment as sociable as could be and proved that he was enjoying himself by his laughter and his sallies.

It was during this visit to Giverny that Mary Cassatt for the first time met Paul Cézanne. In a letter to one of her American friends she described her impressions:

'The circle has been increased by a celebrity in the person of the first impressionist, Monsieur Cézanne—*the inventor of impressionism*, as Madame D. calls him. . . . Monsieur Cézanne is from Provence and is like the man from the Midi whom Daudet describes: "When I first saw him I thought he looked like a cut-throat with large red eyeballs standing out from his head in a most ferocious manner, a rather fierce-looking pointed beard, quite grey, and an excited way of talking that positively made the dishes rattle.' I found later on that I had misjudged his appearance, for far from being fierce or a cut-throat, he has the gentlest nature possible, *"comme un enfant"* as he would say. His manners at first rather startled me—he scrapes his soup plate, then lifts it and pours the remaining drops in the spoon; he even takes his chop in his fingers and pulls the meat from the bone. He eats with his knife and accompanies every gesture, every movement of his hand, with that implement, which he grasps firmly when he commences his meal and never puts down until he leaves the table. Yet in spite of the total disregard of the dictionary of manners, he shows a politeness towards us which no other man here would have shown. He will not allow Louise to serve him before us in the usual order of succession at the table; he is even deferential to that stupid maid, and he pulls off the old tam-o'-shanter, which he wears to protect his bald head, when he enters the room. I am gradually learning that appearances are not to be relied upon over here. . . .

'The conversation at lunch and at dinner is principally on art and cooking. Cézanne is one of the most liberal artists I have ever seen. He prefaces every remark with: "*Pour moi*" it is so and so, but he grants that everyone may be as honest and as true to nature from their convictions; he doesn't believe that everyone should see alike.'

In Giverny Cézanne also met with the sympathy of Clemenceau, who found in the painter a good audience for his jokes. Cézanne, however, had little confidence in the statesman; he explained to Geffroy: 'It is because I am too weak . . . and Clemenceau could not protect me! . . . Only the Church can protect me.' And Monet wrote to a friend: 'How unfortunate that this man should not have had more support in his existence. He is a true artist who has much too much self-doubt. He needs to be bolstered up. . . .'

Cézanne's touchiness and fear of people finally made him suspicious of even his most devoted friends. When Monet, precisely in an effort to bolster him up, gathered a few friends in Giverny, among them Renior and Sisley, he received Cézanne with the words: 'At last we are here all together and are happy to seize this occasion to tell you how fond we are of you and how much we admire your art.' Dismayed, Cézanne stared at his friend. 'You, too, are making fun of me!' were his only words. He turned, took his coat, and left.

Cézanne departed from Giverny so abruptly that he abandoned a number of his unfinished canvases at the inn; Monet picked them up and sent them after him. From Aix Cézanne later wrote him: 'So here I am back again in the South, which I ought, perhaps, never to have left, to fling myself once more into the chimerical pursuit of art. . . . May I tell you how grateful I was for the moral support I found in you and which served as a stimulus for my painting.'

As usual, despair followed periods of enthusiasm for Cézanne, and this moodiness hampered his work and kept him in a state of exasperation. Back in Paris in the spring of 1895 and hopeful of painting a picture which might at last receive a medal at the Salon, Cézanne asked Gustave Geffroy to pose for a portrait in his library (Pl. 72). After having worked on this daily for three months, Cézanne suddenly sent for his easel, brushes, and paints with a note saying that the undertaking was definitely too much for him, that he had been wrong to begin it and excused himself for abandoning it.

At Geffroy's suggestion, Cézanne returned to work on this portrait for another week, but he no longer had faith in it and left for Aix.

Even in Aix Cézanne did not find the peace he sought. Before leaving Paris he had renewed his old friendship with Francisco Oller, whom he had first met more than thirty years before at the Atelier Suisse. After 'numerous tokens of affection and southern warmth,' Oller accepted Cézanne's invitation to accompany him to Aix. A few weeks later, however, Oller wrote to Pissarro: 'My dear, Mr Paul Cézanne is either a *canaille* or he is mad. He has played on me the dirtiest trick you could imagine.'

This is what had happened. Cézanne and Oller had agreed to meet on the train for Aix at the third-class carriages. Unable to find Cézanne there—for the very good reason that he had taken a first-class compartment—Oller did not get on the train at all. With still no Cézanne in view, he decided to take the next train. Arrived in Aix, he sent word of his presence to the 'Jas de Bouffan', and Cézanne replied without delay. 'If this is so, please come right away. I am expecting you.'

The two painters thereupon saw each other for a couple of weeks, but when Oller began to give his friend some advice on painting, Cézanne burst forth with this letter:

> 'Jas de Bouffan, July 5, 1895
>
> 'Sir,
> 'The high-handed manner you have adopted toward me for some time and the rather brusque tone you permitted yourself to use, at the moment you took leave, are not calculated to please me.
> 'I am determined not to receive you in my father's house.
> 'The lessons that you take the liberty of giving me will thus have borne their fruits. Good-bye.
>
> > 'P. Cézanne.'

Oller forwarded this letter to Pissarro, doubtless to ask him to intercede in this painful incident. 'I saw Oller yesterday,' Pissarro wrote his wife from Paris in January 1896. 'He spoke to me a great deal about Cézanne, who, it seems, has been fantastic. He was even worse than with Renoir. He brought Oller to Aix and stuck him there in extraordinary circumstances. I shall tell you about that verbally, it is too long. . . . Dr Aguiard has come to Paris for a few days. He has seen Cézanne; he is sure that he is sick. In short, poor Cézanne is incensed with all of us, even with Monet, who, after all, has been very nice to him.'

Oller also reported to Pissarro disparaging remarks which Cézanne had made about him. 'Pissarro is an old fool, Monet a cunning fellow, they have nothing in them. . . . I am the only one with temperament, I am the only one who can paint a red! . . .'

When Dr Aguiard assured him that Cézanne was not responsible for his fits of rage, Pissarro exclaimed in a letter to his son Lucien: 'Is it not sad and a pity that a man endowed with such beautiful temperament should have so little balance?'

The strange thing about all this is that the year 1895 had offered Cézanne for the first time in many decades some real satisfaction. A young dealer, Ambroise Vollard, had opened in December 1895 a large one-man show of Cézanne in Paris, and though the critics were rather hostile, for many young painters and a few avant-garde collectors this had proved to be the artistic event of the year. But even this success could not dispel Cézanne's sombre mood, and in April 1896 Numa Coste wrote from Aix to Zola:

'I have seen recently and still often see Cézanne and Solari, who have been here for some time. . . . Cézanne is very depressed and is often the prey of melancholy thoughts. He has some self-satisfaction, however, and his work is having sales to which he has not been accustomed. But his wife must have made him do quite a lot of foolish things. He has to go to Paris or return from there according to her orders. To have peace, he has had to give up all he has, and confidential remarks dropped by him reveal that he has only got left a monthly income of about a hundred francs. He has rented a cabin at the quarry above the dam and spends the greater part of his time there.'

In Aix Cézanne still lived with his old mother at the 'Jas de Bouffan'. Her advanced age had little by little deprived her of physical and mental health. Her son cared for her in the most affectionate way.

At the 'Jas de Bouffan', Cézanne found the solitude which he desired. He often worked in the garden, which at every season offered him new and striking aspects: in summer the shady row of chestnuts whose heavy foliage partly hid the house, in winter the bare branches of the trees which allowed the distant silhouette of Mount Sainte-Victoire to be seen and to reflect itself in the pool. Besides these landscapes, Cézanne also painted still lifes and, above all, portraits. He used some peasants and day labourers at the 'Jas' as models for the different paintings of 'Card-players' and of men smoking. A peasant woman was portrayed as a cook, while her son appears in a painting seated at a table with a skull in front of him. Whenever Cézanne's wife and son were in Aix, they too posed for him. To sit for the painter was not an easy matter; he often demanded uncomfortable poses and insisted that they be held for hours on end. His wife was one of the few who consented to go through with this ordeal repeatedly. On many occasions Cézanne also did self-portraits.

Cézanne worked very slowly and needed a week of daily sessions just to sketch on the canvas the contours of the model, a few shadows, and some indications of colour. For his still lifes he was obliged to use paper flowers and artificial fruit, for real flowers wilted and fruit rotted before the work was far advanced. One hundred sittings for a portrait—such as he requested from Vollard (Pl. 73)—were nothing unusual, and even then he was not always satisfied with the result. When he had no model, Cézanne occasionally copied illustrations from his sister's magazines and thus painted a version of El Greco's 'Lady in Ermine'.

Since working with Pissarro at Pontoise, Cézanne's knowledge of technique had greatly developed. He applied his colours less thickly as his brushes more easily expressed his vision. But his canvases still are sometimes covered, at least in part, with several layers of paint that bear witness to long and painful efforts. The technique differs widely in his paintings; in some the limpidity of tone corresponds to the thinness of the pigment and only the dark tones are composed by a multitude of touches of colour. In others Cézanne used the opposite method. The brush strokes are not always the same, either; sometimes they are short and wide, while in other works they are long and narrow. The direction of the brush strokes varies from painting to painting. Cézanne's technique was visibly dictated by the nature of the subject, by the lighting, and possibly also by his mood.

But Cézanne considered technique subordinate to sensitivity. He once remarked: 'Technique grows in contact with nature. It develops through circumstances. It consists in seeking to express what one feels, in organizing sensations into personal aesthetics.' And he told Renoir: 'It took me forty years to find out that painting is not sculpture.' To this Renoir commented: 'That means that at first he thought he must force his effects of modelling with black and white and load his canvases with paint, in order to equal, if he could, the effects of sculpture. Later, his study brought him to see that the work of the painter is so to use colour that, even when it is laid on very thinly, it gives the full result.'

Cézanne summed up his feelings about technique in these words: 'I believe in the logical development of everything we see and feel through the study of nature and turn my attention to technical questions later; for technical problems are for us only the means of making the public feel what we painters feel and of making ourselves understood. The great masters whom we admire can have done nothing else.'

*　　*　　*

After the death of Cézanne's mother in 1897, Marie Cézanne looked after her brother's affairs. In order to settle the estate, and at the insistence of Maxime Conil, the 'Jas de Bouffan' had to be sold in 1899. Cézanne was heartbroken at parting with this beautiful place. It was there that he had found solitude for decades, where he had always worked either in the garden or in the little studio beneath the roof with its view over the vineyards and the hills of Les Lauves. It was there that in the enthusiasm of his youth he had undertaken the decoration of the big salon and there also everything that reminded him of his parents.

Henceforth Cézanne went to live in Aix on the Rue Boulegon where his housekeeper, Madame Bremond, took care of him. Now that he could no longer work at the 'Jas de Bouffan', he returned to the cabin in the Bibémus quarry which he had rented a few years before in search of new motifs (Pl. 81). He also rented a small room in the Château Noir, half-way between Aix and Le Tholonet (Pl. 83). He went often to work there, returning every night to the Rue Boulegon, leaving his canvases and materials in one place or the other. Cézanne even offered to buy the property of Château Noir, but the owner refused to sell. Thus, from 1899 on, Cézanne had no place he could call his own in his beloved country around Aix.

Whether in Aix or in the Ile-de-France, Cézanne led a very retired life. In Paris he went to the Louvre to draw; the city was probably too animated for him to work in the streets or on the quais as he had done in early years, especially in 1875 when he had been Guillaumin's neighbour and had painted in his company. The sketches which he made in the museums were doubtless supposed to take the place of studies on the motif, or even more, from the living model. He began to copy ancient and modern sculpture in the Louvre (Pls. 69, 71), especially the works of Puget, in which he felt the 'breath of the mistral'. He also copied plaster casts in the Trocadero Museum. Among the painters, Rubens and Poussin particularly attracted him, and Cézanne's sketchbooks are filled with drawings after Rubens, whose work, like Puget's, offered him subjects rich in colour and movement.

In Paris, Cézanne now tried to avoid all personal contacts. Paul Signac, for example, walking one day on the Seine quais with Guillaumin, saw Cézanne coming toward them. Ready to greet him, they saw him making gestures, begging them to pass him by; amazed and deeply moved, Guillaumin and Signac crossed the street and went on in silence. Another time, when Cézanne saw Claude Monet, he lowered his head and plunged into the crowd.

Pissarro, too, respected Cézanne's desire for solitude, though in 1898 he encouraged the young painter Louis Le Bail to call on Cézanne when the latter was working at Montgeroult near Pontoise. The two men soon became friends, and one day Cézanne asked his young colleague for permission to work at his side on a motif which Louis Le Bail had discovered. Whereas the young man's canvas was already well advanced, Cézanne impetuously began a large painting. A young peasant girl passing by stopped to look at the two canvases and, pointing to Le Bail's, could not help saying, 'That one is really beautiful.' Cézanne was much upset by this candid remark. When, the next day, Le Bail felt that Cézanne was avoiding him and asked for an explanation, the old painter replied: 'You should pity me; truth comes from the mouths of children.'

Cézanne told Louis Le Bail that he would have been glad to earn six thousand francs a year with his paintings. Vollard was not very liberal, but Cézanne was flattered that he accepted all his canvases, even the unfinished or torn ones. Thus the painter sold his work regularly and this through his son, to whom Cézanne gave 10 per cent. The young man also got 10 per cent from Vollard, a fact fully known to his father. 'The boy is much smarter than I am,' Cézanne said admiringly. 'I have no practical sense.' Young Cézanne even tried to intervene in his father's choice of subjects, urging him, for example, to paint women instead of men, as they were much more salable. But Cézanne's fear of women had grown with age. Although he did propose to work with Le Bail in his Paris studio where they might then have female models, this project was never carried out. The friendly relations of the two men came to a sudden end after a characteristic incident.

Cézanne had asked his young colleague to call him every day at three o'clock after his nap; Le Bail, taking him at his word, and finding Cézanne asleep, entered his room after having knocked several times to wake him. The next day Louis Le Bail received this letter:

'Monsieur:
'The rather discourteous manner with which you take the liberty of entering my room is not calculated to please me. In the future please see that you are announced.
'Please give the glass and the canvas which were left in your studio to the person who comes for them.'

Cézanne's friends eventually understood that he wished them to respect the isolation into which he withdrew more and more. Thus, Auguste Renoir, who was very fond of Cézanne, came to Aix with a young painter to see his friend; at the last minute, however, he hesitated and finally left Aix without calling on him, fearing, as he explained to his companion, an unexpected reaction on Cézanne's part.

His longing for solitude was partially explained by Cézanne in a letter to the Italian collector, Egisto Fabbri, who had written him in 1899:

'I have the good fortune to own sixteen of your paintings. I understand their aristocratic and austere beauty—for they represent what is most noble in modern art. And often when looking at them, I have felt the urge to tell you what emotions they arouse in me. I know, however, that you are importuned by many people and I may appear very indiscreet if I ask permission to come and see you. Nevertheless, I like to think that one day I shall have the pleasure and the honour of making your acquaintance; and however it may be, Monsieur, please accept this expression of my profound admiration.'

To this letter the painter answered: 'I find myself unable to resist your flattering desire to make my acquaintance. The fear of appearing inferior to what is expected of a person presumed to dominate every situation is doubtless the excuse for the necessity I feel of living in seclusion.'

XXI

CÉZANNE ATTRACTS ATTENTION

IN PARIS

NOTWITHSTANDING Cézanne's complete isolation, his works had slowly begun to attract attention in Paris. As early as 1888 J.-K. Huysmans, who had been convinced by Pissarro of Cézanne's value, spoke of the 'too much ignored painter' in an article for *La Cravache*, in which he further stated that Cézanne 'contributed more than the late Manet to the impressionist movement'. The following year Huysmans devoted a whole chapter to Cézanne in his book *Certains*.

In 1889 a painting by Cézanne appeared in the Paris World's Fair, at the insistence of Chocquet, who had refused some other loan unless a canvas by his friend be included in the exhibition. At the end of the same year, Octave Maus invited Cézanne to show in Brussels with the young Belgian group of the 'XX'. In spite of his decision not to exhibit any more because, as he explained to Maus, 'the many studies I made have given only negative results', Cézanne accepted. Sisley and van Gogh having also been invited, Cézanne informed the organizer of the exhibition: 'In view of the pleasure of finding myself in such good company, I do not hesitate to modify my resolve.' Thus three canvases of Cézanne were hung at the Brussels exhibition of 1890.

When Paul Alexis tried in January 1892 to obtain Cézanne's participation in the *Salon des Indépendants*, which had been founded some years before on the principle of no jury and no rewards, the painter at first accepted but then changed his mind. In that same year, Georges Lecomte, a friend of Pissarro's, dealt sympathetically with Cézanne in his book, *L'Art impressionniste*, and the painter Emile Bernard published a short biographical sketch of the artist. A year later, in a study of impressionism, Gustave Geffroy called Cézanne 'the precursor of this art' and even reproduced, probably for the first time, one of his canvases.

But in spite of all this, Cézanne was still almost unknown in Paris and the critic Mellerio could write: 'Cézanne seems to be a fantastic figure. Although still living, he is spoken of as though he were dead. A few examples of his work are owned by a small number of collectors.' Indeed, Cézanne had not exhibited in Paris since 1877, with the exception of the two canvases which had been forced on the official exhibitions of 1882 and 1889.

However, Cézanne's influence was beginning to make itself felt in the works of the new generation. In 1892 the painter Maurice Denis stated at the Salon that it was from 'Monet, Degas, Cézanne, Pissarro, and Renoir, unknown to the public of the openings, that the younger artists borrowed both their art and their vision, without even trying to develop the inheritance of the masters.'

A little later, Gustave Geffroy wrote:

'For a long time, Cézanne has had a curious artistic fate. He might be described as a person at once unknown and famous, having only rare contact with the public yet considered influential by the restless and the seekers in the field of painting; known only by a few, living in savage isolation, reappearing, then disappearing suddenly from the sight of his intimate friends. All the little-known facts about his life, his almost secret productivity, the rare canvases which seem to follow none of the accepted rules of publicity, all these give him a kind of strange renown, already distant; a mystery surrounds his person and his work. Those who are in search of the unfamiliar, who like to discover things which have not yet been seen, speak of Cézanne's canvases with a knowing air, giving information like a password. . . . What did his canvases look like? Where could some of them be seen? Reply was made that the preceding week a canvas had been seen at Tanguy's, the dealer in the Rue Clauzel, but that it was necessary to hurry to find it for there were always collectors quick to pounce upon these prizes which were few and far between.'

Georges Lecomte substantiated this when he stated that canvases by Cézanne were only seen by chance and in a few houses of Cézanne's friends: Zola had, among others, a landscape, Paul Alexis a still life, Duret and Huysmans a sketch each. It was also known that a few of Cézanne's paintings were to be found at Choquet's, at Dr Gachet's in Auvers, at Murer's in Rouen, that Pissarro owned some, that others belonged to Rouart and to the painters Caillebotte and Schuffenecker. Since the founding in 1890 of the new *Mercure de France*, Albert Aurier regularly mentioned in his art column any painting by Cézanne shown at Tanguy's, especially praising 'a still life [pears on a napkin] which is simply an incomparable masterpiece'. Aurier particularly admired the *Portrait of Achille Emperaire*, subsequently bought by Schuffenecker.

The dark little shop of *père* Tanguy was the one place where Cézanne's works could be studied or bought. This humble dealer gave the only information available on the painter and his narrow shop became the rendezvous of all those interested in this artist who would have been taken for a myth had it not been for his canvases in which the new generation sought advice and guidance. To be the only one in Paris to handle Cézanne's work gave a kind of celebrity to Tanguy in the eyes of the younger painters. Bernard later remembered:

'One went there as to a museum, to see the few sketches by the unknown artist who lived in Aix, dissatisfied with his work and with the world, who himself destroyed these studies, objects of admiration though they were. The magnificent qualities of this true painter appeared even more original because of their author's legendary character. Members of the Institute, influential and avant-garde critics, visited the modest shop in the Rue Clauzel, which thus became the fable of Paris and the conversation of the studios. Nothing seemed more disconcerting than these canvases, where the most outstanding gifts were coupled with a childlike naiveté; the young felt the genius, the old the folly of the paradox; the jealous saw only impotence. Thus the opinions were divided and one passed from profound discussions to bitter jeers, from insults to exaggerated praise; Gauguin, confronted with their daubed appearance, exclaimed: "Nothing looks more like a daub than a masterpiece!" Elimire Bourges cried out: "It's the painting of a sewage collector!" Alfred Stevens couldn't stop laughing.'

Imperturbably, *père* Tanguy listened—perhaps often without understanding much—and remained silent. He never tired of showing his treasures. At the request of his visitors, according to Bernard, he went to fetch *the Cézannes*!

'One saw him disappear into a dark room and re-appear a moment later, carrying a package of modest size, carefully tied up; on his thick lips a mysterious smile, damp emotion shining in his eyes. Feverishly he untied the strings and, using the back of a chair as an easel, he exhibited the paintings one after the other, in religious silence. The visitors remarked upon them, pointed out certain parts, became enthusiastic over the colour, the subject matter, and the style; then, when they had finished, Tanguy talked about the artist: "Papa Cézanne," he would say, "is never satisfied with what he does, he always gives up before having finished. When he moves, he is careful to forget his canvases in the house he is leaving; when he paints outdoors, he abandons them in the country. Cézanne works very slowly, the least thing costs him much effort, there is nothing accidental in what he does." Naturally, the curiosity of his visitors was aroused. Whereupon Tanguy would say with a rapt expression: "Cézanne goes to the Louvre every morning".'

Even those who went to Tanguy's to make fun of Cézanne rarely left his shop without a kindly feeling for the good man. An American critic, taken there by some painters in 1892, related:

'Père Tanguy is a short, thick-set, elderly man, with a grizzled beard and large, beaming, dark-blue eyes. He has a curious way of first looking down at his picture with all the fond love of a mother, and then looking up at you over his glasses, as if begging you to admire his beloved children. . . . I could not help feeling, apart from all opinions of my own, that a movement in art which can inspire such devotion must have a deeper final import than the mere ravings of a coterie.'

Among those who visited Tanguy's more or less regularly were Vincent van Gogh and Maurice Denis, Paul Signac and Georges Seurat, Emile Bernard and Paul Gauguin, Jacques-Emile Blanche and Ambroise Vollard. It was there that Egisto Fabbri must have bought his sixteen canvases. Signac also acquired a painting by Cézanne. Denis later explained that what interested the young painters in Cézanne was that he reduced nature to pictorial elements and eliminated all others. All of Cézanne's admirers, however, regretted the silence which surrounded him; he lived, as Geffroy put it, 'on the margin of life.'

Interest in the impressionists was suddenly awakened after the death, in 1893, of Gustave Caillebotte, who bequeathed to the state his magnificent collection of sixty-five paintings by Cézanne, Degas, Manet, Monet, Pissarro, Renoir, and Sisley. Despite Caillebotte's provision that his collection should enter the Luxembourg Museum undivided, the state did not dare accept the bequest as a whole. Renoir, as executor of the will, was forced to yield unless the gift were to be rejected; after long debates, only a fraction of the collection entered the museum.

The Caillebotte bequest aroused vehement protests against 'profanation' of a museum which had been consecrated to 'pure' art and which, by exhibiting impressionist work, became a dangerous place where 'young men could be distracted from serious work'. In the Institute, the Senate, and the Press, protests were made against this donation, which was considered to be 'a heap of rubbish the exhibition of which in a national museum publicly dishonours French art'.

Cézanne's name, however, was never mentioned in all this indignant outcry, perhaps because it was thought that too much honour would be done him even by a derogatory reference. Yet two of his paintings entered the Luxembourg museum in 1895 with the remnants of the Caillebotte collection.

Gustave Caillebotte's death was closely followed by two important events in the history of impressionism: the sale of the Duret and Tanguy collections. In March 1894 Duret, the art critic and Zola's friend, sold his collection, which included three works by Cézanne, at quite good prices. A few weeks later, Tanguy's stock of paintings

55. *Cézanne: View of Gardanne, 1885–6*

56. *Photograph of the same subject*

57. *Cézanne: Turning Road at La Roche-Guyon, 1885. Formerly Coll. Auguste Renoir*

58. *Photograph of the same subject*

59. *Cézanne: View of L'Estaque*, 1882–5

60. *Photograph of the same subject*

61. *Cézanne: The Farm of Bellevue, c.*1892

62. *Photograph of the same subject*

63. *Cézanne: The Jas de Bouffan in Spring, c.*1887

64. *Photograph of the same subject*

65. *Renoir: Mount Sainte-Victoire*, 1889

66. *Cézanne: Mount Sainte-Victoire*, c.1890

67. *Renoir: The Pigeon Tower of Bellevue*, 1889

68. *Cézanne: The Pigeon Tower of Bellevue, c.*1889

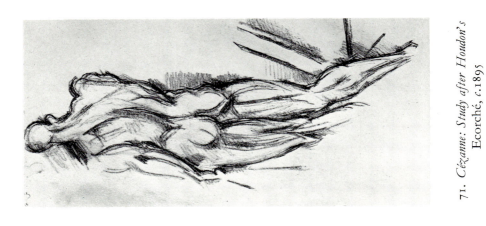

71. *Cézanne: Study after Houdon's*
Ecorché, c.1895

70. *Photograph of Puget's*
Milon de Crotone (*Louvre*)

69. *Cézanne: Study after Puget's*
Milon de Crotone, c. 1895

72. *Cézanne: Portrait of Gustave Geffroy*, 1895

73. *Cézanne: Portrait of Ambroise Vollard*, 1899

74. *Cézanne: Study of Trees*, 1890–5

75. *Cézanne: Study of Trees*, 1890–5

76. *Cézanne: Mount Sainte-Victoire near Chateau Noir, c.*1900

77. *Cézanne: Mount Sainte-Victoire near Chateau Noir, c.*1900

78. *Cézanne: Bibémus Quarry*, 1898

80. *Paul Cézanne having finished his work, 1906*

79. *Photograph of Paul Cézanne at work near Aix, 1906*

81. *Cézanne's cabin at Bibémus Quarry*

82. *Cézanne's studio at Les Lauves*

83. *View of Chateau Noir*

84. *Cézanne: Mount Sainte-Victoire seen from Les Lauves, c.1905*

85. *Photograph of the same subject*

86. *Cézanne sitting in front of his 'Bathers' (small version). Photo,* 1904

87. *Cézanne: Bathers (large version),* 1902–6

was sold at auction, following his death; six canvases by Cézanne sold for between forty-five and two hundred and fifteen francs. Gustave Geffroy availed himself of this opportunity to publish in *Le Journal* a long and laudatory article on Cézanne.

The time seemed ripe for an exhibition of Cézanne's work, to give the public a chance to see for the first time a retrospective exhibit of this much-discussed painter. It was Ambroise Vollard, a young Creole, recently established as an art dealer, who, at the insistence of Pissarro (joined by Monet, Renoir, and Guillaumin), undertook the organization of a one-man show. After numerous difficulties he managed to submit his project to Cézanne who sent from Aix a hundred and fifty canvases. The large number of works intended by the artist himself to represent his efforts between 1868 and 1894, show clearly enough that Cézanne did not consider his paintings merely as rough sketches, as had so often been claimed.

The exhibition took place toward the end of 1895. Vollard, in his small shop in the Rue Laffitte, could not even show all of Cézanne's canvases at once. Nevertheless, this exhibition aroused great interest and lively discussions. Needless to say there were still those who spoke of the 'nightmarish sight of these atrocities in oil which exceed the amount of practical joking legally permissible today'. But Pissarro told his son Georges:

'Vollard is having a Cézanne exhibition; it is really wonderful; there are still lifes, very beautiful landscapes, very strange bathers of extraordinary sobriety. It looks as though it were done in two tones; it is very effective. . . . The collectors are stupefied; they don't understand anything about it, but nevertheless he is a first-class painter of astonishing subtlety, truth, and classicism.'

And to his eldest son, Lucien, Pissarro wrote:

'How rarely do you come across true painters, who know how to balance two tones. I was thinking of H., who looks for noon at midnight, of Gauguin, who, however, has a good eye, of Signac, who also has something—all of them more or less paralyzed by theories. I also thought of Cézanne's show in which there are exquisite things, still lifes of irreproachable perfection, others, *much worked on* and yet unfinished, of even greater beauty, landscapes, nudes, and heads that are unfinished but yet grandiose, and so *painted*, so supple. . . . Why? Sensation is there! Curiously enough, while I was admiring this strange, disconcerting aspect of Cézanne, familiar to me for many years, Renoir arrived. But my enthusiasm was nothing compared to Renoir's. Degas himself is seduced by the charm of this refined savage. Monet, all of us. . . . Are we mistaken? I don't think so. The only ones who are not subject to the charm of Cézanne are precisely those artists or collectors who have shown by their errors that their sensibilities are defective. They properly point out the faults we all see, which leap to the eye, but the charm —that they do not see. As Renoir said so well, these paintings have I do not know what quality, like the frescoes of Pompeii, so crude and so admirable! Degas and Monet have bought some marvellous Cézannes; I exchanged a poor sketch of Louveciennes for an admirable small canvas of bathers and one of his self-portraits.'

In another letter Pissarro mentioned that Renoir and Degas were so enthusiastic about a drawing of some fruit that they drew lots for it.

Pissarro lost no opportunity to win over those who were still not convinced of his friend's qualities. He was incensed when a dealer claimed that Cézanne had always been influenced by Guillaumin. 'Then how do you expect outsiders to understand anything!' he exclaimed to Lucien. 'This monstrosity was expressed at Vollard's. Vollard was blue. Aren't these babblers amusing? You wouldn't believe how difficult it is for me to make certain collectors, who are friends of the impressionists, understand how precious Cézanne's qualities are. I suppose centuries will pass before these are appreciated.'

This time the press contained some respectful and sympathetic articles on Cézanne who, as Thadée Natanson wrote in the *Revue Blanche*, 'assumes in the French school the position of the new master of still life'. And Arsène Alexandre published an article by the significant title, *Claude Lantier*, which appeared in *Le Figaro* on 9 December, 1895:

'When *L'Œuvre*, the romantic epic of painting, appeared, with its exaggeration of types, its wilful distortion of facts, and its lyricism, it seemed to describe very simple things, and some moderately well-informed critics wrote that Claude Lantier, the chief character in the novel, the neurotic and miserable painter who ends by hanging himself in front of his picture, was a portrait of Cézanne. This was all that was necessary for the public, who were interested in the anecdotes and unpublished facts of artistic life, to spread the strangest ideas about the painter who could and moreover would do nothing to contradict them. One might have doubted whether, like Homer, Cézanne really existed.

'The opportunity has arisen for stating that he really does exist, and even that his existence has not been useless to some people. . . . Today it has suddenly been discovered that Zola's friend, the mysterious man from Provence, the painter simultaneously incomplete and inventive, sly and uncivilized, is a great man.

'Great man? Not altogether, if one remains aloof from the enthusiasms of a season, but one of the strangest temperaments, from whom a great deal in the new school has been borrowed, knowingly or not. The interesting thing about this exhibition is the influence he exerted on artists who are now well known: Pissarro, Guillaumin, and later, Gauguin, van Gogh, and others.'

M. Thiébault-Sisson, one of Zola's friends, wrote an article in *Le Temps* which seems to reflect the opinion of Cézanne which was current in Zola's circle. His conclusions could just as well apply to Claude Lantier: 'Incapable of judging himself, he is unable to draw from a concept all the profit that more resourceful people drew from it; too unfulfilled, in a word, to realize completely what he had been the first to discover and give his full measure in definitive works.'

*   *   *

Cézanne suffered profoundly from the lack of understanding with which his art met. He did not even enjoy the favourable comments published on his work. Thus, in May 1896 he wrote to a young poet:

'I curse the X. . . .s and the few rascals who, to write an article for fifty francs, drew the attention of the public to me. All my life I have worked to be able to earn my living, but I thought that one could do good painting without attracting attention to one's private life. To be sure, an artist wishes to raise himself intellectually as much as possible, but the man must remain obscure. Pleasure must reside in study. If it had been given me to succeed, I should have remained in a corner with my few studio companions with whom we used to go out for a pint. I still have a good friend* from those days—well, he has not been successful, despite his being devilishly more of a painter than all the daubers with medals and decorations who make you sick. And at my age you want me still to believe in something! Moreover, I am as good as dead. You are young, and I can understand that you wish to succeed. But as for me, all I can do in my position is to eat humble pie, and were it not that I am passionately fond of the contours of my country, I should not be here.'

Indeed the Vollard exhibition and the enthusiasm of some young admirers drew public attention to Cézanne and at the sale of the Chocquet collection after his widow's death in 1899, thirty-two of his canvases sold for over 51,000 francs, the average price being about 1,600 francs; 'La maison du pendu' brought as much as 6,200. Most of Cézanne's paintings were bought by Durand-Ruel at Monet's behest. The same year, at the sale of Count Armand Doria's collection, one of Cézanne's landscapes went for 6,750 francs. This bid caused quite some excitement and the public, suspecting a manoeuvre, loudly demanded the buyer's name, whereupon the

* Possibly an allusion to Achille Emperaire.

latter rose and declared: 'It's I, Claude Monet,' and the sale went on without further incident.

At the end of 1899 Vollard informed Gauguin with satisfaction: 'I have purchased all of Cézanne's paintings that were in his studio [in Fontainebleau]. I have already held three or four exhibitions of them; they are beginning to catch on with the public.' The same year Cézanne decided at last to send three canvases to the *Salon des Indépendants*. Due to the intervention of Roger Marx, three more of his works were hung prominently at the big centennial exhibition of 1900 in Paris, much to the consternation of the public and the official artists. In 1901 Cézanne again exhibited in Brussels with the 'XX' as well as with the *Indépendants* in Paris, where Maurice Denis showed at the same time a large canvas entitled 'Hommage à Cézanne', representing a group of painters and friends [among them Redon, Vuillard, Bonnard, and Vollard] gathered round a still life by the master. Denis could not portray Cézanne himself because at that time he had not yet met him. His 'Hommage à Cézanne' is one of the first public manifestations in which the new generation of artists expressed their gratitude, admiration, and respect for the 'hermit of Aix'. But these young artists were not as yet followed by the general public in their appreciation of the old painter.

'Although he is no longer scoffed at as in former years,' Gustave Geffroy stated, 'he is still regarded with surprise by certain people who do not make the effort to understand the decorative sense, amplitude of form, brightness of colour which make of this painter a sort of Venetian, possessor of a new style, of a personal gravity.'

And another critic wrote in 1901: 'Cézanne is not known to the masses. . . but for a number of years painters have been following him attentively. Many of them owe to him the revelation of what one might call the intrinsic beauty of painting. In Cézanne the interest of the subject is not in its story . . . but rather in the production of visual delight.'

However unwillingly, Cézanne decided to exhibit again at the *Salon des Indépendants* in 1902, when he wrote to Vollard:

'I have received from Maurice Denis a letter which describes as a desertion my not taking part in the exhibition of the *Indépendants*. I have replied to Monsieur Denis, telling him that I am asking you to place at his disposal the pictures that you are able to lend him and to choose the ones that are calculated to do least harm.

'It seems to me that I find it difficult to dissociate myself from the young people who have shown themselves to be so much in sympathy with me, and I do not think that I shall in any way harm the course of my studies by exhibiting.'

The battle for recognition was slowly being decided in favour of the solitary painter who never made any attempt to answer his critics. Although Manet's work had long been given its just due, and Monet, Pissarro, and Renoir were being recognized as masters, Cézanne alone had not yet imposed himself. Despite the fact that the number of his admirers was constantly increasing, he was still being attacked in the daily press. One of the most vigorous campaigns ever launched against him was occasioned by the sale, in March 1903, of Zola's collection after the novelist's death. Ten of Cézanne's early works, to the surprise of the *Gazette de l'Hôtel Drouot*, obtained bids far above the official estimates. While a landscape by Monet brought 2,805 francs; two paintings by Guillemet, 300 and 600 francs respectively; two canvases by Pissarro, 500 and 920 francs each; and a large painting by Debat-Ponsan (a famous Salon painter), 350 francs, Cézanne's work sold as follows:

'L'Enlèvement' [Pl. 12]	4200 francs
'Nature morte au Coquillage' [Pl. 19]	3000 francs
'Coin d'atelier' [Pl. 15]	2050 francs
'Une lecture chez Zola'	1050 francs
'Paysage de l'Estaque' [Pl. 24]	1050 francs
'Portrait'	950 francs
'Nature morte'	900 francs
'Etude'	720 francs
'Néréide et Tritons'	680 francs
'Portrait de femme' (1864)	600 francs

On the occasion of this sale, Henri Rochefort, a political adversary of Zola, published on 9 March 1903, an article in *L'Intransigeant* on 'The Love of Ugliness', in which he dealt with the novelist's collection. After mentioning the hilarity caused by the work of 'an ultra-impressionist named Cézanne', Rochefort went on to say:

'The crowd was particularly amused by the head of a man, dark and bearded, whose cheeks were sculptured with a trowel and who seemed to be the prey of an eczema. The other paintings by the same artist all had an air of defying no less directly Corot, Théodore Rousseau, and also Hobbema and Ruysdael.

'Pissarro, Claude Monet, and the other more eccentric painters of the plein-air and of pointillism—those who have been called "confetti painters"—are academicians, almost members of the Institute, by comparison with this strange Cézanne whose productions Zola had picked up.

'The experts in charge of the sale themselves experienced a certain embarrassment, in cataloguing these fantastic things and attached this reticent note to each one of them: 'Work of earliest youth!'

'If M. Cézanne was still being nursed when he committed these daubs, we have nothing to say; but what is to be thought of the head of a literary school, as the squire of Médan considered himself to be, who propagates such pictorial madness? And he wrote Salon reviews in which he pretended to rule French art!

'Had the unfortunate man never seen a Rembrandt, a Velasquez, a Rubens, or a Goya? For if Cézanne is right, then all those great brushes were wrong. Watteau, Boucher, Fragonard, and Prud'hon no longer exist and nothing remains as supreme symbol of the art dear to Zola but to set fire to the Louvre.

'We have often averred that there were pro-Dreyfus people long before the Dreyfus case. All the diseased minds, the topsy-turvy souls, the shady and the disabled, were ripe for the coming of the Messiah of Treason. When one sees nature as Zola and his vulgar painters envisage it, naturally patriotism and honour take the form of an officer delivering to the enemy plans for the defence of his country.

'The love of physical and moral ugliness is a passion like any other.'

The repercussions of this article were considerable, especially in Aix, where people were convinced that the Parisians 'admired' Cézanne's work only to make fun of Aix. In his home town, Cézanne was considered an eccentric who, son of an honourable banker, wasted his time and money at 'painting' instead of living like other people. Many were openly delighted to see that there was still someone in Paris who was not afraid to tell the truth. Three hundred copies of *L'Intransigeant* were ordered and, at night, slipped under the doors of all those who had evinced some sympathy for the painter.

All the vicious talk which reached his ears naturally upset Cézanne. Threatening letters and anonymous insults were addressed to him at the Rue Boulegon. His family and few friends were maligned. It was hinted that he ought to relieve of his presence the city he was dishonouring. When his son wrote to him from Paris asking whether he should send him a copy of Rochefort's article, Cézanne answered bitterly: 'It is unnecessary to send it to me; every day I find it under my door, not counting the copies of *L'Intransigeant* sent by mail.'

*　　*　　*

The slanders published about him strengthened Cézanne's hatred of journalism and particularly of art criticism. He despised with equal fervour both attacks on and praise of his art, and when the painter Emile Bernard wished to devote a new study to his work, Cézanne wrote him in 1904: 'Talks on art are almost useless. The work which produces progress in one's own profession is sufficient compensation for not being understood by imbeciles.' And in another letter Cézanne advised Bernard: 'Do not be an art critic, but paint; therein lies salvation.'

Cézanne continued to exhibit, however, and in the summer of 1903 seven of his canvases (mostly loaned by Durand-Ruel) were shown in the impressionist section of the Vienna Secession: in the same year three of Cézanne's paintings were shown in Berlin. In 1904 Cézanne sent no less than nine canvases to Brussels as well as several to the *Salon d'Automne,* an association which had just been founded and in which all the artists who were members took turns at jury duty. The French author, Jules Renard, saw Cézanne's work at this exhibition and noted in his diary:

'At the Salon d'Automne. . . . Cézanne, barbarian. One must first have admired a great many famous daubs before liking this carpenter of colour. . . . The lovely life of Cézanne, all spent in a village in the South. He did not even come to his own exhibition. He would like to be decorated. That is what all these poor old painters want who, after an admirable life see at last, when they are near death, art dealers get rich on their work.'

When Roger Marx reviewed Cézanne's contribution to the *Salon d'Automne* in favourable terms, the painter wrote him from Aix on 23 January 1905:

'I have read with interest the lines that you were kind enough to write about me in the two articles in the *Gazette des Beaux-Arts.* I thank you for the favourable opinion that you express on my behalf.

'My age and my health will never allow me to realize the dream of art that I have been pursuing all my life. But I shall always be grateful to the intelligent amateurs who had—despite my own hesitations—the intuition of what I wanted to attempt for the renewal of my art. To my mind one does not substitute oneself for the past, one merely adds a new link to its chain. With the temperament of a painter and an ideal of art—that is to say a conception of nature—sufficient means of expression would have been necessary to be intelligible to the general public and to occupy a decent position in the history of art.'

And at about the same time Cézanne wrote to a young friend: 'I am still working, without worrying about criticism and critics, as a true artist should do. My work must prove that I am right.'

*   *   *

In 1905 Cézanne sent ten paintings to the *Salon d'Automne* and again the same number in 1906. But he did not exhibit his work only in Paris during the last years of his life. In Aix a 'Society of the Friends of Art' had been formed around the turn of the century with Cézanne's old fellow-student, Villevieille, as president. As a member of the society, Cézanne exhibited in 1902 a landscape of the 'Jas de Bouffan' and a still life, and in 1906 a view of Château Noir. In the little catalogues of these exhibitions Cézanne had himself listed as 'Pupil of Pissarro'. Thus the old painter whose name was beginning to be honoured in the art world, paid a debt of gratitude to the man who had guided his early efforts and given him boundless encouragement, the magnificent example of a high artistic conscience, and deep kindness.

Thanks to all these exhibitions, the public was now able to study and appreciate Cézanne's art. Yet the painter and his work continued to be maligned, especially after Rochefort's article had reminded the critics that Cézanne had been Zola's friend.

'Cézanne, for a short time victor, with Zola, may now definitely be classed with the vanquished,' wrote Max Nordau with ill-concealed satisfaction, and in 1904 an anonymous critic of *La Lanterne* spoke of the painter as though he were dead: 'Cézanne was nothing but a lamentable failure; perhaps he had some ideas but he was quite incapable of expressing them'. And later the same expert wrote: 'Why are they still bothering us with M. Paul Cézanne? Has his cause really not been heard? Do not all those who have seen his works consider him a complete failure? So much the worse for the dealers who, at Zola's word, thought they could make a killing with his works.'

Calling Cézanne 'victor with Zola', insinuating that it was the novelist who had pushed the painter's work, was a complete distortion of the truth. All that Zola had written about Cézanne was, in 1867, that he 'respected' his strong and individual talent; in 1880, that the painter was still trying to find himself; and sixteen years later, that Cézanne was an 'abortive genius'. But in spite of this evidence, and in spite of the fact that nobody ever dared suggest that Manet, whom Zola had so frequently praised, owed his fame to Zola, the journalists began to insist that 'Cézanne has Zola to thank for his reputation.'

Now that Zola was dead, Cézanne became the victim of his friendship. After having suffered so much from his friend's lack of understanding, Cézanne was haunted at the end of his life by Zola's ghost, always called forth to attack him.

XXII

CÉZANNE AND HIS ADMIRERS

THE EXHIBITIONS and criticisms drew the attention of the younger generation to the old painter, but, curiously enough, it was at first chiefly writers and poets who entered his solitary life. His friend Philippe Solari introduced his son, Zola's godson, who intended to become a novelist. Together they took long walks and even climbed Sainte-Victoire. In 1896 through another schoolmate, Henri Gasquet, Cézanne met the latter's son, the poet Joachim Gasquet, who became for a while Cézanne's most intimate friend. Joachim Gasquet in turn introduced some of his youthful colleagues, such as Edmond Jaloux, Xavier de Magallon, and Louis Aurenche to Cézanne. They were joined around 1900 by the poet Léo Larguier, and the painter Charles Camoin, who were then doing their military service in Aix.

With these young people Cézanne, so timid and suspicious by nature, came out of his shell, touched by the sincere respect and admiration which they vouchsafed him. One now sometimes saw him on the terraces of the cafés on the Cours Mirabeau, surrounded by these young writers, or met him at the Hôtel de la Croix de Malte where he went to eat with them when he did not invite them to the Rue Boulegon.

'If I was interested in being with you,' Cézanne explained in 1902 to Louis Aurenche, 'it was egotism, since I found myself with new friends in the wastes of this good town of Aix. I was unable to open my heart to anyone here.'

But despite his pleasure at finding himself surrounded by youthful admirers who tried to compensate him for the contempt he had been shown by his own generation, the friendship of these young men caused the old painter almost as much anxiety as real enjoyment. Although he was often happy and cordial with them, Cézanne could not master his occasional fits of rage, his sudden and offensive reactions. He could, for example, make a terrible scene when someone touched him by accident, but at other times he permitted intentional contact. A fear of persecution, which from time to time obscured his judgment, caused him to speak ill of those who were not present. Almost all of those who knew him during the last years of his life, report that Cézanne made unpleasant remarks about all the others. Thus he said cruel and unjustified things about Gasquet, Geffroy, Gauguin, Zola, the young painters he knew, and even the art of Claude Monet. In spite of the fact that Cézanne referred to Zola as 'a phrase-maker', to Monet as a 'black-guard', and to Renoir as a 'pimp', one must not attach undue importance to these epithets, especially since at the same time Cézanne often spoke very warmly and with real emotion of his former comrades. It is true that Pissarro thought Cézanne's friendship had cooled at the time of the Dreyfus affair, but after Pissarro's death in 1903 Cézanne never let an occasion pass to render homage to this artist who was his friend from the beginning, who had never lost confidence in his genius, and whom he considered his teacher.

*   *   *

The young men who met Cézanne in Aix, though they were not always conscious of his genius, were without exception struck by something in the old painter that led them to feel his greatness. Edmond Jaloux, who lunched with Cézanne at Gasquet's, later remembered:

'Suddenly the door opened. Someone came in with an exaggerated air of prudence and discretion. He had the face of a petit bourgeois or a well-to-do peasant, sly and rather formal. He was slightly round-shouldered and had a tanned complexion, a high forehead, long dishevelled white hair, small piercing, and ferret-like eyes, a slightly red Bourbon nose, a short, drooping moustache, and a military goatee. That was Paul Cézanne. . . . I can hear his speech, nasal, slow, meticulous, with something careful and caressing about it. I can hear him discourse on art or nature with subtlety, dignity, and profundity.'

Louis Aurenche, who also met Cézanne in Gasquet's house, had a similar impression:

'Dressed in a dark jacket, with a black silk string-tie tightly knotted, holding his hat in his hand, Cézanne seemed to me extremely unhappy. He remained stiff after the first step, silent, intimidated, almost confused. His globular eyes stared anxiously at one after the other of us. With a completely feminine grace, Madame Gasquet took us up to him and introduced each one of us in turn. At every introduction Cézanne bowed deeply, stammering a few unintelligible words; then a long silence fell. At table, Cézanne answered mainly his neighbour, Madame Gasquet, and sometimes I saw him interrupt himself suddenly and blush. Imagining that a slightly crude word might have shocked one of the guests, he remained silent a long moment. He left us before three o'clock so as not to be late for vespers at Saint-Sauveur.'

As to Gasquet's own relations with the painter, not much is known, in spite of the book of souvenirs which he published many years later. It seems certain, however, that after one or even several quarrels, the two men avoided each other, and that on Cézanne's part a fairly pronounced disdain took the place of a sincere friendship. It may have been that Gasquet was lacking in tact and showed a too evident desire to obtain some of Cézanne's canvases. Though the painter was often happy to present his works to the few friends who admired them, he did not appreciate a too obvious wish to receive them as presents. Thus when the young painter Hermann-Paul quite innocently asked the price of a canvas, he got the unexpected answer: 'I have no reason to make a gift of them to anyone.'

Cézanne ceased to see Gasquet, not only because of his suspicion of the poet's motives, but also, as he explained to a young painter, because: 'I have no business in their salon, I am always saying *Nom de Dieu*!' However, he remained on good terms with several of Gasquet's friends, such as Léo Larguier and Louis Aurenche, who often came to dine at 23 Rue Boulegon. Léo Larguier in particular, who spent two years in Aix, was a regular Sunday visitor. He has told in his recollections of Cézanne that the painter was, contrary to the legend, better and more comfortably dressed than most people in Aix and was, moreover, very cordial. During dinner Cézanne would tell the most innocent stories and, when he had finished, drop his hands and exclaim with a sigh: 'Life is frightening'. He admitted to the young soldier that he considered himself 'a weakling', that he found Larguier 'very well balanced', and that he should come often since he gave him 'moral support'. The same moral support Cézanne found in Charles Camoin, a young painter from Marseilles who, like Larguier, was doing his military service in Aix, and became one of Cézanne's favourite companions. This shy young man would listen with such ardent admiration that Cézanne willingly spoke to him of his art, feeling himself understood by this colleague who was so full of good will. In the letters which he later wrote to Camoin, Cézanne gave him advice on painting in a particularly affectionate and paternal tone.

The same cannot be said of Cézanne's relations with the young painter, Emile Bernard, who came to Aix early in 1904 and stayed there for a month. Bernard, who had published a pamphlet on Cézanne twelve years before, was very well received by the old painter and even invited to come and work in a room below his own studio. While he painted there he used to hear Cézanne walking up and down in his studio and frequently interrupting his work, descending into the garden, then rushing up again.

Together, Cézanne and Bernard visited the museum of Aix or took long walks into the beautiful countryside. They also painted side by side. They had long discussions on art and continued these discussions in a fairly consecutive correspondence. However, Cézanne's letters to Bernard do not always show the same cordiality as those which he wrote Camoin. Indeed, the old painter seems often tired of Bernard's numerous questions on his artistic theories and somewhat resented having to answer them with abstract thoughts. 'The man of letters expresses himself in abstractions,' he wrote Bernard, 'whereas the painter gives concrete shape to his sensations and perceptions by means of drawing and colour.'

It was apropos of one of Bernard's letters that Cézanne wrote to his son: 'I can scarcely read his letter but I think it is right, though the good man absolutely turns his back in practice on what he expounds in his writings. His drawings are merely old-fashioned rubbish which stem from his dreams of art suggested not by the emotion of nature, but by what he has been able to see in museums, and more still by a philosophic mind which comes from the too great knowledge he has of the masters he admires.'

Camoin and Bernard were not the only ones to visit Cézanne in Aix. Other painters, such as Maurice Denis, K. X. Roussel, and Hermann-Paul made the pilgrimage to Aix to render Cézanne the homage of their admiration. They came to see him in his studio or accompanied him to the motif, listening to his theories on art. 'What we sought in his work and his words,' Maurice Denis later admitted, 'was that which seemed opposed to impressionist realism, and the confirmation of our own ideas, those which were *dans l'air*. Cézanne was a thinker, but he did not always think the same thing every day. All those who approached him made him say what they wanted to hear. They interpreted his thought.'

However, even those who approached Cézanne without preconceived ideas were astonished by the ease with which he seemed to contradict himself. A young artist, Francis Jourdain, heard him say: 'Impressionism, it's no longer necessary. It is nonsense!' and then promptly pay a moving tribute to Pissarro, whom he called the true master, the incontestable leader of the impressionists. After remarking, before his large canvas of 'Baigneuses', done without models, that 'painting is in here' and tapping his forehead, Cézanne surprised his young friend by insisting that his purpose had always been to convey the real distance between the eye and the object, and that true progress could only be based on nature. Their admiration notwithstanding, Cézanne's visitors sometimes had to admit that consistency was not the greatest virtue of his remarks.

*   *   *

Cézanne's position in Aix had remained somewhat ambiguous, and if he desired so ardently to be accepted at the official Salon or to be decorated with the red ribbon of the Legion of Honour, it was doubtless to prove to his compatriots that his art was more than the pastime of an old maniac. But neither of these dreams were to be fulfilled; on the contrary, fate seemed determined to deny even the least satisfaction to his pride. When, in 1905, Monet, who was already world-famous, declared his admiration for Cézanne in an interview, saying that he considered him one of the great painters of the epoch, his words were published with a footnote specifically for that remark: 'The review *L'Art et les Artistes* is open to all sincere opinions, it is free of any bias, and it is not to be held responsible for the aesthetic judgments of its contributors.' It is not surprising, therefore, after innumerable such experiences, after the protests unleashed by the Caillebotte bequest, after the calumnies at the time of the Zola sale, after so many daily vexations, that Cézanne finally believed that there was some plot against him and became suspicious even of good news. Thus the announcement that one of his paintings had been hung in the Berlin National Gallery had the unfortunate consequence of making him fear that such a gesture by the Germans might forever close to him the doors of the French museums. However, in 1906, when the German collector, Karl Ernst Osthaus, founder of the Folkwang Museum, came to see him in Aix, he was very well received at the Rue Boulegon. Osthaus wrote of his visit:

'When the door was opened we entered an apartment that in no way betrayed the exceptional qualities of its inhabitant. There were no pictures anywhere on the walls. Cézanne received us without formality. Standing, we told him that we had been glad to take the opportunity of a trip south to bring him the homage of our respect, that our admiration for his art dated from far back, and that we hoped very much to buy one of his works.

'Cézanne put us several questions about our collection. The names represented gained us his esteem. He became communicative and began to expound his thoughts on painting.

'He explained his ideas in front of several canvases and sketches which he fetched from all over the house. They showed masses of brush, rocks, and mountains all intermingled [Pl. 78]. The principal thing in a painting, he said, was to find the distance. It was there that one recognized the talent of a painter.

'And saying this, his fingers followed the limits of the various planes on his canvases. He showed exactly how far he had succeeded in suggesting the depth and where the solution had not yet been found; here the colour had remained colour without becoming the expression of distance.

'Then he spoke to us of painting in general. Was it courtesy towards his German interlocutors which caused him to place Holbein at the head of the list of all the masters? In any case, he did so with such emphasis that it was not permissible to question his convictions.

' "But one cannot equal Holbein," he exclaimed, "that is why I took Poussin as an example!"

'Of the moderns, Cézanne spoke warmly of Courbet. He admired Courbet's unlimited talent which mastered all difficulties. "Great as Michelangelo," he said, but with this restriction: "He lacks the elevation!"

'He only mentioned van Gogh, Gauguin, and the neo-impressionists. "They make things a little too easy for themselves," he said. Finally, he delivered an enthusiastic eulogy of his comrades of former years. In the pose of a great orator, raising his finger in the air, he exclaimed: "Monet and Pissarro, the two great masters, the only ones!"

'Before saying good-bye to us, Cézanne urged us to come to see him after lunch in his studio in the country, where he was working on a painting. When we arrived, he was awaiting us. He had us enter the simple two-storey house which contains, in addition to a few bare rooms, only the large studio which is also bare. On his easel was a still life he had just begun and the chief work of his old age, the 'Baigneuses'. The tall shafts of the trees were already bending, forming an arch under which the bathing scene was unfolding [Pl. 87]. We spoke of the painting of nudes. Cézanne then complained of the narrow provincial attitude which prevented him from having a female model. "An old invalid poses for all these women," he explained.'

At the end of this visit, the collector purchased two canvases, one of them a landscape from Bibémus quarry [Pl. 78], doubtless the painting of brush and rocks Cézanne had shown him at the Rue Boulegon. The painter even promised to send some works to Germany, a promise which he was not able to keep.

Only on his return to Paris, where Herr Osthaus spoke of the courteous reception given him by Cézanne, did he learn that the painter was considered, even by some of his admirers, as perfectly impossible to approach. According to rumour it was better to avoid him if one ever ran into him.

XXIII

CÉZANNE'S THEORIES ABOUT ART

THE YOUNG PAINTERS who sought Cézanne's advice in Aix were sure of a cordial reception. He was always ready to speak of his work and would ask whether the others had made the same observations on nature. 'I think the young painters are much more intelligent than the others,' he wrote to his son. 'The old ones see in me only a dangerous rival.'

Realizing that it was too late for him to form pupils, Cézanne decided to leave to posterity what might be called a system of painting. Despite his frequently expressed contempt for theories, he now did not hesitate to formulate some of his own, glad to be sought after and to have his advice esteemed. 'I owe you the truth about painting,' he wrote, a year before his death, to Emile Bernard, 'and I shall tell it to you.' And to Charles Camoin he promised: 'I shall speak to you about painting better than anyone else.'

* * *

If Cézanne had recognized his own words and gestures in Claude Lantier, as well as his difficulty in realizing his sensations, Lantier did not express Cézanne's ideas. What Cézanne thought about art, the theories which he communicated to his young painter-friends, he had found expressed by Balzac in the short novel *Le Chef-d'œuvre inconnu* and he had not hesitated to identify himself with its chief character, the painter Frenhofer. The spiritual similarity between Cézanne and Frenhofer is such that one cannot determine whether Cézanne found in Frenhofer an echo of his own ideas or whether he gathered these ideas from Balzac's character.

For example, Frenhofer speaks of this 'mass of ignorant people who fancy they can draw correctly because they carefully make a sharp line'. He then explains his own method: 'I have not coldly outlined my figure and emphasized each minor anatomical detail, for the human body is not limited by lines. . . . Nature comprises a series of curves which interlace. Strictly speaking, drawing does not exist. . . . line is the means by which man takes account of the effect of light on objects; but there is no line in nature, where everything is full: it is in modelling that one draws, that is to say, one detaches things from their environment—the daylight alone gives the body its appearance! . . . Perhaps it would be better not to draw a single line, but rather to begin a figure in the middle, starting with the protuberances which receive the most light and proceeding thence to the darker parts. Is that not the method of the sun, the divine painter of the universe?'

Cézanne, like Frenhofer and all the impressionists for that matter, denied the existence of line in nature. 'Pure drawing is an abstraction', he said. 'Drawing and colour are not separate and distinct, as everything in nature has colour.' And Cézanne remarked to Emile Bernard: 'While one paints, one draws; the more the colour harmonizes, the more precise becomes the drawing. When the colour is rich, the form is at its height. The contrasts and relations of tone comprise the secret of drawing and form' for 'the form and contour of objects are conveyed to us through the opposition and contrast resulting from their individual colours.'

Frenhofer's theory that one should attack a figure by starting with the most illuminated protuberances is found again in the advice which Cézanne gave Emile Bernard, to whom he wrote: 'In an orange, an apple, a ball, a head, there is a culminating point and this point is always—despite the tremendous effect of light and shade and sensation of colour—the closest to our eye. The edges of objects recede to a centre placed on our horizon.'

For a better grasp of his model, Cézanne advised Bernard to 'see in nature the cylinder, the sphere, the cone, putting everything in proper perspective, so that each side of an object or a plane is directed toward a central point. Lines parallel to the horizon give breadth, that is, a section of nature. . . . Lines perpendicular to this horizon give depth. But nature, for us men, is more depth than surface, whence the necessity of introducing in our vibrations of light—represented by reds and yellows—a sufficient quantity of blue to give the feeling of air.'

This theory, which preoccupied Cézanne during his last years, is the outcome of his study of planes and volume. In Cézanne's work, however, one finds neither cylinders, cones, nor parallel and perpendicular lines, the line never having existed for Cézanne except as a meeting place for two planes of different colour. One might thus be permitted to see in this theory an attempt to express his consciousness of structure beneath the coloured surface presented by nature. It was this awareness of form that detached Cézanne from his impressionist friends. But nowhere in his canvases did Cézanne pursue this abstract concept at the expense of his direct sensations. He always found his forms in nature and never in geometry.

It was chiefly Emile Bernard who, by his numerous questions and long discussions, pushed Cézanne to formulate theories. As he wrote his son: 'With Bernard one can develop theories indefinitely, for he has the temperament of a logician.' But Cézanne did not much like this temperament which lead to interminable controversies, sometimes interrupted by sudden rages of the old painter. When Bernard asked too many questions, Cézanne, instead of answering, would say: 'I am not in the habit of reasoning so much.' And when the young man continued his queries in his letters, Cézanne complained that he spoke of so many different things all related to art that he could not 'follow his reasoning'.

'I am sorry not to have him in my power,' Cézanne wrote about Bernard in 1906 to his son, 'so as to infuse into him the idea which is so healthy, so comforting, and the only correct one of the development of art through contact with nature.'

This was the best piece of advice he thought himself capable of giving to young painters, besides urging them not to neglect the old masters. 'Go and study Veronese and his technique in the Louvre,' he told Louis Le Bail, while speaking of the vibration of colour. He also liked to hold forth about Chardin, the brothers Le Nain, Poussin, Rubens, and particularly Delacroix, in whose honour he dreamed of painting an 'Apotheosis' uniting Pissarro, Monet, Chocquet, and himself. Ultimately, he considered himself closest to the French school of the eighteenth century, yet at the same time he feared that the young painters might pursue their study of the old masters to the detriment of the observation of nature, and this danger he constantly exhorted them to avoid. 'Since you are now in Paris,' he wrote to Camoin, 'and the masters of the Louvre are attracting you, make, if you feel like it, some studies after the great decorative masters Veronese and Rubens, but just as you would do after nature—a thing I was only able to do incompletely myself. But you do well to study above all from nature.'

*　　*　　*

Cézanne's advice would have been incomplete if he had not shown his method of work, brush in hand, avoiding all the dangerous abstractions which he so disliked. He could say, for instance, to Louis Le Bail as they were starting off together to the motif: 'We are going to put our absurd theories into practice.' He cared little for theory if it was not justified in the work. And he insisted: 'I do not want to be right in theory but in nature.' For, as he said in a letter to Emile Bernard, theories 'are always easy; it is only the proof of what one thinks that presents serious obstacles'. Thus, while painting a portrait, Cézanne once exclaimed: 'If I make a success of this fellow, the theory will have been right!' However, Cézanne would not have hesitated to reject any theory if in its realization he did not find complete satisfaction. 'All things, particularly in art,' Cézanne wrote to Camoin, 'are theory developed and applied in contact with nature.' And another time he told him: 'I have nothing to hide in art. Primary force alone, *id est* temperament, can bring a person to the end he must attain.'

One rainy day, Louis Le Bail watched Cézanne compose a still life: a napkin, a glass containing a little red wine, and peaches. 'The cloth was very slightly draped upon the table, with innate taste,' he later remembered. 'Then Cézanne arranged the fruits, contrasting the tones one against the other, making the complementaries vibrate, the greens against the reds, the yellows against the blues, tipping, turning, balancing the fruits as he wanted them to be, using coins of one or two sous for the purpose. He brought to this task the greatest care and many precautions; one guessed that it was a feast for the eye to him.'

When he had finished, Cézanne explained to his young colleague: 'The main thing is the modelling; one shouldn't even say modelling, but modulating.'

Questioned by a young artist on what, in his opinion, was the most necessary study for a beginner, he replied without hesitation: 'Copy your stovepipe.' And he gave his reasons for attaching the greatest importance to a profound knowledge of the play of light on a form and the means of expressing this form by reproducing that play: the most luminous point, the gradation of light, half-tone, shadow, reflection.

To Renoir, Cézanne once remarked that good painting required that 'the angle of the shadow be equal to the angle of light'. And Emile Bernard noted how Cézanne painted a still life: 'He started with the shadow and with a brush-stroke, then covered it with another, larger one, then a third, until all the spots of tones, forming a kind of screen, modelled the object in colour.' To give him an idea of his approach, Cézanne advised Bernard 'to begin lightly and with almost neutral tones. Then one must proceed by steadily climbing the scale and tightening the chromatics.' In order to accomplish this, Cézanne, instead of mixing a lot of colours, had ready on his palette an entire scale of tone gradations.

Cézanne's palette, according to Bernard and memos found in the painter's notebooks, consisted of the following:

YELLOW:	brilliant yellow	GREEN:	Veronese green
	Naples yellow		viridian
	chrome yellow		green earth
	yellow ochre	BLUE:	cobalt blue
RED:	raw Sienna		ultramarine
	vermilion		Prussian blue
	red ochre		

RED: burnt Sienna   peach black
     madder lake
     carmine lake
     burnt lake

From about 1890 on, watercolour played an important role in Cézanne's work. Since this medium does not permit any correction of brushstrokes, Cézanne, who for so long had been unwilling to part with a canvas until he had gone over it time and again, must have acquired a complete confidence in the spontaneous reaction of his sensibility before taking up watercolours. In general he did not use this medium to add colour to his drawings but as a self-sufficient means of expression, in which all lines and forms spring from colour alone. Never before had the technique of watercolour been used with such purity or been so reduced to its essence.

Cézanne, who filled notebook after notebook with sketches, sometimes hasty, sometimes developed, was not, strictly speaking, a draughtsman; that is to say, drawing does not seem to have been an end in itself to him. When he took up his pencil it was, so to speak, for his personal use, to retain forms and movements, to fix an idea, to exercise his eye. He hardly ever did preliminary sketches, since his canvases are not the products of a long, abstract reflection but the result of direct observation which did not allow such preparations. That which meant most to Cézanne was precisely the colour which is lacking in drawings.

The draughtsman Cézanne, who, in studies of objects which had little colour (sculpture, skulls, etc.) endeavoured to render the form by a range from pure white to black, proceeded in a completely different fashion in the presence of nature: he hardly ever tried to suggest depth, a task which devolves on colour; he was satisfied with indicating the contours, setting off all their purity. The bare trees become living arabesques, the roofs of L'Estaque form nothing more than a mosaic of geometric figures. But even when Cézanne consciously renounced colour, he generally could not help substituting patches and strokes of the pencil for it, indicating the different values. Some of his drawings look as though they had been made one day when the painter had forgotten his box of colours. While in his watercolours he was satisfied with a very light pencil sketch without much detail (the brush would later fix with precision the joint of a branch or the roundness of a trunk), these drawings are all composed of little dashes in different directions, each one seemingly representing a brushstroke. The colour seems to be 'invented' by the pencil (Pl. 74).

However, drawings without colour are found less and less in the work of Cézanne's old age, precisely because colour became increasingly the dominant element in his art. In the watercolours or oils the drawing is no longer even the scaffolding, the frame for the colour; it is hardly more than an indication of masses. It has no longer the right to encroach upon the domain of colour; the strokes of the pencil have no plastic value, so that the colour may freely weave that astonishing and dense texture presented by the last works of Cézanne (Pl. 75).

Watercolour was for Cézanne a means which permitted him quickly to retain coloured impressions or to enliven his studies, still lifes as well as studies for portraits, landscapes, and groups of bathers. Sometimes he was satisfied to add colour to a sketch, dashes of violet blue doubling contours, a few spots indicating the nature of the object (Pl. 74). It was these studies which inspired Rilke to write: 'They are very beautiful; they reveal as much assurance as the paintings and are as light as the others are massive. Landscapes, brief pencil sketches upon which, here and there, as though to emphasize or to confirm, falls a trace of colour, casually; a succession of dashes, admirably arranged with a sureness of touch, like the echo of a melody.'

Besides these, as it were, high-lighted drawings, Cézanne did watercolours the technique of which is reminiscent of his oil paintings. Proceeding only by very light spots, he covered the white sheet with several successive layers. To prevent the wet spots running into each other, this procedure demands that each one dry completely before the next one is applied. It is thus a very slow method, which Cézanne used, however, without sacrificing the spontaneous charm of the medium, endowing his watercolours with a luminous beauty never before attained. For unlike oils, the various layers of watercolour as used by Cézanne remain transparent; they do not imprison forms or define them but rather indicate their shapes in such a loose way that each patch seems to move when looked at. The richness of tones and nuances of these works is equalled only by the simplicity with which Cézanne uses this complicated procedure to fix the roundness of a few apples on a white plate or to give a dreamlike atmosphere to a scene of bathers.

The influence of oils on Cézanne's watercolours corresponds to a reciprocal influence of his watercolour technique on his oil painting. He placed large strokes without hesitation, giving to the canvas itself, which often appears, the role of the white paper, that is to say, as a bond between the scattered touches. However, in his very last years, Cézanne made use of a technique which one might call 'impasto' if this term were not reminiscent of his early works or of his Auvers period, for this new impasto is one of the first layer. Cézanne worked with a full brush on canvases often hardly prepared and which rapidly absorbed the oil of the pigment, thus robbing the colour of its brilliance. All preliminary drawing seems to have disappeared and the canvas is covered with a dense tissue of spots which, from close to, offer the eye nothing but a mosaic of tones (Pl. 77).

In his last years, Cézanne had found that sureness which permitted him to work more or less spontaneously. When, for example, he began a new canvas, he drew with a brushful of ultramarine diluted with a lot of turpentine, sketching with vigour, without hesitation. His paintings are in general only covered with a single layer of pigment, and the canvas often shows through. It was apropos of these bare spots that Cézanne wrote to Emile Bernard in 1905: 'Now, being old, nearly seventy years, the sensations of colour, which give light, are the reason for the abstractions which prevent me from either covering my canvas or continuing the delimitation of objects when their points of contact are fine and delicate; from which it results that my image or picture is incomplete. . . .'

'It is very painful to have to register,' Cézanne told Emile Bernard, 'that the improvement which manifests itself in the understanding of nature, as regards the form of the painting and the development of the means of expression, should be accompanied by old age and a weakening of the body.'

XXIV

THE LAST YEARS

1900 – 1906

DURING the last years of his life, Cézanne seldom left the Midi. 'When I was in Aix,' he had written to Solari from Talloires, near Annecy, in the summer of 1896, 'it seemed to me that I should be better elsewhere; now that I am here I miss Aix. Life for me is beginning to be of a sepulchural monotony. . . . I paint to divert myself; it is not very amusing, but the lake is very nice with the big mountains all round. . . . It is not worth our country, though—without exaggeration—it is fine. But when one was born down there, it is no use, nothing else seems to mean anything.'

In Aix, Cézanne had taken the habit of hiring a carriage to drive him to the motifs, which were all situated in the surroundings of the city, preferably in spots far from the roads and on heights, so that the painter could see in time anyone who came to interrupt his work. Yet Cézanne could not always paint where he wished, as he sometimes did not receive permission to work on private proper-ties, either because of his reputation of being a little touched, or because he was too timid to insist.

Up to 1899, Cézanne often went to the picturesque Bibémus quarry, where the orange-coloured rocks contrasted their strange forms with the bushes and the pines, the whole dominated from afar by Sainte-Victoire. Not far from the quarry, Cézanne also worked in the forest which covered the rough hillside rising behind Château Noir. He did some watercolours there, and set up his easel in the road which leads to the buildings themselves; here he caught the aspect of the trees, never trimmed, through which appeared the light walls, with gothic windows, of the two houses.

'The world does not understand me,' he sometimes said to his driver, with whom he liked to chat when, on the hills, he got out and walked. 'And I do not understand the world,' he continued. 'That is why I have withdrawn from it.' And it would frequently happen that, deep in his thoughts, Cézanne forgot to climb back into the carriage when they had reached the top of the hill; medi-tating or talking to the driver, he reached their destination on foot.

When in a mood for company, Cézanne liked to go for walks

with his old friend, Philippe Solari, talking all the time and explaining to him his ideas on art and on nature. At other times he would invite him to dinner at the Rue Boulegon and their heated discussion on art would sometimes stop the passers-by in the street. 'The poor man,' wrote Cézanne to Solari's son, speaking of his father, 'I have saturated him with theories on painting. He must have a good constitution to have withstood it.'

For some time already Cézanne had avoided L'Estaque, and he gave his reasons in a letter to his god-daughter, Paule Conil, who was spending her vacation near there: 'I remember perfectly the once so picturesque coast of L'Estaque. Unfortunately, what is called progress is nothing but the invasion of bipeds who will not rest until they have transformed everything into hideous quais with gas lamps, and—what is even worse—electric lights. What times we live in!'

In November 1901, Cézanne bought some land on the Chemin des Lauves north of Aix and commanding a magnificent view of the town, the belfry of its cathedral, and the range of mountains on the horizon. Here he had a house built (Pl. 82), according to his instructions, consisting of several small rooms and a large studio with tall windows looking south on the city and another, enormous one, with a north light.

From 1902 on, Cézanne worked almost exclusively in this studio. He arose very early and arrived there at six every morning. He would stay until half past ten, when he went down to the Rue Boulegon to eat, unless he preferred to have his lunch brought up to Les Lauves. In this studio, surrounded by a garden in which he had his gardener, Vallier, pose for him, Cézanne painted, besides the 'Baigneuses' canvases, a great many still lifes of fruits, flowers, skulls, or plaster statuettes. Working very slowly, a single canvas could take him several months, as revealed by some letters to Vollard about a painting of a bunch of roses. The artist first wrote on 23 January 1902: 'I continue working at the bouquet of flowers which will doubtless take me until about the 15th or 20th of February.' But early in April, Cézanne wrote again to announce:

'I find myself obliged to postpone sending you the picture of your roses to a later date. Although I should have greatly liked to send something to the Salon of 1902, I am putting off the execution of this plan again this year. I am not satisfied with the result I have obtained. On the other hand, I shall not give up this study which will have caused me to make, as I like to believe, not unproductive efforts.'

A year later, however, in January 1903, the painter mentioned in a letter to Vollard: 'I have had to drop your flowers, with which I am not very satisfied.'

One can understand how, in such conditions, Cézanne could only do his still lifes from artificial flowers.

While Cézanne spent his mornings painting in his studio, he often returned after lunch to work 'on the motif' near-by (Pls. 79, 80). He would then climb farther up the hill until he reached the height of Les Lauves, whence he could see the wooded valleys in front of Sainte-Victoire, whose back slopes away gently from its steep and cliff-like front. Many were the watercolours and canvases on which Cézanne depicted this new aspect of the mountain (Pl. 84).

In age, Cézanne could not, of course, maintain as rigorous a routine, but his work was not interrupted. When, in 1906, the great heat of the summer months did not permit him to work on motifs where he would be too exposed to the sun, the painter would have himself driven to the banks of the Arc, the little river that had been the scene of so many happy bathing and fishing parties in his youth. Near the picturesque bridge of Les Trois-Sautets, not far from the road to Palette, he found some shade and coolness; he set up his easel opposite a big mill, behind which the grey wall of Sainte-Victoire could be seen.

In these later years Cézanne also suffered from poor health. His diabetes had been aggravated by excessive nervous strain from overwork, and it made rapid progress during the summer of 1906. Cézanne felt this, and in almost all his letters to his son he complained about his health. 'Being in pain exasperates me so much,' he wrote, 'that I cannot get over it and it forces me to live a retired life; that is what is best for me.' Illness and old age accentuated the morbid traits in his character, and what was once only sensitivity and suspicion turned sometimes into a real persecution mania. More than ever before he feared getting into the clutches of others, and especially those of priests and art dealers.

In spite of his frequent moods of discouragement, Cézanne knew his own value, and although in general his opinion was that 'the feeling of one's own strength makes one modest,' he did not hesitate, when the occasion arose, to express himself openly. 'There is only one living painter—myself!' he declared, and another time he interrupted a political argument by saying, 'There are two thousand politicians in every legislature but there is a Cézanne only every two centuries.' This awareness of his own superiority, however, did not prevent Cézanne from saying often that he was still far removed from the goal which as an artist he dreamed of attaining. 'I have a lot of work to do,' he wrote to Louis Aurenche. 'It is what happens to everyone who is someone.'

When the painter Louis Le Bail asked him which were his favourite paintings, Cézanne replied: 'Mine, if I had managed to achieve what I am still seeking.' And in 1903 Cézanne informed

Vollard: 'I am working obstinately; I am beginning to see the promised land. Shall I be like the great leader of the Hebrews or shall I be able to enter it? . . . I have made some progress. Why so late and with such difficulty? Is art indeed a priesthood which demands the pure in heart, completely dedicated to it?' To a young friend he explained: 'My painting is getting along so-so. I sometimes have magnificent bursts of enthusiasm and even more often painful disappointments. That is life.'

Cézanne's temperament led him always to waver between the extremes. Kind and generous, even extravagant, he discharged his driver in the autumn of 1906 when the latter demanded higher wages. From then on he went on foot to the outskirts of the town, carrying his watercolour equipment on his back. But in general he seemed less conscious of the value of money. He was often sent unfortunates who could be sure that they would not leave his house without generous alms. And he gave not only because he did not know how to refuse but also for the pleasure of giving, to see the joy of the country children to whom he would throw a few sous when they ran after his carriage. It even seems that his sister, who, with Madame Brémond, looked after his household, was careful not to let him go into town with anything but a very small sum of money in his pocket, although, for that matter, he did not often go.

*   *   *

Toward the end of May 1906, a bust of Zola by Philippe Solari, left unfinished at the sculptor's death, was unveiled at the Bibliothèque Méjanes in Aix, in the presence of a large crowd. Among those attending the ceremonies were noted, in the reserved section, near Madame Zola, the members of the Municipal Council; the director of the Aix Academy; the director of the library; the senator Louis Leydet, a former schoolmate of the painter; Emile Solari, son of the sculptor; and Paul Cézanne.

It was the mayor of the town, M. Cabassol, son of Louis-Auguste Cézanne's partner in the bank Cézanne & Cabassol, who made the first speech, and pointed out the considerable role played by the town of Aix in the novels of the master. Paul Cézanne, visibly moved, heard the mayor evoke the youth of Zola, heard him speak about the 'Jas de Bouffan', which Zola had described in L'Œuvre as 'the mosque-like whiteness, in the centre of the vast grounds'. Cézanne listened as the mayor told how in 1858 Zola had parted from Cézanne ('since become the great modern painter, as we know,' in the words of the orator), and, hearing him speak of the three inseparables, his youth arose before his eyes.

Cézanne's emotion became even more profound when the mayor

was followed by their old friend, Numa Coste, who paid tribute to the memory of the departed and described the days of their youth together:

'We were then at the dawn of life, filled with vast hopes, desirous of rising above the social swamps in which impotent jealousies, spurious reputations, and unhealthy ambitions lie stagnant. We dreamed of the conquest of Paris, the possession of that intellectual home of the world, and outdoors, in the midst of arid and lonely spaces, by the shaded torrents or at the summit of marmorean escarpments, we forged the armour for this gigantic struggle. . . . When Zola had preceded the group to Paris, he sent his first literary efforts to his old friend, Paul Cézanne, at the same time letting all of us share his hopes. We read these letters amidst the hills, in the shade of the evergreen oaks, as one reads the communiques of a campaign that is beginning.'

The painter, always so easily moved, could not resist this flood of memories. Tears came to relieve the nostalgia which had taken possession of him, and the other guests saw that the old man was crying, no longer able to hide his emotion.

Numa Coste, continuing his address, now spoke of the later Zola. 'As he often said,' Coste remembered, 'one thinks one has revolutionized the world, and then one finds out, at the end of the road, that one has not revolutionized anything at all. . . . Men remain the ephemeral creatures they have been since they appeared on earth.'

But what does it matter whether the world has been revolutionized or not, as long as one has worked with all one's might to attain an end, as long as one has succeeded in adding a new link to the chain of the past? Had not Cézanne, like Zola, lived a life completely dedicated to work, so absorbed by the artistic effort that even the oldest friendship, the most profound affection of his life, had had to be thrown aside?

Through the tears that veiled his eyes, Cézanne saw Madame Zola embrace Numa Coste in grateful emotion when he had finished his speech by extolling the 'work which consoles and makes one forget the sorrows'.

* * *

Work consoles and makes one forget the sorrows. Cézanne had expressed the same thought when he wrote to Gustave Caillebotte on the death of his mother, begging him to devote his time and his energies to painting 'as being the surest way of distracting our sadness'.

Again and again Cézanne spoke of this constant preoccupation in his last letters to his son in Paris. They permit one to follow the life of the painter almost day by day from the end of July 1906 to his death on 22 October of that same year. Although his failing health put serious obstacles in the way of work, Cézanne continued indefatigably his 'research'.

In the month of August, suffering greatly of the heat, Cézanne wrote:

'It oppresses my brain considerably and prevents me from thinking. I get up early in the morning and hardly live my normal life except between five and eight o'clock. At that time the heat becomes stupefying and exerts such a cerebral depression that I cannot even think about painting. . . . I regret my advanced age, in view of my colour sensations. . . . It is unfortunate not to be able to produce many examples of my ideas and sensations; long live the Goncourts, Pissarro, and all those who have the love of colour, representative of light and air.'

A little later he excused himself:

'If I forget to write to you it is because I am losing my sense of time to a degree. . . . My nervous system must be very much enfeebled, I live somewhat as in a void. Painting is what means most to me. I am very annoyed at the cheek with which my compatriots seek to compare themselves with me as an artist and try to lay their hands on my studies. You should see the messes they make. . . . I am going up to the studio; I got up late, after five o'clock. I am still working with pleasure, but sometimes the light is so horrible that nature seems ugly to me.'

In still another letter he explained:

'. . . As a painter I am becoming more lucid in front of nature, but the realization of my intentions is always very painful. I cannot attain to the intensity which is revealed to my senses. I have not the magnificent richness of colouring which animates nature. Here, on the banks of the river, the motifs are plentiful, and the same subject, seen from a different angle, provides a subject for study of such powerful and varied interest that I believe I could occupy myself with it for months, without moving, by leaning once a little more to the right, once a little more to the left.'

As a result of fatigue and the heat, Cézanne had to give up going to his studio on the Chemin des Lauves, and only took a short walk in the morning; the carriage came in the afternoon to drive him to the banks of the Arc. Toward the end of September the heat passed. 'The weather is magnificent, the country superb,' he exclaimed, but soon his fears took possession of him again, and he continued: 'As for me, I must remain alone. The meanness of people is such that I should never be able to get away from it—it is theft, complacency, infatuation, violation, the seizing of your work. And yet nature is beautiful. I still see Vallier, but I am so slow at realizing my ideas that it makes me very sad.'

A little later he wrote again: 'Sketches, paintings, if I were to do any, would be merely constructions after nature, based on methods, sensations, and developments suggested by the model.'

In the last letter to his son, on 15 October, he said:

'In order to give you news as satisfactory as you desire, I would have to be twenty years younger. I repeat, I eat well, and a little moral satisfaction—but only work can give me that—would mean a lot to me. All my compatriots are hogs compared with me.'

This letter also contains a phrase which he used again and again: 'I continue to work with difficulty but in spite of that something is achieved.' A few weeks earlier, Cézanne had written to Emile Bernard: 'I am old and ill, and I have sworn to die painting rather than to waste away vilely in the manner which threatens old men who allow themselves to be dominated by passions that coarsen their senses.'

Life, which had brought Cézanne so many disappointments, now gave him a first and last satisfaction: a death as he had desired it. On Monday, 15 October, a storm overtook him while he was working on a landscape near his studio and he remained exposed to the rain for several hours. He had to be brought back to the Rue Boulegon on a laundry cart and it took two men to carry him to his bed. At dawn the following day he arose and went into his garden to work on a portrait of his gardener, Vallier. He came home in a state of collapse; yet from his bed he still wrote a line to his colour merchant, on Wednesday, the 17th:

'It is now eight days since I asked you to send me ten burnt lakes and I have had no reply. What is the matter?

'A reply, and a quick one, I beg of you.

'Accept, Monsieur . . .

'Paul Cézanne.'

On Saturday the painter's sister, Marie, wrote anxiously to her nephew: 'You know your father, it is a long story. . . .' And she insisted: 'I repeat that I find your presence here necessary.' Two days later, on 22 October, Madame Brémond telegraphed to wife and son: 'Both come immediately, father very ill.' They were too late.

APPENDICES

BIOGRAPHICAL OUTLINE

1839, 19 Jan., birth of Paul Cézanne, 28 Rue de l'Opéra, Aix-en-Provence. 22 Feb., baptism at the church of Sainte-Madeleine.

1841, 4 July, birth of Marie Cézanne, 55 Cours Mirabeau, Aix.

1844, 29 Jan., marriage of Louis-Auguste Cézanne and Anne-Elisabeth Aubert in Aix.

*c.*1844–9, Paul Cézanne at Primary School, Rue des Epinaux in Aix.

1848, 1 June, establishment of the Bank Cézanne & Cabassol in Aix. Louis-Auguste Cézanne stands unsuccessfully for the municipal council under the short-lived Second Republic.

*c.*1849–52, Paul Cézanne at the Ecole Saint-Joseph in Aix.

1852–8, Cézanne at the Collège Bourbon in Aix; friendship with Emile Zola and Baptistin Baille.

1854, 30 June, birth of Rose Cézanne, 14 Rue Matheron, Aix.

1858, Feb., Zola leaves Aix for Paris but returns there for his summer vacation. In July Cézanne fails at the baccalaureate; passes the examination on 12 Nov. From Nov. 1858 to Aug. 1859 Cézanne works at the Drawing Academy in Aix.

1859, Cézanne studies law at the University in Aix. His father acquires the 'Jas de Bouffan'. Zola again spends his holidays in Aix. From Nov. 1859 to Aug. 1860 Cézanne once more works at the Drawing Academy; he dreams of becoming a painter. At about this time he is called for military service but his father buys him a substitute.

1860, Cézanne continues his law studies more and more reluctantly. His father agrees to his departure for Paris, where Zola impatiently awaits Cézanne, but the latter's teacher at the Drawing Academy advises against the trip. From Nov. 1860 to the spring of 1861 Cézanne again works at the Drawing Academy.

1861, abandons his law studies. From Apr. to the autumn, first sojourn in Paris, Rue Coquillière, later Rue des Feuillantines. Visits the Salon. Meets Pissarro at the Atelier Suisse. Paints portrait of Zola. Returns discouraged to Aix in Sept.; enters his father's bank. From Nov. 1861 to Aug. 1862, works once more at the Drawing Academy.

1862, leaves his father's bank. Takes up painting again. Friendship with Numa Coste. Returns to Paris in Nov. Apparently fails in examinations for the Ecole des Beaux-Arts.

1863, in Paris probably during the entire year. Exhibits at the Salon des Refusés; visits the exhibition with Zola. Works at the Atelier Suisse where he meets Guillemet, Oller, and Guillaumin.

1864, rejected at the Salon. Copies painting by Delacroix. Returns to Aix in the summer.

1865, spends most of the year in Paris, 22 Rue Beautreillis. Rejected at the Salon. Works at the Atelier Suisse. Returns to Aix toward the end of autumn; friendship with Valabrègue, Marion, and the German musician Morstatt. Zola publishes *La Confession de Claude*, dedicated to Cézanne and Baille.

1866, Guillemet spends Jan. in Aix. Cézanne returns to Paris in Feb., lives again Rue Beautreillis. Is complimented by Manet on his still lifes. Rejected at the Salon despite intervention of Daubigny; writes a letter of protest to the Director of Fine Arts. Zola publishes Salon reviews in *L'Evénement*; has to suspend series of articles later issued as pamphlet dedicated to Cézanne. In July with Zola, Valabrègue, Baille, Solari, etc., at Bennecourt. Plans large paintings. From Aug. to Dec. in Aix. Guillemet spends Oct. and Nov. in Aix, obtains higher allowance for Paul from his father. Cézanne begins to show interest in working out of doors.

1867, Jan. to June in Paris, Rue Beautreillis. Rejected at the Salon. Zola defends Cézanne in the press. Spends summer in Aix. A painting exhibited in Marseilles has to be withdrawn so as not to be torn to pieces by the crowd. Returns to Paris in the autumn.

1868, rejected at the Salon. From May to Dec. in Aix, works at the 'Jas de Bouffan'. Friendship with Alexis. Often paints in company of Marion.

1869, spends most of the year, if not all, in Paris. Rejected at the Salon. At about this time meets Hortense Fiquet, born 1850. Zola begins work on the *Rougon-Macquart* series.

1870, 31 May, is witness at Zola's wedding in Paris; lives 53 Rue Notre-Dame-des-Champs. 18 July, declaration of the Franco-Prussian war. Works in Aix, later in L'Estaque, where he lives with Hortense Fiquet. They are joined for a while by Zola. Cézanne avoids the call-up. 4 Sept., proclamation of the Third Republic. Cézanne's father retires from the bank, is nominated member of the municipal council of Aix. Cézanne himself is elected on 18 Nov. member of the commission for the Drawing Academy but does not participate in the work of this commission which is dissolved on 19 Apr. 1871.

1871, Armistice signed 28 Jan. Paris *Commune* from 18 March to 28 May. Cézanne leaves L'Estaque in Mar., apparently returns to Aix. Is back in Paris in the autumn, impatiently awaited by Zola. Lives 5 Rue de Chevreuse, the same house as Solari. Moves in Dec. to Rue de Jussieu, opposite the Halle aux Vins, where Emperaire stays shortly with him.

1872, 4 Jan., Hortense Fiquet gives birth to a son recognized by his father and christened Paul Cézanne. All three move to Pontoise, where Cézanne works at Pissarro's side and sees Guillaumin frequently. He lives at the Hôtel du Grand Cerf at Saint-Ouen-l'Aumône, across the river at Pontoise. Copies a landscape by Pissarro.

1873, early in the year leaves Pontoise and settles in near-by Auvers-sur-Oise, where he remains throughout the year. Friendship with Dr Gachet. Duret becomes interested in Cézanne's work. Zola publishes *Le Ventre de Paris* in which appears a painter, Claude Lantier, resembling Cézanne.

1874, in Auvers. Participates in the first impressionist group show, 15 Apr. to 15 May; exhibits three paintings. Pissarro does Cézanne's portrait. Returns to Aix in June but is back in Paris in the autumn, 120 Rue de Vaugirard.

1875, in Aix part of the year. Through Renoir meets Chocquet after the latter bought a canvas of his at *père* Tanguy's. Paints Chocquet's portrait. Lives in Paris, 15 Quai d'Anjou, neighbour of Guillaumin in whose company he sometimes works.

1876, in Aix and L'Estaque for the greater part of the year. Rejected at the Salon. Declines to join the impressionists for their second group show.

1877, probably in and around Paris most of the year; lives 67 Rue de l'Ouest. In Apr. participates in the third group show of the impressionists with sixteen works, mostly still lifes and landscapes; also exhibits his portrait of Chocquet. Is praised by Renoir's friend Rivière but mocked by all the other critics. Works with Pissarro in Pontoise, appears shortly in Auvers, Chantilly, Fontainebleau; also works in Issy near Paris. Zola spends the summer in L'Estaque.

1878, back in Aix at the beginning of the year; works in Aix and L'Estaque during the entire year. Has difficulties with his father and is helped financially by Zola. Rejected at the Salon. Is ready to show with the impressionists, but no group exhibition is organized that year. Zola buys a house in Médan.

1879, works in L'Estaque. Is rejected at the Salon despite intervention of Guillemet, now jury member. In March returns to Paris; from Apr. to Dec. in Melun. In autumn pays visit to Zola in Médan.

1880, from Jan. to Mar. in Melun. Probably again rejected at the Salon. From Mar. to Dec. in Paris, 32 Rue de l'Ouest. Zola mentions Cézanne in an article in which he begins to detach himself from his painter friends. In August Cézanne pays visit to Zola in Médan, where he meets Huysmans. Renoir does Cézanne's portrait.

1881, until Apr. in Paris, Rue de l'Ouest. Probably again rejected at the Salon. From May to Oct. with Pissarro in Pontoise; lives 31 Quai de Pothuis. There meets Gauguin. In June his sister Rose, who has just married Maxime Conil, comes to Paris with her husband. In Oct., Cézanne visits Zola in Médan. Returns to Aix in Nov. Is caricatured in a short novel by Duranty, published posthumously.

1882, works in L'Estaque with Renoir, whom he nurses in Feb. during an attack of pneumonia. From Mar. to Oct. in Paris, 32 Rue de l'Ouest. Is admitted to the Salon as 'pupil' of Guillemet; exhibits a portrait of a man. Spends five weeks in the autumn at Zola's in Médan. Returns to Aix in Oct., works at the 'Jas de Bouffan'. Makes his last will which he entrusts to Zola.

1883, works mostly in and around Aix. Is probably again rejected at the Salon. Apparently in Paris for Manet funeral, 4 May. In L'Estaque from May to Nov.; sees Monticelli often. In Dec. meets Monet and Renoir in the south.

1884, works mostly in and around Aix. Is rejected at the Salon despite intervention of Guillemet. The young Signac buys a landscape by Cézanne at Tanguy's.

1885, probably again rejected at the Salon. Works in L'Estaque and Aix until May. Has mysterious love affair. Visits Renoir with Hortense Fiquet and their son in La Roche-Guyon during June and July. Short stays in Villennes and Vernon. Pays visit to Zola in Médan, returns to Aix in Aug. Works in Aix and Gardanne during rest of the year. At about this time his brother-in-law, Maxime Conil, acquires the estate of Bellevue near Aix. Zola writes *L'Œuvre*.

1886, in Paris during Feb.; spends most of the year in Gardanne with Hortense Fiquet and their son. In March, Zola publishes *L'Œuvre*; Cézanne, deeply hurt, breaks with him. Probably again rejected at the Salon. On 28 Apr., marries Hortense Fiquet in Aix in the presence of his parents; religious ceremony, 29 Apr., at the church Saint-Jean-Baptiste with Marie Cézanne and Maxime Conil as witnesses. Cézanne's father dies 23 Oct., aged eighty-eight; the painter inherits sizeable fortune.

1887, probably in Aix most of the year.

1888, in Paris, 15 Quai d'Anjou. Works in Chantilly and in the outskirts of Paris.

1889, in Paris, Quai d'Anjou. Chocquet manoeuvres to have Cézanne's *Maison du pendu* shown at the Paris World's Fair. In June pays short visit to Chocquet in Hattenville, Normandy. Spends latter part of the year in Aix; Renoir comes there, rents Montbriant from Maxime Conil. Cézanne is invited to exhibit with the Belgian group, Les XX, in Brussels.

1890, in Paris, Quai d'Anjou; later, Avenue d'Orléans. Shows three canvases in Jan. with Les XX in Brussels. Spends five months during the summer with his wife and son in Switzerland (Neufchatel, Berne, Freyburg, Vevey, Lausanne, Geneva). During the autumn in Aix, works at the 'Jas de Bouffan', probably at his *Cardplayers* series. Begins to suffer from diabetes.

1891, at the beginning of the year in Aix, where he sees Alexis frequently. Considers exhibiting at the *Salon des Indépendants* but changes his mind. Obliges his wife and son to settle in Aix, later leaves for Paris. At about this time becomes a devout Catholic.

1892, in Aix and in Paris, 2 Rue des Lions-Saint-Paul. Works in Fontainebleau Forest. The painter Emile Bernard publishes a pamphlet on Cézanne.

1893, in Aix and in Paris, Rue des Lions-Saint-Paul. Works in Fontainebleau Forest. Death of Caillebotte.

1894, in Aix and Paris. Spends autumn in Giverny with Monet, where he meets Clemenceau, Rodin, Gustave Geffroy, and Mary Cassatt. Leaves suddenly for Aix. Death of *père* Tanguy; at the auction of his belongings, Cézanne's canvases bring between 45 and 215 francs. Plans to paint an Apotheosis of Delacroix. Ambroise Vollard who, in Jan., has opened a small gallery in Paris, Rue Laffitte, follows Pissarro's advice and seeks out Cézanne to organize a one-man show of his work.

1895, in Paris from Jan. to June, Rue Bonaparte. Paints portrait of Geffroy. Spends the autumn in Aix; excursions to Bibémus quarry and Mount Sainte-Victoire with Solari and the latter's son. Conflict

with Pissarro's friend, the painter Oller. In Dec. Vollard opens
Cézanne's first one-man show; the painter sends him some hundred-
and-fifty works. With the Caillebotte bequest, two paintings by
Cézanne enter the Luxembourg Museum.

1896, in Aix until June, works at Bibémus quarry. In Apr. meets the poet
Joachim Gasquet, son of one of his former schoolmates. Through
him meets Edmond Jaloux and Louis Aurenche. Zola spends some
days at Numa Coste's in Aix but does not see Cézanne. In Vichy
during June, then in July and Aug. at Talloires, on the Lac
d'Annecy. Spends autumn and winter in Paris, living in Montmartre, Rue des Dames. Zola, in a new article, calls Cézanne an
'abortive genius'.

1897, in Paris, 73 Rue Saint-Lazare, until Apr. Spends May in Mennecy,
Fontainebleau Forest. Before he leaves, Vollard buys the entire contents of his studio. From June until the end of the year in Aix, works
frequently in nearby Le Tholonet and at the Bibémus quarry. 25
Oct., death of Cézanne's mother, aged eighty-two. Two of Cézanne's
paintings are hung in the Berlin National Gallery but banned by the
Kaiser. During the Dreyfus affair, Cézanne disapproves of Zola's
stand.

1898, spends most of the year in Aix, works at Château Noir. Returns in
the autumn to Paris, 15 Rue Hégésippe-Moreau. Works in Montgeroult and Marines near Pontoise, sometimes in company of the
young painter Louis Le Bail.

1899, spends most of the year in and around Paris. The Italian collector,
Egisto Fabbri, owning sixteen canvases by Cézanne, meets the artist
in May. Paints portrait of Vollard. Returns to Aix in the autumn.
In order to settle the estate of Louis-Auguste Cézanne and at the
insistence of Maxime Conil, the 'Jas de Bouffan' has to be sold, much
to the regret of Cézanne, who then tries to buy the domaine of
Château Noir, half-way between Aix and Le Tholonet. His offer is
rejected; he rents an apartment, 23 Rue Boulegon, in Aix. Exhibits
three paintings at the *Salon des Indépendants*. At the sale of the Chocquet collection Cézanne's paintings average 1,700 francs. Monet buys
Cézanne landscape at Doria Sale.

1900, spends the year in Aix. Due to the intervention of Roger Marx, three
of Cézanne's paintings are shown at the Centennial Exhibition in
Paris.

1901, spends the year in Aix. Maurice Denis exhibits at the *Salon* an
'Hommage à Cézanne'. Cézanne shows two paintings at the *Salon
des Indépendants* and one in Brussels with the group of La Libre
Esthétique. In Nov. he buys some land on the Chemin des Lauves,
on a hill dominating Aix, to build a studio. Frequently meets the
poet Léo Larguier and the painter Charles Camoin, both doing their
military service in Aix.

1902, works in Aix and Le Tholonet while his studio is being constructed.
Apparently spends several weeks on Gasquet's estate in Eguilles
near Aix but soon afterwards their friendship cools. Exhibits three
paintings at the *Salon des Indépendants*, upon the insistence of
Maurice Denis. Shows two paintings in Aix with the 'Société des

Amis des Arts'. The dealer Bernheim buys in Aix some paintings from Cézanne's son. In the autumn visits the Larguier family in the Cévennes. 29 Sept., death of Zola in Paris.

1903, spends the year in Aix; works in his new studio. 7 Mar., sale of Zola's collection; ten works by Cézanne average 1,500 francs, but the painter is violently attacked in the press. Seven paintings by Cézanne are exhibited at the *Secession* in Vienna and three in Berlin. 12 Nov., death of Pissarro in Paris.

1904, spends most of the year in Aix, is visited there by Emile Bernard with whom he corresponds after his departure. Bernard prepares a new article on Cézanne. Sojourn in Paris, works in Fontainebleau Forest. Exhibits nine paintings with La Libre Esthétique in Brussels and others at the *Salon d'Automne* in Paris. The Galerie Cassirer in Berlin organizes a one-man show of Cézanne. Camoin, Francis Jourdain, and the painter-dealer Gaston Bernheim visit Cézanne in Aix.

1905, in Aix during almost the entire year. Is visited by Maurice Denis and K. X. Roussel. In Fontainebleau briefly during the summer. Shows ten paintings at the *Salon d'Automne*. Monet expresses publicly his admiration for Cézanne.

1906, in Aix. Is visited during the spring by the German collector Karl Ernst Osthaus who buys two paintings for his Museum. Exhibits a *View of Château Noir* with the 'Société des Amis des Arts' in Aix; lists himself in the catalogue as 'pupil of Pissarro'. Suffers an attack of bronchitis in Aug. Works near the bridge of Les Trois-Sautets. Is again visited by Camoin. Shows ten paintings at the *Salon d'Automne*. Dies in Aix, 23 Rue Boulegon, on 22 Oct.

BIBLIOGRAPHY

THIS bibliography is limited to the more important publications on Cézanne, special emphasis being put on books or articles of documentary interest. More complete bibliographies may be found in Lionello Venturi: *Cézanne, sa vie, son œuvre*, Paris, 1936; and in John Rewald: *Cézanne, sa vie, son œuvre, son amitié pour Zola*, Paris, 1939. A classified and annotated bibliography is included in John Rewald: *The History of Impressionism*, New York, 1946.

ALEXIS, Paul: *Emile Zola, notes d'un ami*, Paris, 1882.

Anonymous: 'Compte-rendu de l'inauguration du buste d'Emile Zola à la bibliothèque Méjanes,' Aix-en-Provence, 27 May, 1906.

AURENCHE, Louis: 'Lettre', *Tablettes d'Avignon*, December 1932.

AURIANT: 'Duranty et Zola', *La Nef*, July 1946.

BARNES, A. C. and MAZIA, V. de: *The Art of Cezanne*, New York, 1939.

BARR, A., Jr. and SCOLARI, M.: 'Cézanne in the Letters of Marion to Morstatt, 1865–8,' *Magazine of Art*, February, April, May, 1938.

BAZIN, Germain: 'Cézanne et la montagne Sainte-Victoire', *L'Amour de l'Art*, December 1938.

'Cézanne devant l'impressionnisme', *Labyrinthe*, 15 Feb. 1945.

BERNARD, Emile: 'Paul Cézanne', *Les Hommes d'Aujourd 'hui*, 1892, vol. III, No. 387.

'Paul Cézanne', *L'Occident*, July 1904.

'Souvenirs sur Paul Cézanne et lettres inédites', *Mercure de France*, 1 and 15 Oct. 1907.

'Julien Tanguy', *Mercure de France*, 16 Dec. 1908.

'La méthode de Paul Cézanne', *Mercure de France*, 1 Mar. 1920.

'La technique de Paul Cézanne', *L'Amour de l'Art*, December 1920.

'Une conversation avec Cézanne', *Mercure de France*, June 1921.

Souvenirs sur Paul Cézanne, Paris, 1921, 1925, 1926.

'L'erreur de Cézanne', *Mercure de France*, 1 May 1926.

BERNEX, J.: 'Etude sur Philippe Solari', *Méditerranée*, September 1911.

'Zola, Cézanne, Solari', *Les Cahiers d'Aix-en-Provence*, p. 49, 1923.

BURGER, Fritz: *Cézanne und Hodler*, Munich, 1913.

CAMOIN, Charles: 'Souvenirs sur Paul Cézanne', *L'Amour de l'Art*, January 1921.

CÉZANNE: *Letters*, edited by John Rewald, Paris, 1937; London, 1941.

CHAPPUIS, Adrien: *Dessins de Paul Cézanne*, Paris, 1938.

COQUIOT, Gustave: *Paul Cézanne*, Paris, 1919.

DENIS, Maurice: 'Cézanne', *L'Ermitage*, 15 Nov. 1905.

'Cézanne', *L'Occident*, September 1907.

'Cézanne', *Burlington Magazine*, January, February, 1911.
Théories, 1890–1910, Paris, 1912.
'L'influence de Cézanne', *L'Amour de l'Art*, December 1920.
Nouvelles Théories, 1914–21, Paris, 1922.
'Le dessin de Cézanne', *L'Amour de l'Art*, February 1924.
'L'aventure posthume de Cézanne', *Prométhée*, July, 1939.
DOITEAU, Dr V.: 'La curieuse figure du Dr Gachet', *Æsculape*, August, September, 1923.
DORIVAL, Bernard: *Les étapes de la peinture française*, vol. I, 1883–1905, Paris, 1943.
DURANTY, Edmond: *Le pays des arts*, Paris, 1881.
DURET, Théodore: *Les peintres impressionsnites*, Paris, 1878.
Manet and the French Impressionists, Philadelphia, 1910.
DURET, WERTH, JOURDAIN, MIRBEAU: *Cézanne*, Paris, 1914.
ELDER, Marc: *Chez Claude Monet à Giverny*, Paris, 1924.
FAURE, Elie: 'Cézanne', *Portraits d'Hier*, No. 28, Paris, 1910.
'Paul Cézanne', *L'Art Décoratif*, 5 Oct. 1911.
Les constructeurs, Paris, 1914.
'Toujours Cézanne', *L'Amour de l'Art*, December 1920.
L'Arbre d'Eden, Paris, 1922.
History of Art, vol. III, New York, 1924.
P. Cézanne, Paris, 1926.
FRY, Roger: *Cézanne, A Study of His Development*, New York, 1927.
GASQUET, Joachim: *Paul Cézanne*, Paris, 1921, 1926.
GAUGUIN, Paul: *Avant et Après*, Paris, 1919, 1923.
GEFFROY, Gustave: *Histoire de l'Impressionnisme*, Paris, 1894.
'Paul Cézanne', *Le Journal*, 25 Mar. 1894.
Claude Monet, vol. II, Paris, 1922.
GOLDWATER, Robert: 'Cézanne in America', *Art News*, 25 Mar 1938.
HUYGHE, René: *Cézanne*, Paris, 1936.
HUYGHE, R. and REWALD, J.: *Paul Cézanne*, special issue, *L'Amour de l'Art*, May 1936.
HUYSMANS, J.-K.: *Certains*, Paris, 1889.
JALOUX, Edmond: *Fumées dans la campagne*, Paris, 1918.
'Souvenirs sur Paul Cézanne', *L'Amour de l'Art*, December 1920.
JEWELL, E. A.: *Paul Cézanne*, New York, 1944.
JOËTS, Jules: 'Les Impressionnistes et Chocquet', *L'Amour de l'Art*, April 1935.
JOHNSON, Erle Loran: 'Cézanne's Country', *The Arts*, April 1930 (see also: Loran, Erle).
JOURDAIN, Francis: 'A propos d'un peintre difficile', *Arts de France*, No. 5, 1946.
LAFARGUE, Marc: 'Souvenirs sur Paul Cézanne', *L'Amour de l'Art*, January 1921.
LARGUIER, Léo: *Le Dimanche avec Paul Cézanne*, Paris, 1925.
Paul Cézanne, Paris, 1936.
LE BLOND-ZOLA, Denise: 'Zola et Cézanne, d'après une correspondance retrouvée', *Mercure de France*, January 1931.
Emile Zola, raconté par sa fille, Paris, 1931.
'Paul Alexis', *Mercure de France*, 1 Mar. 1939.

LECOMTE, Georges: *L'art impressionniste*, Paris, 1892
    Paul Cézanne, Catalogue of the Blot Collection, Paris, May 1900.
LEROY, Louis: 'L'exposition des impressionnistes', *Charivari*, 25 Apr. 1874.
LÉVY, S.: 'Lettre sur Cézanne', *L'Amour de l'Art*, December 1920.
LHOTE, André: 'L'enseignement de Cézanne', *Revue Française*, November 1920.
LORAN, Erle: *Cézanne's Composition*, Los Angeles, 1943. (See also: Johnson, Erle Loran).
MACK, Gerstle: *Paul Cézanne*, New York, 1935.
MAGLIONE, A.: *Monticelli intime*, Marseilles, 1903.
MAUS, M.-O.: *Trente années de lutte pour l'art*, Brussels, 1926.
MEIER-GRAEFE, Julius: *Paul Cézanne*, Munich, 1910; New York, 1927.
    Cézanne und sein Kreis, Munich, 1922.
MONTIFAUD, Marc de: 'L'exposition du Boulevard des Capucines', *L'Artiste*, May 1874.
MOORE, George: *Reminiscences of the Impressionist Painters*, Dublin, 1906.
NOVOTNY, Fritz: *Cézanne*, London, 1937.
    Cézanne und das Ende der wissenschaftlichen Perspektive, Vienna, 1938.
ORS, Eugenio d': *Paul Cézanne*, Paris, 1930.
OSTHAUS, K. E.: Article in *Das Feuer*, 1920.
PACH, Walter: *The Masters of Modern Art*, New York, 1924.
    Queer Thing, Painting, New York, 1938.
PFISTER, Kurt: *Cézanne, Gestalt, Werk, Mythos*, Potsdam, 1927.
PISSARRO, Camille: *Letters to his Son Lucien*, edited by John Rewald, New York, 1943.
PROVENCE, Marcel: 'Cézanne chrétien', *Revue des Lettres*, December, 1924.
    'Cézanne collégien', *Mercure de France*, 1 Feb. and 1 Aug, 1925.
    'Cézanne et ses amis: Numa Coste', *Mercure de France*, 1 Apr. 1926.
RAPHAEL, Max: *Von Monet zu Picasso*, Munich, 1913.
RAYNAL, Maurice: *Cézanne*, Paris, 1936.
REWALD, John: 'Cézanne au Louvre', *L'Amour de l'Art*, October 1935.
    'Une copie par Cézanne d'après le Greco', *Gazette des Beaux Arts*, February 1936.
    'A propos du catalogue raisonné de l'œuvre de Cézanne et de la chronologie de cette œuvre', *La Renaissance*, March-April 1937.
    'Achille Emperaire, ami de Paul Cézanne', *L'Amour de l'Art*, May 1938.
    Cézanne, sa vie, son œuvre, son amitié pour Zola, Paris, 1939.
    'As Cézanne recreated Nature', *Art News*, 15-29 Feb. 1944.
    'The Camera verifies Cézanne's Watercolours', *Art News*, 1-30 Sept. 1944.
    'Proof of Cézanne's Pygmalion Pencil', *Art News*, 1-15 Oct. 1944.
    The History of Impressionism, New York, 1946.
REWALD, J. and MARSCHUTZ, L.: 'Cézanne et le Château Noir', *L'Amour de l'Art*, January 1935.
    Cézanne et la Provence, special issue, *Le Point*, August 1936.
REY, Robert: *La renaissance du sentiment classique*, Paris, 1931.
RILKE, R. M.: *Briefe aus den Jahren 1906 bis 1907*, Leipzig, 1930.
    Lettres sur Cézanne, edited by Maurice Betz, Paris, 1944.

RINTELEN, Friedrich: *Reden und Aufsätze*, Basle, 1927.

RIVIÈRE, Georges: *L'Impressionniste, Journal d'Art*, No. 1, 6 Apr. 1877.
  Renoir et ses amis, Paris, 1921.
  Le maître Paul Cézanne, Paris, 1923.
  'La formation de Paul Cézanne', *L'Amour de l'Art*, 1 Aug. 1925.
  Cézanne, Paris, 1933.

RIVIÈRE, R. and SCHNERB, J. F.: 'L'atelier de Cézanne', *La Grande Revue*, 25 Dec. 1907.

ROCHEFORT, Henri: 'L'amour du laid', *L'Intransigeant*, 9 Mar. 1903.

ROUX, Marius: 'La Confession de Claude, par Emile Zola', *Memorial d'Aix*, 3 Dec. 1865.

ROYÈRE, Jean: 'Sur Paul Cézanne', *La Phalange*, 15 Nov. 1906.

STERLING, Charles: Catalogue of the Cézanne exhibition, Paris, Musée de l'Orangerie, 1936.

STERLING, JAMOT, TOLNAY, VERGNET-RUIZ, COMBE: *Cézanne*, special issue of *La Renaissance*, May-June 1936.

VAUXCELLES, Louis: 'Un après-midi chez Claude Monet', *L'Art et les Artistes*, March 1905, October 1906.

VENTURI, Lionello: 'L'Impressionismo', *L'Arte*, March 1935.
  'Paul Cézanne', *L'Arte*, 1935.
  'Impressionism', *Art in America*, July 1936.
  Cézanne, son art, son œuvre, 2 vols., Paris, 1936.
  Paul Cézanne—Water Colours, London, 1943.

VOLLARD, Ambroise: *Paul Cézanne*, Paris, 1914, 1919, 1924, 1938; New York, 1926.
  Recollections of a Picture Dealer, Boston, 1936.

WAERN, C.: 'Notes on French Impressionists', *Atlantic Monthly*, April 1892.

ZOLA, Émile: *La Confession de Claude, Paris*, 1865.
  Mon Salon, augmenté d'une dédicace et d'un appendice, Paris, 1866 (later incorporated in *Mes Haines*).
  'Letter to "Le Figaro",' *Le Figaro*, 12 Apr. 1867.
  Thérèse Raquin, Paris, 1867.
  'Mon Salon', *L'Evénement*, 2, 10, 19, 24 May, 1, 9, 16 June 1868.
  Le Ventre de Paris, Paris, 1873.
  Nouveaux Contes à Ninon, Paris, 1874.
  'Le Naturalisme au Salon', *Le Voltaire*, 18-22 June, 1880.
  Nos auteurs dramatiques, Paris, 1881.
  L'Œuvre, Paris, 1886.
  'Peinture', *Le Figaro*, 2 May 1896.
  Correspondance, Lettres de Jeunesse, Paris, 1907.
  Correspondance, Les Lettres et les Arts, Paris, 1908.
  Documents litteraires, Paris, 1912.
  Contes et Nouvelles, Paris, 1928.

---

* These works have been re-issued in Zola's *Œuvres complètes*, with notes and commentaries by Maurice Le Blond, Paris, 1928.

INDEX